THE UNCOILING PYTHON

The *Uncoiling* *Python*

SOUTH AFRICAN STORYTELLERS AND RESISTANCE

Harold Scheub

OHIO UNIVERSITY PRESS   ATHENS

Ohio University Press, Athens, Ohio 45701

www.ohioswallow.com

© 2010 by Ohio University Press

All rights reserved

Printed in the United States of America

Ohio University Press books are printed on acid-free paper ⊗ ™

18 17 16 15 14 13 12 11 10   5 4 3 2 1

Library of Congress Cataloging-in-Publication Data

Scheub, Harold.
  The uncoiling python : South African storytellers and resistance / Harold Scheub.
    p. cm.
  Includes bibliographical references and index.
  ISBN 978-0-8214-1921-2 (hc : alk. paper) — ISBN 978-0-8214-1922-9 (pb : alk. paper) — ISBN 978-0-8214-4332-3 (electronic)
  1. Storytelling—South Africa. 2. Oral tradition—South Africa. 3. Folklore—Political aspects—South Africa. 4. Apartheid—South Africa. 5. South Africa—Social life and customs. 6. South Africa—Politics and government. 7. South Africa—Colonization. I. Title.
  GR359.S343 2010
  398.20968—dc22
                      2009051808

I am a part of all that I have met . . .

Alfred Lord Tennyson

CONTENTS

ILLUSTRATIONS

PREFACE AND ACKNOWLEDGMENTS

Why should one study the history of a people when they are moving dramatically and decisively into a new sense of identity? Because that new sense of identity is firmly rooted in that history, because one cannot understand one's "new" identity in the absence of that identity of the past.

Why is it important, in a new millennium, to study the history of apartheid in South Africa? It seems faded and dated: after the dramatic changes that occurred in South Africa in 1990 and 1994, the 350 years of apartheid seem to sink into history. But those years are not a history to be forgotten or ignored. In fact, the way South Africa survived those centuries is an augury of how well it will survive successive years.

Bishop Desmond Tutu, the chair of the Truth and Reconciliation Commission,[1] wrote, "It is this contemporary history . . . it is this history with which we have had to come to terms. We could not pretend it did not happen. Everyone agrees that South Africans must deal with that history and its legacy."[2]

The problem for South Africa in the 1990s was how to forge ahead in time without history dragging it back—how, in short, to deal with those years of apartheid. The Truth and Reconciliation Commission was one way of attempting this: the stories of the past would, it was hoped, enable South Africans to put the past behind them. But making that attempt had its own risks. Those 350 years and the way South Africans lived those years are the rich soil that will provide growth possibilities for future generations. The years must not, can not, shall not be forgotten.

How did a Zulu family endure? How did a colored child move into his future? How did a white family struggling with ideas of race manage to cope? As a carefully designed system based on racial separation was developed and then ruthlessly enforced from Pretoria, what enabled the African people to survive?

One looks behind and sees the shadow of history. There are times when one wants to avoid that shadow and its implications. But the shadow can never be eliminated, never be forgotten: it is woven into life itself. The stories of that past are the means of catharsis.

And we are left with this question: How do a people and a country move ahead into a new sense of identity if the past is forgotten? Whatever South Africa's future, it flows—whether we wish it to or not—from its history, from its stories. And that future will be strengthened when one considers that history, when one considers how a people maintained their identity and strength in the face of astonishing odds, in the face of a police state that divided people rigorously on the basis of skin color. Everything that South Africa is to become in the new millennium is tied tightly to its history, to its survival of 350 years of apartheid.

Tutu wrote, "Racism came to South Africa in 1652; it has been part of the warp and woof of South African society since then."[3]

EUROPEANS AND THE "NATIVES"

The Xesibes are said to be indolent but they are no more averse to hard labour than any other natives. They have a very good sense of humour and always enjoy a joke.

—Author and date unknown

The Xesibes were a brave and moral race, loyal to their Chiefs, superstitious as all native tribes are, and this is the stumbling block of all natives and been the cause of disintegration of many a tribe and family, they are a fine race, the constant raids and wars kept them in hard training and in the children reared it was always the survival of the fittest, there were few opportunities for over indulgence in beer. They were said to be indolent, but they were no more averse to hard labour than other natives.

—W. Power Leary, 1904

The tribes in the vicinity are law-abiding and have made great strides in civilization.

—Captain G. D. Ward, compiler, 1878

Observers often disparage the stories in the oral traditions of African people.[4] On the surface, these stories seem to be typical fairy tale–type narratives, with the usual folkloric motifs, the ogres and the fantasy helpers, the Cinderella characters moving up from their status as least likely heroes. And that is the way many of those in the white ruling class of apartheid South Africa viewed these stories. They were the activities of the subjugated

Africans and were not to be taken seriously, certainly not as weapons in the antiapartheid struggle. But when I conducted research in the rural areas of southern Africa in the late 1960s and in the 1970s, I learned otherwise.

I collected oral stories from the Xhosa, Zulu, Swati, and Ndebele peoples. The Xhosa and Zulu live in South Africa, the Swati in Swaziland, and the Ndebele in the southern part of Zimbabwe. During each of four year-long trips, I walked some 1,500 miles up and down the southeastern coast of the continent, working with storytellers, historians, poets, and philosophers in the oral traditions of those areas.

These materials were collected at a critical moment in South Africa's history, during the lowest moments of apartheid. In the end, the thousands of stories that I collected documented the way a severely repressed people survived 350 years of racist rule. They are a testament to the power and lasting effects of storytelling. The collection is therefore of historical moment. But it is also significant as far as the study of story is concerned, at any time and in any age. Here is a gamut of storytellers and historians and poets, from the commonplace practitioners to the Homers of southern Africa. In southern Africa, there are no professional storytellers (although there are professional bards, such as poets in the retinue of kings): everyone is a potential storyteller. So I worked with storytellers in all aspects of life, mainly in the rural areas, from elder to young, from people who were wholly in the African tradition to those who were more influenced by the West and by Christianity, including schoolchildren. In most cases, I taped and filmed storytelling sessions that I had nothing to do with setting up: I was invited to such sessions. And I learned lessons that go far beyond obvious Aesop's fable–type moralizing. I learned that these oral stories were a major part of the Africans' success in surviving 350 years of apartheid.

HISTORICAL BACKGROUND

10,000 BC—Khoi and San. The history of South Africa begins with the story of the Khoi and the San, the original inhabitants of the southern part of the continent. San civilization can be glimpsed in the rock paintings found throughout the region. These indigenous people would later be decimated. The Khoi would be destroyed by the Dutch and by epidemics; many of the San would be killed by the Dutch, and the remainder would be forced into the Kalahari Desert by the whites and by the Africans who came down from the north.

AD *1500—Bantu-speaking Africans.* Large numbers of Bantu-speaking Africans moved down from the great lakes area of East Africa. They were farming and cattle-raising people, moving into southern Africa seeking new grazing and farm lands. They would become the Zulu, Xhosa, Swati, Ndebele, Sotho, Tswana, Tsongo, and Venda peoples.

1652—The Dutch. The Dutch came to South Africa as a part of the Dutch East India Company, seeking a refreshment station so that ships could obtain fresh fruits, vegetables, and meat on the voyages from Europe to India and Malaysia. When San and Khoi people refused to work on Dutch farms, Malays were brought to South Africa. Dutch farmers had children by the Khoi and by Malays, and so began the "colored" population of South Africa. Dutch farmers in search of land began to trek from Cape Town to the north. Inevitably, they came into contact with the Africans who were moving south, also seeking land. This gave way to one hundred years of sporadic wars between blacks and whites, a struggle for the land.

1806—The British. Because of wars in Europe, the British took over the administration of South Africa early in the nineteenth century. The Dutch (also called Boers [farmers] and later called Afrikaners, speaking a Dutch-based language called Afrikaans) left the Cape because they were unhappy with British rule.

1820—British settlement. British settlers were brought to South Africa and were settled between the warring Boers and the Xhosa.

1836—Great Trek of the Boers. The Boers were seeking land and independence from the British. British forces followed the Boers, and when the Boers settled in an area—in Natal, in what would become the Orange Free State, or in Transvaal—the British annexed these territories.

1867, 1886—Gold and diamonds. The British were halfhearted about this colonizing activity until diamonds and gold were discovered in the 1860s and 1880s. Then South Africa (until then considered in London a colonial backwater, merely an agricultural country) became much sought after, and the British decided to stay. The struggle between the two groups of whites—the Dutch and the English—for hegemony in South Africa resulted in two wars, one of them a major one at the turn of the century (1899–1902): the Anglo-Boer War. Many Africans also died in this war, conscripted on one or the other of the two sides. The British won the war and in 1910 unified the four colonies (Cape, Natal, Orange Free State, Transvaal) into the Union of South Africa.

1912—African National Congress. To the whites, the Africans of South Africa were a ready-made labor force for extracting the minerals from the earth: the blacks would, in the minds of the whites, forever remain servants. But the Africans persisted in their struggle for freedom, and they established the South African Native National Congress, later to become the African National Congress (ANC).

1920s—Labor strikes on the Rand. In the 1920s, the Africans continuing their struggle for their rights withheld their labor and went on strike on the Rand, that part of South Africa where the many mines were located—mines that were worked by Africans.

1948—The Nationalists in control. Until 1948, the Afrikaner Nationalist Party had to share power with the British. But in the election of 1948, after the Second World War, the Afrikaner-dominated Nationalist Party won elections in which only whites could vote, and the Nationalists took control of the government. For the next two decades, apartheid laws came into existence as racism became a part of the law of the land, and Africans were made permanently a part of a servile labor class. This government rejected the United Nations Declaration of Human Rights (1948) and brought into effect the Suppression of Communism Act (1950). The Registration Act (1950) classified all South Africans into separate categories—African, "colored," Asian, white—to prevent all crossing of the color line. The Bantu Education Act (1953) was meant to ensure that African education remained inferior to the education of white children. The Immorality Act (1957) forbade sexual relations between the races. The Universities Apartheid Act (1959) prevented most Africans from attending South Africa's universities.

1960s, 1976, 1985—Continued African resistance. African resistance continued, resulting in anti-pass demonstrations at Sharpeville, an African location outside the city of Vereeniging (near Johannesburg), in which sixty-nine Africans were killed. The event became known internationally as "the Sharpeville Massacre." In 1962, the Sabotage Act came into effect, and Nelson Mandela, an ANC leader, was arrested and imprisoned on Robben Island, South Africa's prison for political prisoners. The struggle continued intermittently, then exploded again during the "children's revolution" in urban areas throughout the country, a rebellion that began in Soweto (Soweto is an acronym for "SOuthWEst TOwnship," an

African ghetto fifteen miles outside Johannesburg). At least five hundred children would be killed during that year, 1976. By the mid-1980s, open revolt had become general, and the government brought into effect a state of emergency.

1990, 1994—Freedom. The whites could no longer govern South Africa, and the authorities were forced to release Nelson Mandela from prison and to legitimize such organizations as the ANC and the Pan-Africanist Congress in 1990. In 1994, the first full elections were held in South Africa; the ANC won the election, and Nelson Mandela became president of South Africa.

ACKNOWLEDGMENTS

I am grateful to the University of Cape Town Libraries for permission to use San stories and poetry and for the use of the photographs of ||kábbo and Díä!kwăin. My thanks go to Lesley Hart, the manager of Special Collections Information Services, University of Cape Town Libraries.

PRELUDE

The Uncoiling Python

And Michal took an image, and laid it in the bed,
and put a pillow of goats' hair for his bolster, and
covered it with a cloth.

— *1 Samuel 19:13*

The python is the operative image in this discussion of the place of oral traditions in the 350-year struggle against apartheid in South Africa. The Zulu people, Axel-Ivar Berglund has written, "are convinced that" the python is "the coolest of all the animals in the whole world," a result of "the coolness of water, especially that of deep pools"; in addition, "there is the coolness related to calmness and an even temperament. A python is said to have no *amawala* (careless, hasty and haphazard action)."[1]

How did the Africans endure the sustained assaults on their liberties? The secret to survival is to be found in the imagery of transformation and rebirth in the traditions of the San and Nguni peoples. The uncoiling python is an apt poetic mirror of this transitional process.

An informant told Berglund, "This animal is never seen working hastily or in anger. It is always slow and steady, thinking a long time before it does something. So it is clear that it has no *amawala* at all. That is why we say that it is cool." Berglund further noted, "The python is also the symbol of great power, expressed in physical strength and ability. A man in the uMhlatuze valley where pythons are found said: 'It is the strongest of all, only he (the Lord-of-the-Sky) being stronger. It is stronger than all the animals, being able to kill anything. Even bulls are killed by it.'" Its physical strength is linked with its coolness: "The python itself

I

is said to be very difficult to kill 'because of its coolness all the time, even when it is facing death.'" Berglund quoted a diviner as saying, "It remains peaceful, doing nothing. So many times people think that it is dead and commence working (i.e. removing the skin). But when they look inside (the skin) they find that it is living. They fear very much and take it very quickly to the shadow of a tree. There they cut off the head, letting the blood run out on the earth under the tree, the animal all the time just remaining quiet and doing nothing." In addition to coolness and quietude, Berglund noted, "pythons symbolize togetherness, undivided oneness."

> The thought-pattern of togetherness is the underlying idea in the use of a python's skin in the *inkhatha yesizwe,* the emblem of national unity and loyalty. It is only when the *inkhatha* has been enveloped with the skin of a python that it is really and truly the national emblem, even though it could lack other ingredients. But under no condition may the skin of the python be omitted. "How else could we say, 'We are the children of Mageba and Zulu" if this thing was not there, binding us together."[2]

The python is a poetic example of rebirth. In the praises of kings and other significant figures, this is a common image, as is evident in the following poem directed to Ofisi Kona:[3]

> *Ovuk' emini akabonanga nto,*
> *Kub' akayibonang' inamb' icombuluka.*
> The person who rises late has seen nothing,
> Because he has not seen the python uncoil.

The same is true in this poem for Mhluti Tini:[4]

> *Phumani bantu baseBhotwe anibonanga nto*
> *Kub' aniyibonang' inamb' icombuluka.*
> Come out, people of the palace, you have seen
> nothing
> Because you have not seen the python uncoil.

Magagamela Koko created a poem for his son using the same imagery:[5]

> *Ndiza kuphinda ke ndibonge*
> *Into yam enkulu*[6]
> *uBantwana bayaxathula*[7]
> *Abanye bafund' ukuhlala*
> *Abanye bafund' ukuhamba*

Abanye bafund' ukuthetha
Ovuk' emin' akabonanga nto
Kub' akayibonang' inamb' icombuluka . . .
I will praise again
My senior son,
Children-walk-in-shoes,
Some are only beginning to sit,
Some are only starting to walk,
Some are only learning to speak.
The late-riser has not seen anything,
He has not seen the python uncoil.

And Nongenile Masithathu Zenani, speaking of her craft as a poet, recalled how, in the old times among the Xhosa, the poet addressed the king:[8]

Hoyiiiiiini na! . . . hoyiiiiiini na! . . . ovuk' emini ngobudenge
akabonanga nto . . .
ngokuba yen' engasoze wayibona inamba xa icombuluka
Hoyiiiiiiiini na! Hoyiiiiiiiini na!
The late-riser has foolishly seen nothing . . .
Because he will never see the python uncoil!

Mditshwa Diko, a Mpondomise king, was compared to the python:[9]

Ulala ngemva kulal' ingwenya yakwaMajola ngaphambili.
He sleeps behind, the Majola python sleeps in front.

As was Sarhili Hintsa, a Gcaleka king:[10]

Yinamb' enkul' ejikel' i-Hohita.
Ovuk' emini akabonanga nto,
Kub' engayibonang' inamb' icombuluka.
It is a big python that surrounds the Hohita,
The one who rises late has seen nothing,
For he has not seen the python uncoil.

And Gumna Sandile:[11]

Yinamba yakwaNzunga
Eyajikel' eKubusi mhlana yafika.
He is the python of Nzunga
That encircled Kubusi when it arrived.

Surviving 350 Years

I have been preparing to write this book ever since I began collecting oral traditions in southern Africa in July 1967. In a trilogy,[12] I attempted to explain the complexities of performance of oral stories in southern Africa; in *The Tongue Is Fire*,[13] I presented historical stories and commentaries that deal more directly with apartheid in South Africa. My experiences collecting these materials[14] and the writing of these books were the foundation for this book, in which I attempt to show how the oral poets and storytellers, through their traditional materials, dealt with the day-to-day inhumanity of the racist system and kept their audiences from succumbing to the daily tedium and irrational weight of this system.

How did the African people survive 350 years of apartheid? They did not have the weaponry with which to confront the interlopers. Many went to the cities and farms to work for the whites. But most remained in the rural areas, continuing to farm as they had for generations. Some were nomadic, migratory; others were sedentary. And they told stories, stories that were ancient—fairy tales, the stuff of the "noble savage," primitive, animistic, and obvious, hardly an adequate shield against the daily onslaught of the colonial powers.

When I began my research in July 1967, I was not prepared for the real force of those oral traditions. I was aware of the motifs, the surface themes. What I did not fully anticipate was the active role played by the audience, the pivotal role of the storyteller, and the startling and subversive use made of ancient and seemingly hackneyed images. As I learned more and storytellers and audiences provided me with the tools that I needed, I was able to move beneath the obvious and unthreatening surfaces of these stories. And I slowly became aware of something extraordinary, something splendidly seditious; I gained insight into the way the African peoples protected themselves, how they were able to survive the years of apartheid.

At the same time, I inevitably became sensitive to the daily incivility of the system under which Africans lived. In a journal entry dated January 26, 1976, I wrote of the comments by a Xhosa woman named Nongenile Masithathu Zenani on race relations in South Africa. The black man, she says, is better off as a fly or dog. The white calls the black a "kaffir," *inkawu*.[15] She fears that whites will fly over in airplanes and bomb the blacks, so that the blacks die a fearful death. However, when Hitlani, the young autocratic headman of this area, extorts a fifth of brandy from her, she is furious but complies, for she wants no problems. She does not like whites but fears black rule if Hitlani is to become a ruler. Similarly, on February 11, 1976, I wrote more about Masithathu's life-experience. She tells of the *imantyi,* the white magistrate, who would not accept that she is seventy years old and therefore qualified for a government pension (her deceased husband worked for the government years ago, and at the time Masithathu qualified for a pension of about fourteen dollars a year). He made her bare her head, to see whether her hair was gray; this act was an ignominious one because, she explains, a mature woman never bares her head in the presence of a man who is not her husband.

In Soweto, I had been playing tapes of some of the stories that I had collected in the South African rural countryside, and doubting young Africans argued that the lack of any clear statements about apartheid revealed that these traditions were antiquated and not relevant to contemporary issues and history in that country. When I returned to the countryside, I told some of the storytellers what the youthful Africans had said. One storyteller said, "Our traditions were here long before apartheid came to South Africa, and our traditions will be here long after apartheid is gone. How do you think we have survived these three hundred and fifty years? It is the truths embodied in the images of the stories that helped us to endure. The stories deal with eternal truths, not with the exigencies of the moment."[16]

A. C. Jordan, the Xhosa writer, told me of how, when he was an education supervisor, he moved from town to town in the African areas of South Africa, always accompanied by white officials who, Jordan said, made certain that nothing subversive was being said. Jordan was regularly able to circumvent these watchdogs by telling stories to his audiences, stories that seemed on their surface to be simple traditional tales but that were, if one understood the language of storytelling, deeply subversive and significantly important in the sense that they enabled members of audience to continue to bear the world they lived in. Jordan, using "oral tradition as a political weapon," was able to

> attack[ ] the white rulers in an oblique fashion, creating *iintsomi* in Xhosa, the meaning of which would not escape the Xhosa members of his audiences. He told of the contest between the birds, for example, how the birds met together to participate in a contest to discover who could soar highest in the sky. That bird would become the king of the birds. The eagle flew highest—or so it appeared. But unknown to the eagle, a tiny bird was hiding in its feathers. And when the eagle had reached the apex of its ascent, and started descending, the little bird flew a few feet higher, then itself glided to the earth.[17]

The oral and written traditions of the Africans of South Africa have provided an understanding of their past, particularly the way the past relates to the present and the continued shaping of the past by the present (and vice versa). When colonial forces first came to this region in 1487, those traditions were also a bulwark against what would become 350 years of colonial rule, characterized by the racist policies of apartheid. The people retreated into themselves, finding a harbor in tradition.

From the indigenous San and Khoi populations of southern Africa to the fifteenth century, when Bantu-speaking peoples moved into the southern part of the continent, people later to become known as the Xhosa, Zulu, Swati, Ndebele, Sotho, Tswana, and Tsonga, this part of Africa was a rich amalgam of interacting peoples. The coming of the whites added to and dramatically altered these interactions. Although they did not initially consider themselves a colonizing power, the whites became determined from an early period to bring the African peoples under their rule. With superior firepower, and through one hundred years of war, the subjugation was made permanent.

The Africans did not submit to colonial rule from the beginning. There were open insurrections and also subversive means whereby the Africans effectively contented with the whites. Probably the most effective and least apparent of these has never been wholly understood: the indigenous storytelling and poetic traditions of the Africans gave them the means whereby they could withstand the daily humiliations of colonial rule. In areas where there were no radios or television sets, no computers or iPods, the storytellers were the daily news broadcasters, conveying the daily news in extraordinarily penetrating ways: through the traditional stories of the people. The storytellers were by turns or simultaneously Walter Cronkite and Jon Stewart,[18] placing the contemporary world into the context of the traditions of the people.

This book is an effort to understand the force and the effectiveness of these traditions, virtually unknown and never appreciated or understood by the white overlords. The whites viewed the Africans as "noble savages," a view that derived from an eighteenth-century doctrine of simplicity and innocence unencumbered by the complexities of civilization. If the Africans had a religion, it was the concept of animism, emphasizing a "preliterate" belief in a natural world in which plants and animals have souls, as do humans. These concepts persist in contemporary times, especially when considering the San and other African groups.[19] This may seem to explain the simple oral traditions of such people—the fairy tales and repetitive poetry—but those who view these people as "simple" have no understanding of the complexities of the people and their traditions.

Noble savage? Animist? No, there was something more, something that escaped the racist Western clichés. When I listened to the oral stories of the Nguni peoples and read the Bleek and Lloyd collection of San poetry and stories,[20] I knew that I was in the presence of extraordinary intellectual and imaginative works, not something that could be dismissed in such a flippant and ugly fashion. I was determined, from the first stories that I heard (among the Mpondomise people of the Transkei), to attempt to reveal the complexity of a people who have been dismissed as merely simple.

The first thing that I needed was an analytical method that would enable me to study more closely what I was witnessing every day. I adopted the method that was taught to me by storytellers and their audiences, as this became something of a detective story for me and has preoccupied me for fifty years.

This volume is an effort to reveal some of this subversive activity. I have selected San poems and tales along with Nguni and Sotho poems and tales from the nineteenth and twentieth centuries, some of which I collected in the late 1960s and the 1970s. Mainly, I have allowed the poets and storytellers to speak for themselves, but I have added analytical commentaries from time to time.

It is the seamlessness of all of creation that the San artists speak of: the movement from human to tree, from human to bird, from human to cloud, and back again. The San creators of rock paintings had this in mind also, as they created images of humans, placing these images against images of gods, so that there was a visual interplay between them. That interplay is what characterizes the art of the San and lies at the heart of the oral traditions of the Nguni peoples of southern Africa. It is also touched upon in contemporary written works when the authors have the sensitivity to comprehend what the San artists had been portraying centuries earlier.

The metaphor is created by a series of links (just as a loom is created) as a human becomes enmeshed with a tree, a bird, a cloud. The poet slowly connects the two, and in the end it is no longer a metaphor, because the two have become one. The process is metaphorical, but the result is a union that defies metaphor. When the process is complete, one does not have a claim to the country,[21] for there is no difference between the human and the country: a poetic metaphorical journey has moved us to that union. The poetry and the stories reveal the relationship between the people and the land—and reveal how it is that Africans survived 350 years of apartheid.

The interplay of history and story has been a pulse through time. The one informs the other; the one is composed of shards of the other and is then developed into a fictional metaphor of the other. The San and the Khoi people, early inhabitants of South Africa, and the Nguni and Sotho people, later residents of the region, were at war with the whites for centuries, first with the Dutch, then the British, as the San were driven into the Kalahari Desert and the Nguni and Sotho engaged in sporadic warfare with the whites. Initially, it was the land that they fought over; later it was diamonds and gold. From the beginning, the whites enforced restrictions on the Africans that would later be codified into the laws of apartheid. Africans were destroyed, imprisoned, forced to work for the whites, and forcibly relocated to the least favored lands of the region. Deprived of essential rights and not allowed to vote, they were considered in every way lesser than the white masters.

How could they endure these decades that rotted into centuries? They were considered savages, primitives, and barbarians, and their imaginative and intellectual lives were thought to be less than civilized. True, they did have storytelling traditions, but these were not taken seriously by the Europeans. Nevertheless, these traditions were a part of the strength of the Africans, means whereby they were able to tolerate the persistent onslaught. On the surface, the poems and stories seem harmless enough.

What I have attempted to do is reveal the uncoiling python.

FROM A NOTEBOOK

June 22, 1975. The reasoning process takes place against a regular background characterized by repetition (I have variously called this background a "grid," "expansible image," etc.). But *why* repetition? How do the images *work* with repetition? How do the images work *generally*? The image and narrative— discursive reasoning: How does it work? Why the image? *The image and feeling:* the image evokes and holds feeling, but it is not feeling itself, it is not *composed* of feeling. Is it held together by feeling? or is its function limited to *evoking* feeling? It evokes feeling; is it evocative rather than creative? What precisely is the image? How is it constructed? And of what? How is it retained in the tradition over the years? How does it change over time? How does it *hold feeling?* Is the holding of feeling within an image the purpose of repetition of image? Once trapped in the image, feeling is kept there through repetition of the image? Is this what happens? And what then does repetition do to the feeling trapped in the image? Heighten it? Dissipate, dull, dilute it? Repetition of the feeling-trapped-in-image: this image is then blended with yet other images which evoke and hold yet other (related?) feelings.

A San Poem

A MAN BECOMES A TREE

By | | kábbo

The man here climbs the mountain,
he plays the goura.[22]
The girl looks at him as he comes,
he stands fast; as he comes,
he holds the goura in his hand,
he holds the goura in his mouth,
it is he who stands playing the goura.

As he stands, the sun has set,
as he stands; he still stands,
as he holds it,
he holds in his mouth the goura,
for it is the girl,
she listens to the goura with her ears,
the man stands,
he still stands,
he has his legs,
he has his feet,
he is a man,

he was a man,
he becomes a tree,
and his feet, they are,
he has his arms,
because the maiden looks at him
with the maiden eye.
The maiden looks,
fastening him to the ground,
and it is so:

Bleek Archive, http://lloydbleekcollection.cs.uct.ac.za/data/stories/184/index.html, Lloyd Book II-2, 295–305; July 1871. I have made some changes in Lloyd's original translations.

his legs are those of a
man,
he is a tree,
his arms are those of
a man,
he holds the goura
with his mouth,
he is a tree,
he has his eyes,
because he was a
man,
he has his head,
he has his head-hair,
because he is a tree
which is a man,

he is a man,
he is a tree,
he has his feet, he is shod,
he has his nails,
he has his mouth,
he has his nose,
he has his ears,
he is a tree,
because he is a man,

he is a tree,
and it is so that he plays the goura,
he is a tree,
he plays the goura
while he is a tree,
he is a man,
he plays the goura,
and it is so that he is a tree
which playing the goura stands,

because he does look, with his eyes,
and it is so that he does play the goura,
because he does look.
And another fast stands:
he carried the arrows,
he held the bow,
he was returning,
holding a jackal's tail's hair,
the maiden looked at him,
and it is so that he stands fast,
and it is so that he still stands,
as he holds the jackal's tail's hair,
he did hold it, standing fast,
as he stood; he also held the bow,
he stood,
because he did still stand,
and it was so that he did become a tree,
as he stood,
he held the hair,
for he was a man,
and it was so that he did hold the hair,
he is a tree,
he stands,
he has his legs,
because he formerly had his feet,
and it is so that he does indeed stand,
he was shod in gemsbok skin sandals,
he has his legs,
he has his feet,
he has his arms,
he has his nails,
he has his eyes,
he has his nose,
his head remains,
he has his head-hair,
he has his ears,
he has his spear,
he has his tinderbox.

Another man mounts the mountain
he is seeking,[23]

he comes over the mountain:
as he comes,
as he carries the quiver
and it is so that the maiden looks at him
as he comes,
he also, he stands,
as he carries the quiver on his shoulder,
he stands,
holds the bow,
he stands,
he holds the stick,
he stands,
it is so that he still has his legs,
and it is so that he still stands,
he carries the quiver,
he is a tree,
he is a man,
he carries the quiver,
he has his arms,
and it is so that he indeed still carries the bow,
he still holds the stick,
because he still has his hands,
he still has his nails,
he still has his eyes,
he still has his nose,
his eyes remain,
he is a tree,
he has his head,
he has his head-hair,
he talks,
he is a tree,
for it is he who was a man who talked,
and it is so that he talks,
while he is a tree,
he waits standing on the mountain,
he carries the quiver,
he is a talking tree,
which talked standing,
for he was a man,
the maiden looked at him,

and it is so that he became indeed a tree,
and it is so that he talks,
for he was a man,
and it is so that he became a tree which talked,
for he was a tree,
he looked,
he talked,
his mouth sat,
his tongue remained,
to indeed talk with,
he is a tree which has his head-hair,
he also has his eyes,
he looks, he is a tree which looks,
he is a tree,
he looks,
he has his flesh,
because he was a man,
and it is so that he stands. . . .
he is a lion,
he has hands,
he talks. . . .

COMMENTARY

"Metaphor," wrote Aristotle, "is the application of the name of a thing to something else, working either (a) from genus to species, or (b) from species to genus, or (c) from species to species, or (d) by proportion."[24] During the millennia since that definition was first written, metaphor has been broadened somewhat: "Metaphorical thought is normal and ubiquitous in our mental life, both conscious and unconscious. The same mechanisms of metaphorical thought used throughout poetry are present in our most common concepts."[25] Zoltán Kövecses observes, "In the cognitive linguistic view, metaphor is defined as understanding one conceptual domain in terms of another conceptual domain."[26] Michael Spitzer writes, "A rhythmic pattern allows the mind to hold distant points of time together, to survey a temporal event as if it were an object or a concept."[27]

"The maiden" is the poet in the San poem. She encounters three men: under her gaze, the men are transformed into trees, fastening them to the earth. Each is still a man, but he is in the process of becoming a tree. "Man is a tree" is the metaphor, but what we experience in this poem is the transformation from the one to the other, the man remaining a man even as he becomes a tree. Metaphor has to do with the process, the act of becoming. It thus involves more than the two stark sides, involving the transformation itself. The rhythmical patterning in the poem expresses this act of becoming. And always, both sides of the metaphor are joined: the metaphorical process links the two inexorably.

The storyteller is also the San artist who, in an ancient rock painting, depicted a youth's quest for birds by means of a dramatic pattern: replicating the birds and in the process revealing the quest. This is also what happens in the spoken tale.

The San oral storyteller creates a metaphor in the presence of the audience. As the man becomes a tree, the audience can experience the transformation as the image shifts from man to tree and back again; in the process, a metaphor, a dancing metaphor, is born. A man becomes a bird, a man becomes a cloud, a man becomes a tree: the San oral poet attempts through words, images, and patterning to reveal a metaphor in the process of becoming. In that rhythmical verbal dancing, the audience is woven into the transformation just as the poet and the transforming man are. This is the mythic center, the place where the various components of metaphor come to a boil, the place of the dancing metaphor. It is the trope laboratory.[28] The audience is necessarily involved in the metaphorical process; its anticipation and prediction during that process is integral to the success of metaphor.

Metaphor becomes process: the audience is emotionally locked into the evolvement of the metaphor. In stories, neither of the two sides of the metaphor is reality. But one side is masquerading as the real part of the metaphorical equation. The other side is typically fantasy, mythic, often clearly *un*real. The storyteller manages the movement from the one to the other, erecting a temporary artifice: the storyteller is always a trickster, bringing the audience to a brief shimmering sense of reality that is all smoke and mirrors. Within that smoke and mirrors, the storyteller reveals a defense against external bombardment, a defense woven of the emotions of the members of the audience. A world is created and a domain established[29] that is impenetrable by alien forces, composed as it is of images and image-linkages known only to those initiates who remember and reconstitute them.

WALTER BENSON RUBUSANA

Walter Benson Rubusana was born February 21, 1858, at Mnandi, in the Somerset East district of Cape Colony. His father was Rubusana kaMbonjana, a councilor of the paramount chief, Sandile kaNgqika. Walter Rubusana was influenced by the Christian missionaries; he was educated at Lovedale College, the Free Church of Scotland mission school. He received the Cape Teachers' Certificate with distinction in 1878. In 1880, he was a teacher and an assistant pastor at the Peelton mission station. In 1883, he married Deena Nzanzana, and he later became the father of a son and five daughters. In 1884, he was transferred to East London, where he remained for the rest of his life. He was given an honorary Ph.D. from McKinley University in Chicago. He was an executive committee member of the South African Native National Congress and in 1909 was elected president of the South African Native Convention. When South Africa became the Union of South Africa in 1910, Rubusana was among those to protest before the king of England. He was the first black member of the Cape Provincial Council, representing the constituency of Thembuland. He was a pastor at the Congregational church in Newsam's Town, East London, in 1888. In 1892, when Africans were forcibly removed from this area, he founded the East London branch of the Native Vigilance Association. He helped to establish the newspaper *Izwi Labantu (The Voice of the People)* in East London. His collection of Xhosa poetry and stories, *Zemk' Inkomo Magwalandini (Away Go the Cattle, You Cowards!* or *There Goes Your Heritage, You Cowards!)*, was published in 1911. Rubusana died April 19, 1936, at the age of seventy-eight. He was buried in East London.

1

METAPHOR

Inevitable Encounters, Tools for Analysis

*W*hen I was witnessing performances of oral stories in southern Africa, I slowly became aware of how meaning is generated. Storytellers and their audiences acquainted me with two essential aspects of analysis: a complex form of metaphor and a basic transformational movement. These, I learned, were the basic tools that lead to understanding.

METAPHOR

Of the tools for understanding how stories work, none is more important than metaphor. A Ndebele story reveals the metaphorical process: two men, one from the west and one from the east, are bound to move from the one to the other. This is the metaphorical state of human existence— humans always moving to their other side, their lives composed of this process of movement, a move to completion. Metaphor is more than a connection of two unlike images: it is the process of connection to two images that, while apparently unlike, are in fact precisely the same. Metaphor is that mysterious inevitable movement.

A Ndebele Story
"STRANGE ENCOUNTERS"

By Agnes Ncube

Agnes Ncube creates a story about two friends whose closeness results in "Strange Encounters." One goes to the west and settles. He makes a difficult journey to visit his friend, then goes back to his home in the west. When he decides once again to return to the east, with the help of two men he cuts brush and fights ogres along the way. Then the other man sets out to visit his friend in the west. The two meet during their journeys. Strangely, they have identical thoughts of following ashes on the path. They meet in the mythic center . . . out there, far from their homes, in a land of heavy brush and ogres, ashes point the way.

Two men had been friends for a long time. Then one day one of the men set out to hunt, going toward the west. While on the hunt, he came to a place that had a lot of game. So he settled there, and he built a homestead for himself.

After a time, he thought, "I left my friend behind back there. I'd like to go back to see him, but how can I leave my homestead here?"

This friend of his was thinking the same thing: "How will I ever see my friend again? Which way should I go to see him?" While he was thinking about this, it began to rain hard. He considered setting out, but he thought, "I'll have trouble crossing overflowing rivers along the way."

Then, one day, this man who had set out from where they had originally lived, the one who had built a homestead for himself, became the first to make the journey. While he was traveling, he said, "When a person sets out on a journey like this, he should go toward the east, where he came from." So he went straight in that easterly direction. He traveled on, persisting in his journeying, not knowing what to expect.

Then, suddenly, he was there with his friend, who was very surprised at their meeting after so many days and years.

"Where have you come from?"

They greeted each other, rejoiced with each other. All was well, and this one told him that he had found a beautiful site and had built a homestead.

After a time, the man's sojourn came to an end. He had to return to his homestead. So he set out—going west, sleeping along the way, stopping as he went along. At length, he arrived at his home.

The *inganu* (2S-2349) was performed by Agnes Ncube, a Ndebele woman, about thirty-five years old, on Tuesday, November 14, 1972, in her home at Lukatsi, Matopo/Gulati, at about 9:30 am, before an audience of one woman, one man, and three children, all Ndebele.

After a time, he began to consider again whether he should return to his old home in the future. But he knew now that where he wanted to go, that place in the east, was a long distance. "I might come across wild animals and ogres." Then he thought, "On the other hand, if I don't get up and go back there, what will happen?"

So the man looked back and prepared to set out, knowing that to the east of his homestead was much fearsome, grassy land. He decided that he must have two men to accompany him. The men agreed. He said, "Let's take axes, men, and as we go we'll cut the bushes. We'll try to go precisely in an easterly direction. That's the only way to get to where my friend is." So they cut the bushes, and moved on and on.[1]

In the meantime, the other man felt saddened that his friend had taken such a long trip and had traversed long roads to get there, that he had spent such a long time on the road. "I will begin a long, arduous journey toward the west. It might be that I shall find my friend who comes from the west, I may find him striving with all his strength to reach my home, the home of his friend."

At the same time, the one who came from the east was striving with all his strength, seeking the help of other people. They chopped down the bushes to open the way. Having cleared a long path, they could see that the homestead toward which they were moving was getting closer. So they cut down more bushes.

As the one who came from the west was asleep one day, the one who came from the east said, "I can see in front of me what appears to be my old homestead drawing closer and closer. I desire therefore that I should enter secretly, so that I may see whether what I see in front of me is actually my home."

He pushed ahead with his plan, terribly afraid, thinking of wild animals and ogres, knowing that they ate people up completely. As he continued on his journey, as he traveled on, he began to see ashes appearing on his path. It was toward evening. He pushed ahead, however, following the ashes, even though he had thoughts sometimes about ogres. He pressed on.

When he arrived at the place where the ashes came from, he found that friend of his, also traveling. He was very happy, and he greeted him. They asked each other questions.

This man said, "Thoughts came to my mind as I slept. I decided to continue cutting down the bushes, going toward the east. It was as if I had a peculiar sense of where you might be. The first time I went in the direction of the west, and traversed long slopes and ridges. When I returned, I journeyed over quite a few slopes, cutting down as I went, opening up a path."

The other said, "I have been involved in a similar undertaking. What is it that has caused identical thoughts to come to us?"

They were taken aback.

So it was that they had cut down the bushes until they met, having opened up a way that was short, beginning with the idea that they should visit the home of the man who lived in the west. When they arrived there, an ox and a goat were slaughtered. And there was a huge celebration.

And there was festivity in the homestead of the friend who had remained behind. There was a great slaughtering and wonderful merrymaking. There was feasting. Everything was done, there was rejoicing because they had received thoughts that were identical, thoughts that had had a happy issue. It was wonderful.

COMMENTARY

Stories are regularly composed of two characters who, taken together, reveal the two sides of one individual. Typically, one of those characters is mythic. In this case, the two characters seem to be real-life figures, but they meet in the mythic arena between their two homes. For this storyteller, the strangeness of the encounter is sufficient: "What is it that has caused identical thoughts to come to us?" In the end, "there was rejoicing because they had received thoughts that were identical, thoughts that had had a happy issue."

Metaphor occurs as the two characters merge into union.

TRANSFORMATION

Stories deal with transformation. The theme of transformation weaves through this book; the oral stories and poems of the San and Nguni peoples of southern Africa are essentially constructed around transformation patterns. This constant theme of transformation reveals the way the people of the region survived the onslaught of colonialism. Because we have been dealing with the uncoiling python, consider three stories about snakes . . .

A Zulu Story

MAMBAKAMAQULA

By Kholekile

Two sisters, a cripple, and Mambakamaqula are the crucial characters in the story, with the cripple testing and instructing the girls, one of whom succeeds, while the other fails. The success of the elder sister is revealed by her doppelgänger, the snake-man. The other sister is cast aside. The two sisters and Mambakamaqula are the same being: the two sisters, the two sides of the same character; Mambakamaqula, the fantasy shadow whose move from animal to human mirrors the princess's move from girl to woman. The mystical aspects of the storytelling performance involve an inner movement that is energized by emotions at the same time that it organizes emotions, and so moves metaphor from vehicle to tenor.[2] The uncoiling snake is the storyteller's artistic device to reveal a transformation at the same time that metaphorical connections between humans and the animated world around them are being made.

It happened that a king of his people begot female children. They grew up until they were older girls.

They heard that there was a king, Mambakamaqula. The elder one, the crown princess, left. She went to be married to Mambakamaqula.

She went out and arrived there. At the river of that place, she found a cripple fetching water and carrying it on her hips.

The cripple said, "Where are you going, mother? Come here, and you shall put this burden upon me." She asked, "Where are you going?"

Kholekile, "Umambakamaqula, The Bewitched King," collected by O. Stavem, *Folk-Lore Journal* 1, no. 5 (September 1879): 102–9. Mambakamaqula means "Mamba of the Pools." The journal editors note, "The translation of the title *Umambakamaqula* is, Mr. Stavem tells us, 'The Umamba (a kind of snake) of Maqula'" (100). In a letter, dated Umvoti, September 18, 1879, the following comment was made by Stavem: "The name of the native man, who related to me most of the tales . . . is Ukholekile, and he is one of the most clever Zulus. He had been a Zulu diviner previous to my acquaintance with him, but he learned to understand the folly of the 'smelling' and he gave up that practice."

The princess answered, "I am going to be married to Mambakamaqula."

She said, "Yo! Sit down and let me tell you." And she proceeded, "He is a snake, child of man." She went on, "Don't be frightened, don't be seized by fear. If you are, he will kill you. When you have come to the kraal, take out some millet, and crush and grind it. He has already heard of you, because he is herding, it is he who is herding. You shall go and pour milk from the large pots, and put some at both sides of the kraal and some in the cattle path. Then he will come, you will hear him by the whistling. When the cattle are returning, he will commence with the sour milk on the path. The cattle will be entering the kraal." The cripple said to her, "You shall go into the house and sit down. He will come through from above, but don't be afraid, or he might hurt you and kill you, because he is going to wind about you."

She came to the kraal, and did what the cripple had told her. Mambakamaqula ate, and came to the kraal. He crawled along one side of the kraal. Then he bent over the house, discovered the bride, and pierced the top of the house, wound around her body, and embraced her again and again; he put his head just at her heart, the woman being perfectly quiet all the while.

He unloosened himself from her body and went to creep alone, and he lay by himself. Then the snake went out, and he slaughtered cattle for his wife.

He summoned his people, as he was going to have a dance. Then the woman danced her bridal dance.

The bridal dance was over.

Then he buffed clothing for her at the river, making her begin by putting on the skin of a goat. Then he buffed her petticoat, the hide of a cow, and trimmed it with brass and the skin of the goat.

Then she started, saying, "Now I shall go home."

When she arrived at home, the people, as they did not know to whom she had gone to be married, began praising the garments that she had on.

When their younger girl saw the splendor of her sister, she ran away to get married, without asking to what kind of a man her sister had been married.

She came to the river of that place and met with that cripple.

The cripple said, "Come here, and put my burden upon me."

She refused, saying, "You are carrying on your hips, and you think that your burden should be put upon you by me?"

The cripple said, "Go on, my mother, I was only about to tell you something."

She went on, came to the kraal, and found that the snake had gone out to herd.

He returned, he heard of her when he was with the cattle in the field. As he was coming in the afternoon, he found her sitting in the house. At the moment she heard him piercing the house, she started and ran away from the kraal.

People belonging to the kraal said, "Why do you run away from your husband?"

He went out and chased her. And although he reached her body, he did not bite her.

She ran until she arrived at her own home, while the snake followed her all along.

When she arrived, her sister asked her, "Where do you come from?"

She answered, "I come from my wedding. The man I was going to be married to is a snake."

The elder sister said, "Indeed! Do you come from playing with my husband?"

The snake had now come near the kraal, and he was crawling at the river. Then the younger sister went out. She was going to fetch water from the river, and she discovered the snake.

He said, "Why did you jump and jump and stop at once? Did you happen to see the situation with your sister?"

She returned to the kraal, and when she reached it she said, "There is something great at the river."

Her sister said, "Oh! The king who is at the river is my husband." And so she told her father that he should be brought to the kraal.

Then cattle were driven to be killed at the river. The cattle came down and were slaughtered. At the kraal, food was cooked.

Mambakamaqula went up to the kraal.

His wife said that the things should be taken out of the house, since he was not a man, but a snake. (He had been a man, but he became a snake. I think his own relatives were using witchcraft.)

He was brought into the house, and then he was crawling alone at one side of the house. Now all the people of the kraal went inside, and they sat down in one part of it. Food was brought inside, and he ate. They were sitting there until it became dark.

His wife said that he was asking them to bring wood for her, that she might make a fire for her husband. A big fire was made in the house, and the people walked out. He was left lying alone in the house.

His wife shut the door, having gone outside. She drew branches from the fence of the kraal, and she gathered grass and piled up heaps of such things at the house. Then she filled even the holes of the house, and she put fire to the material, and it burned.

Then even the house burned. How it burned! it burned!

When it was quite consumed by the fire, the bones remained, and she said, "Leave them to cool."

When everything had cooled, she took her medicinal herbs, and she bruised them over and over again. She caused skins of game to be brought, and gave them to her brothers, saying that they should cut a back dress and a front dress for a man. She gathered the bones carefully, and she dug a deep hole outside the kraal. She poured down the medicinal herbs, and made a fire in the hole. A fire blazed and was burning. She put the bones into the hole, placing many medicinal herbs on top of them, and then she filled the hole with soil. And she remained there.

In the afternoon, the ground where she had buried the bones burst. She saw him coming out, first appearing with his face, then with his chest, and so the whole body came out.

Then the woman asked, "*Hawu!* Where are you coming from?"

He said, "*Awu.* Do I know?"

She gave him the dress, and said, "Put it on."

She helped him to wash, and made him limber by means of fat.

Then she returned, and they went into the kraal. Cattle were now slaughtered inside. He was presented with them by the father of the girl.

Then she said, "Go, leave for your village, as you are now a man."

But he refused, saying, "We shall both leave together." Then they left.

And he said, "Now it is you who shall give birth to my successor."

The father and the girl went to his daughter. And then all his people went as well, when much cattle had been buried. At last, places were cleared for the kraals of her father.

A Zulu Story

MAMBA

By Lydia umkaSethemba

The emergence of Mamba from the snakeskin is equivalent to the emergence from the belly of a swallowing monster. And the young woman becomes identified with Mamba, so that his transformation shadows her own: in the end, they are the same. The mother of Mamba, complicit in the disguising, is the frame of this transformation. The negative shadows are the jealous co-wife and her son, Nsimba, reproducing in negative form the queen mother and her son, Mamba. And a young woman (like the co-wife and Nsimba not up to the stature of the other woman) becomes Nsimba's wife. The story therefore occurs on two levels, each a counterpart of the other—one being positive, the other negative. The negative aspect of the jealous co-wife is revealed in the initial pattern, when she kills the three children of the queen mother. The rivalry between the mothers provides the context for the rivalry between Mamba and Nsimba. Mamba and the woman he will marry both have an ordeal: Mamba living his life in pain as a snake, the woman in a patterned way removing the skin from the glistening body of the young man.[3]

There was a certain king who married many wives. When his wives were very many, he married two women, the daughters of another king. One of these he made the queen; the other was jealous because she also wished to be the queen. When the dowry was provided, both danced the marriage dance.

It happened in the process of time that all the king's wives were pregnant. They gave birth to their children, but the queen was long in giving birth.

When they heard that she had given birth, her sister went to her house. On her arrival, she said, "Bring me the child, that I may see it."

They gave her the child. She took it and looked at it. But while it was in her arms, it died.

Lydia umkaSethemba, "Mamba," in Henry Callaway, *Nursery Tales, Traditions, and Histories of the Zulus* (Springvale, Natal: John A. Blair, 1868), 321–31.

All the people said, "How did you handle the child?"

She said, "No. As soon as I took it, it died."

All the people wondered.

Again, they had children. And the queen's sister took the second child also, and it too died.

Three children at length died in this way.

And all the people said, "They were killed by the queen's sister."

Again, they were pregnant. The mother of the king said, "If your sister had not touched the children who are dead, they would not have died. But she kills them because you place them in her hands."

Again, she gave birth to a child. But she told no man that she was in labor. In the morning, all the people heard that she had a child. They went to see it. When they came, they said, "Just let us see the child."

She replied, "No. I have not given birth to a child this time, but to a mere animal."

They said, "What animal?"

She replied, "A mamba."

They said, "Just uncover it, so that we may see."

She showed it to them. They wondered when they saw a mamba.

Her sister gave birth to a boy. She rejoiced because she gave birth to a human being, and her sister had given birth to a snake.

Both grew up.

The king said, "As regards these children, the name of one is Mamba,[4] and of the other Nsimba."

But Mamba went on his belly.

When she gave birth to Mamba, and he grew up and did not die, the people said, "See then, this child did not die because he is a snake. The others were killed by the mother of Nsimba, because she wants Nsimba to be king."

But the father of Nsimba said, "If you see the medicine with which she killed the children, bring it to me, that I may take it in my hand. Then I'll touch her with my hands, and she too will die, for you say, 'She touches the children with her hand and they die.' And I too see that it is so, for the children who are human beings die, yet the snake is not dead. But for my part, I do not know if they were killed."

It happened when the two were grown up, women came to choose their husbands. When the people asked them whom they came to choose, they replied, "Nsimba."

Others came to choose Mamba. But when they saw that he was a snake, they fled, saying, "We thought he was a real man."

The father was greatly troubled, for he loved Mamba. But all the young women were afraid of him because he was a snake.

The father said, "You, Nsimba, shall not be married before Mamba, for he is your superior."

But Nsimba laughed because he saw that the women rejected Mamba, and he said, "Since the girls reject Mamba and love me, what is to be done?"

The mother of Mamba said, "You, Nsimba, your father is merely laughing. Was there ever anyone who was prevented from marrying because it was said he rivals one who is deformed?"

It happened later that two young women came from another country to choose a husband; one was the companion of the other.

They asked one of them who she had come to choose.

She replied, "Nsimba."

They placed them in a house.

The father agreed that Nsimba might marry.

Cattle were killed, and many people assembled, because the king's child was an elected bridegroom.

In the evening, many young men came in to get the young women to point out those they liked best. When the young men had come in, Mamba also came. And the young women fled, screaming, to the upper end of the house.

The king said, "Tell them not to run away, for that is my child."

The people who were in the house said, "Sit down, do not run away, for this is the king's child."

He took his mat and sat on it.

The young women said, "But how did he become a snake?"

They said, "His mother lost her children by death, and at last he was born."

They greatly wondered.

The young women were made to point out their favorites among the young men.

The sister of the bride pointed to Mamba.

Nsimba did not like it that his sister-in-law pointed to Mamba, wishing her to point to himself.

They asked her again, "Who do you point out as your favorite?"

The young woman replied, "Mamba."

But the young men said, "You mean Nsimba."

The young woman said, "No, Mamba."

The young men said, "You mean Nsimba."

The young woman replied, "No, Mamba."

Nsimba said, "No, just leave her alone, for although she has chosen Mamba, she will soon reject him because he is a snake." Nsimba said, "What are your names?"

The young women said, "She who has come to marry is Nhlamvu-yobuthlalu.[5] And her sister's name is Nhlamvu-yetusi."[6]

But Nsimba did not love Nhlamvu-yobuthlalu very much, he loved Nhlamvu-yetusi.

When the young women had finished pointing out their favorites, Nsimba went to his house, and Mamba went to his.

The young men said, "Let us take the bride to Nsimba's house."

Nhlamvu-yobuthlalu went.

They told Nhlamvu-yetusi to go to the house of Mamba.

She went and entered the house and sat down.

She saw Mamba resting on his mat, and Mamba's sister was also sitting there in Mamba's house.

Mamba's sister said, "Since the women pointed out their favorites, and you pointed out a snake as yours, do you agree to be his wife?"

She laughed and said, "Does he devour men?"

Mamba said, "Is there anyone who chooses a snake?"

Nhlamvu-yetusi said, "As you do not devour men, what is there in me that you should devour me?"

Mamba's sister went out.

Mamba said, "Arise, and close the doorway."

Nhlamvu-yetusi said, "Why do you not close it?"

He replied, "I have no hands with which to close it."

Nhlamvu-yetusi said, "Who closes it every day?"

He replied, "The lad who sleeps with me closes it."

Nhlamvu-yetusi said, "And where has he gone?"

Mamba answered, "He has gone out on your account, my love."

Nhlamvu-yetusi arose and closed the doorway.

Mamba said, "Spread the mat for me."

Nhlamvu-yetusi said, "Who spreads it for you each day?"

Mamba replied, "My lad."

Nhlamvu-yetusi arose and spread the mat for him.

He said, "Take the pot of fat and anoint me. Then I shall sleep well."

Nhlamvu-yetusi said, "I am afraid to touch a snake."

Mamba laughed.

They went to sleep.

They awoke in the morning, and the people wondered. They said, "We have never met a child possessed of such courage as to sleep in a house with a snake."

In the morning, Mamba's mother took some very nice food and cooked it and took it to the young woman, talking with herself and saying, "If I too had given birth to a real human being, he would have married this child of the people."

In the evening, they again went to retire, to rest. The sister of Mamba again went into the house. They sat with her. Again, she went out.

Mamba said, "Go and close the doorway."

Nhlamvu-yetusi arose and closed it.

Mamba said, "Yesterday you refused to anoint me. Do you not see that I move with pain, because I go on my belly? It is pleasant to lie down after having been anointed. Then my body is soft, and I sleep well. Just help me, and anoint me today. I devour no one. My lad anoints me, and I do not devour him."

Nhlamvu-yetusi took the pot of fat and a stick.

Mamba said, "No, my fat is not taken out with a stick, it is just shaken out into the hand, it is soft."

Nhlamvu-yetusi said, "Anoint yourself. I do not like to anoint you."

Mamba said, "No. I devour no man. Just anoint me."

Nhlamvu-yetusi took the fat and poured it into her hand, and anointed Mamba. But when she anointed him and felt the body of the snake very cold, she was afraid.

But Mamba said, "No, just anoint me, I devour no one."

When she had anointed him, she left him.

Mamba waited a little while, then said to Nhlamvu-yetusi, "Lay hold of me here very tight, and stretch me, for my body is contracted."

But Nhlamvu-yetusi said, "I am afraid."

Mamba said, "No. I shall do you no harm. I devour no one. Lay hold of the pillar, and look at the upper end of the house.

Do not look at me. And drag with all your might, for my mode of going hurts me. Therefore, I like, when I am lying down, that someone should stretch me."

She laid hold of the pillar, and dragged with all her might. She felt the skin come into her hand. She threw it down quickly, and started, thinking it was the snake.

When she turned her eyes and looked, she saw that Mamba was very beautiful, and his body was glistening.

She rejoiced exceedingly and said, "What was the matter with you?"

Mamba said, "My mother had for some time lost all her children by death, and the people said that the children of our house were killed by my mother's sister. Before giving birth to me, my mother went to her people and told her brother to catch a small mamba and to take its skin. And when I was born, I was put into the skin. But none of our people knew that I was a human being. They thought I was truly a snake, for my mother did not tell them that I was a man. And don't you tell anyone."

Nhlamvu-yetusi said, "On other days do you take off this skin?"

Mamba said, "Yes, my lad anoints me with fat and takes it off."

They retired to rest.

In the morning, Nhlamvu-yobuthlalu said, "I now wish to go home."

They picked out twenty head of cattle.

Mamba said, "I too, father, wish to take twenty, that I might go and choose this young woman at her father's."

The father assented, and he went with many cattle and young men to make the marriage settlement.

So they set out.

When they were leaving home, Mamba told them to take his pot of fat. Nhlamvu-yetusi carried it. When they were on the high land, Mamba went slowly after the rest, and told Nhlamvu-yetusi also to go slowly.

All the people went on in front, but they two went in the rear.

Mamba said, "Let us sit down. Anoint me with fat and take off the skin, for I am troubled. The grass hurts me when I go on my belly."

They sat, and she anointed him with fat, and dragged him. The skin came off.

Mamba rose and walked. They went behind the others. When they were near the people, Mamba put on the skin again.

They reached the young woman's home and went in. But all the people of the place fled, being afraid of the snake.

They said, "There is the wedding party of Nhlamvu-yobuthlalu coming with a snake."

The young women said, "Do not say that. That is the bridegroom of Nhlamvu-yetusi."

The people wondered and said, "How is it that she is not afraid, since it is a snake?"

They had many cattle killed for them. When the meat was eaten, the bridegrooms' party returned to their people. After a time, they sent a man to wait for the marriage party.[7] The marriage party was summoned. Much beer was made, and they were told to go and bring the marriage company. They came with it.

In the morning, many people assembled, but some laughed because Mamba did not know how to dance. They said, "Since he is a snake, how will he dance?"

The line of wedding guests entered, and the brides and the young women and men of their people danced.

When the marriage company had stopped dancing, the bridegrooms' party went to adorn themselves.

Mamba went to his house, and his lad anointed him with fat and took off the skin.

He said, "Go and call my mother, that she may bring my things."

His mother came with his things.

He adorned himself, and said to the lad, "See if Nsimba has already left his house."

The lad replied, "Yes, he has already left it."

Mamba took a great skin, put it on, and went on, going on his belly.

When the people saw him, they all said, "Now he is very great, because he has been anointed with fat."

He went to the cattle-pen and sat down.

When all the bridegrooms' men stood up, Mamba wriggled himself, and his lad came and laid hold of his head, and took off the skin.

And all the people were unable to look on him because of his glistening appearance.

Nsimba went to his house, afraid because he saw that Mamba was a human being. He was very angry.

All the people wondered when they saw that he was now a man. They laid hold of him, saying, "What has been done to you all this time?"

His father refused to allow them to dance on that day. He said, "You shall dance tomorrow, for I wish to look at him today."

Then the mother rejoiced because her child had taken a wife. The people returned to the house and sat down. In the morning, they danced.

But Nsimba was much troubled, because he saw that Mamba was a human being.

They all remained, rejoicing. The father rejoiced exceedingly when he saw that Mamba was a human being.

Mamba built his own village, and lived there with many people who wished to live with him.

And when he had sewn on the head-ring,[8] he married many wives, and lived happily and prosperously with them.

A Zulu Story

TALE OF AN IMAMBA

By Umpengula Mbanda

Here, the relationship between the uncoiling snake and the beliefs of the people is at the surface of the story. The characteristic subtleties of the storyteller give way to a more openly didactic view of the uncoiling snake.

The account of the *imamba*[9] which is the *ithongo*[10] of our people among the amaPepete. The chief of that nation was Maziya. That chief became an *imamba* when he went out of his human body. He was killed by the abaMbo. When the people were scattered from the country of the amaZulu, they wished to come here to the English. But he had been dead for some time. It was his son, Myeka, who remained in his father's place, and his brother too, Mgwaduyana, died, and left two sons, one named Madikane, and the younger one, Bafako.

But at the time of the scattering of the people the lad Bafako had a bad sore on his thigh; they were then living in

---

Umpengula Mbanda told his "Tale of an Imamba" in 1868; the story was published in Henry Callaway, The Religious System of the Amazulu (Springvale, Natal: J. A. Blair, 1870), 204–11.

the open country and had quitted their homes, when he was ill with that sore; and it had been already treated with medicines; but the medicines would not adhere, and the sore increased continually. At length it happened one day, as they were living in the temporary booths erected in their flight, an *imamba* entered; the child was asleep; the people started up and were frightened when they saw the beast enter the house, but it neither took any notice of them nor was in the least afraid, but pressed onward to go up to the child.

The mother now cried out, "The snake will kill the child."

But it was already known that it was the chief. But they had not any courage on that account, for he had now a different body, to which they were not accustomed—the body of a beast. It reached the child and placed its mouth on the sore, and remained still a little while, and then departed and went out of the house.

After that they went to the diviners that they might hear what was the meaning of so great an omen. But the doctors said, "It is your chief. He comes to heal the child of his son."

So the people waited in patience; and the sore contracted, and at length healed.

And it used constantly to happen, when they were traveling towards this country, when they had set out, the *imamba* too was seen where they crossed at the fords of rivers; it used to cross lower down constantly, until they reached Table Mountain, where it still was when his son, Myeka, went down to the Inanda, flying from the Dutch.

But the chief refused, saying, "I will not go to a country by the sea. I shall stay here, and eat grasshoppers." And so indeed it was.

At length, Myeka was very ill, and it was said to him in a dream, "Why did you forsake your father? He is calling the people; let them return."

But they would not agree, fearing their feud with the Dutch, for Myeka had stolen their cattle.

So it was until our eldest uncle went up to our father, who was younger than our own father. Our father departed, leaving our eldest uncle, and returned to the old site of our chief's great kraal. But he was on the other side of the stream; he did not build on the old site, but dug there only. Then, on a certain day, our father whilst asleep dreamt the chief was talking with him. And as at that time it was winter, and the water was very cold, he said to him, "Ngqokqwane, it would be well for you to make a bridge for me, that I may cross on it and come home; for I am cold, and the water makes me colder still."

And truly I heard my father calling me and saying, "My child, come, let us go yonder to the ford which leads to the old site of Umzimvubu, the village of the Nembala chief, and make there a bridge for the chief to cross over." And truly we cut down many mimosa trees and elephant trees, and laid them across the stream, and poured earth on the top of them.

A few days after, for I was then the herd-boy who closed the cattle pen, I put off for a long time going to close it, until it was dark; and did not set out to do it until the usual time had passed. As I was going, I saw yonder something glistening on the poles with which the gateway was closed. But I did not trouble myself as to what it was. I went in a hurry, wishing to close the gateway at once, for I left them about to eat *amasi*[11] in the house. Therefore I wished to close the gateway at once. But I took the first pole; it was heavy, I could not raise it; and it was the same with another. The poles were too heavy for me. I began to examine intently into the cause why the poles were too heavy, since they were old poles. I looked intently, and forsooth it was a great snake which was lying on them. I shouted.

They came out of the house, and asked what it was.

I replied, "Here is a snake."

My father came immediately, and looked intently, and said, "Do not close the gateway."

I enquired, "What is it?"

He said, "It is the chief."

I said, "What, this snake?"

He said, "Yes."

We returned to the house.

In the morning he told us, "The chief asks why you were afraid of him. Did he not tell us to make a bridge, that he might cross?"

Then my father gave praises, praising the snake with the laud-giving names which the chief had whilst living; praising in concert with our grandmother, the mother of my father. For such is the custom with us. The *ithongo* dwells with the great man, and speaks with him; and when worship is performed at a house, it is the chief man, and the oldest old woman, who knew those who are dead, who worship.

Under these circumstances, one from the chief's kraal at length came up to where we were living, and we lived together till Ngoza came and turned us out by the direction of Somseu. We were scattered, and went to other places. That, then, is a thing which I saw.

After that Myeka, the chief, came up.

The people said, "Let us go to the old dwelling to call the chief, the present chief's father; for the village is perishing because the chief did not consent to go down to the coast."

So then they brought a dun-colored cow in the afternoon; and all the chief men, both old and young, were assembled. They sang a song of their father which used to be sung on great festivals, to arouse him to the recollection that his children were truly in trouble because he was not among them. This is the song which was sung:

> "Dig for the chief, and watch our gardens which are at
>   Isiwandiye.
> Those words are naught.
> Dig for the chief, and watch our gardens which are at
>   Isiwandiye.
> Those words are naught.
> Which are at Isiwandiye, I-i-i-zi—which are at Isiwandiye.
> Those words are naught."

A large circle was formed outside the old site. They danced. There were there also all the women with beer, and the damsels. At length, they separated when the sun was going down and it was raining, and they went home to our village, for the abundance of beer was fearful. So they consumed beer and meat, and sang hut-songs.

In the midst of these doings, one of the young men, named Mathlathi, went out. On his return, he said, "The chief has come, even whilst we are singing. There he is, coiled up on the house."

A hole was made in the house, that he might look on at the singing.

They sang until it was near morning, rejoicing exceedingly because it was said, "The *idlozi*[12] of our people has now united with us; our village will stand."

Thus then it was.

That is the end of the tale.

COMMENTARY

Yatyap' ingweny' ukuthetha banaThwa.
The python did well to speak with the San.
Rubusana, "Mditshwa Diko," 348, line 10

In these three stories, the skin of the snake becomes the means and the symbol of transformation at the same time that the snake and the human undergoing change are seen as metaphorically the same. The storytellers thus reveal the oneness of a human and the world that human inhabits. A transformation therefore becomes a reassurance of and an emphasis on that tight relationship. This is not animism, nor is it evidence of the "noble savage": it is, rather, evidence of a human's universe, the stories' routine reinforcements and assurances of that unity. That unity cannot be broken, the stories assert, and so the storytellers provide the strength to their audiences that enables them to endure assaults on that unity from without.

The performer's line[13] brings two young people into a relationship with each other, with the relationship that each has with the other being dependent on the movement into a new identity.

At the core of these stories is transformation, the essential metaphorical movement. That movement runs a gamut in these stories, from realistic to mystical.

In the story by Kholekile, the transition has to do with the ritual movement from child to adult, with the two sisters representing the two sides of this equation. The fantasy level of this tale is the movement of Mambakamaqula from snake to human, a mythic transformation that mirrors the movement from one girl to another. The cripple, made a cripple to move her to the margins, is on the borders, between the girls and the dualistic snake, manipulating the girls.

In the version by Lydia umkaSethemba, the relationship between Mamba and Nsimba reveals the movement of the girl to womanhood. The transformation of Mamba from snake to human is a mirror of the girl's movement. The young woman, with fear initially, transforms Mamba into a man, the way prepared by the pattern of "the lad," and this activity is her ordeal as she moves into womanhood. In the background is a dualistic rivalry between mothers, a reflection of the rivalry between Mamba and Nsimba even as it mirrors the girl's transformation from one state to another.

METAPHOR AND TRANSFORMATION

The connection between the stories of Kholekile and Lydia umkaSethemba is somewhat complex but can readily be seen. However, if one needs a key, one need only turn to the Mbanda tale, in which one character becomes identified with another as, through the pulse of the tale, the storyteller metaphorizes one character by bringing that being into a relationship with another. The figure in the welter of words involves this metamorphosing, in-process paralleling of characters. That core relationship, the joining of two characters into one, is made possible by the addition of another aspect, a mythic aspect, of the human: a serpent, an old woman, an old man. This complex set of relationships is the result not of the linear movement of the story but of the rhythmical line. The story is told in the form established by that poetic line. The rhythm of the story has to do with the parallel revealed between patterns, the various expansions of parts of those patterns, and ultimately, the joining of the patterns that is made possible by the deftly drawing finger of the storyteller. The line grows out of the separate patterns, then joins them. The metaphorizing activity occurs as rhythmically, through patterns, one character becomes another. This is the poetic complexity of the tale. Through the regular dancelike movement of the story, the tale-teller unites characters, superimposing one over the other. This metaphorical activity is chiefly an emotional activity, the windowpane of José Ortega y Gasset.[14] From the literal, cause-and-effect movement of the story emerges the poet's line, which commences to link characters, establishing a relationship between them—frequently within a mythic context.

The storyteller is also a sculptor, controlling the emotions by masking and mirroring the real. As Samuel Taylor Coleridge put it, "everywhere / Echo or mirror seeking of itself."[15] Mask makers always have in mind the idea of what masking involves—the work of art and the human beneath the mask. Storytellers never tell stories in the absence of an audience: the story is a mask within and without, and the audience is the basic material that is being masked. A piece of sculpture, three-dimensional, contains within itself the imagined form: it is never an end but is always in progress, in the process of becoming. Story, mask, and three-dimensional sculpture: all are in the process of becoming.

The dramatic image is the uncoiling python—and the dangers of "rising late," for if one does so, one will not see the python uncoil. The uncoiling python becomes the poetic image of the slowly uncoiling resistance to what was happening in South Africa. And the snake's further significance becomes evident in tales in which the snake is a symbol of transformation—of the transition of young people from childhood to adulthood. Underlying this critical rite of passage, another transformation occurs: from the shackled to the free. The stories, as the young revolutionaries in Soweto complained, did not deal with that transformation in a confrontational way, but deal with it they did. In the end, the storytelling and poetic traditions were a part of the sustaining apparatus of the African people.

FROM A NOTEBOOK

June 9, 1975. How do these *intsomi* images trap, hold, lock significant cultural experiences, artists' (society's) feelings regarding these experiences? Feeling-experiences. *Gestures:* Are they *physical* only? Or do they also move beyond representation to thought and abstraction and symbol? The narrative images, repeated often and apparently very old: Why are they remembered? What do they really *mean* for the culture? Does that meaning change through the generations? Does alteration of *meaning* require alteration of *image*? Or does the ancient image continue to trap and hold similar human *feelings*, yet adapt them to current contemporary realities? And, therefore, the old question about the relationship between the *intsomi* image and reality. How are the gestures related to the verbal aspects of performance? Even those that are purely complementary? And how do abstract gestures differ from representational gestures in their relationship to the word? Why do these images continue to stir audiences? Why are they so universally remembered among the Xhosa over long periods of time, pretty much intact? What human feeling do they express? reflect? hold? Sound, structure, image, statement (Langer). Sensuous beauty. The body, its normal movement versus its movement in the *intsomi:* How do they differ? One is functional, the other virtual reality? an abstraction? Functional movement now consciously altered by an artist, the superfluous omitted, the symbolic included. Now a closed world, whereas functional movement occurs in an open world. Gesture now harnessed to a thought, not to a physical deed. Gesture now harnessed to an imaginary *story,* not to the bewildering chaos and open-endedness and uncertainty of real life.

The narrative images are very familiar, securely familiar, touchstones—artistic touchstones offering security, familiarity, the warmth of the familiar. Life in the world of the *intsomi* flows evenly and predictably along ancient cultural lines and molds. The narrative images capture and hold human feeling in these lines and molds, providing security and order to an insecure and potentially disordered existence.

The narratives accomplish this, but they also transmit data. They are not only a secure and well-lighted place; they also communicate information. They mold our feelings in our youth; they nourish those feelings as we move beyond youth. The narratives trap feeling and give it meaning in our youth; they continue to trap feeling and affirm that meaning as we grow beyond youth.

The stories deal with diffuse human feelings, uncertainties, fears, joys, hopes, dreads. They trap and hold these feelings: when this has been done, it becomes possible to manipulate these feelings and give them meaning, to manipulate them by bringing them into relationship with yet other feeling-locked images, and in that juxtaposition endow (imbue) them with meaning.

The familiar narrative images thus first indoctrinate (i.e., educate), then affirm—give meaning and shape to diffuse experience: shaping feelings, thereby giving them meaning. The images are the repositories of feeling. They call up feelings, purposely dealing with feelings of fear and dread, trapping those feelings, immersing us in images thereby, and then juxtaposing those feeling-packed images with other feeling-packed images. *Meaning* is the result. It is meaning achieved through images which molds our feelings. So it is that often nameless fears find form in the *zim*[16] or the *imbulu*.[17] These feelings are given form thereby, become understandable, controllable in a cultural sense, in a performance.

Feelings (particularly concerning such transformations as the great rites of passage) are thus stamped with cultural identity, meaning. The artist calls up images through her own feelings, and traps the feelings of the members of the audience in those images. The movement is from diffuse and nameless feeling to thought, idea, cultural ideal. The process is made possible by the image.

The move is to the abstract, to the symbolic, from the representational image to nonrepresentational thought. The material acted upon is the feelings of the members of the audience. The molding process is the activity of image-evocation and manipulation. The concrete image takes the diffuse feelings, the many *different* feeling experiences of the members of the audience, gives them form, and thereby ensures a common experience.

The *zim* "holds" a certain feeling, evokes a certain feeling, for the Xhosa audience, as does, for example, a hapless girl, an *imbulu,* an ox. Bring a hapless girl image (trapping a certain feeling) together with a *zim* image (also trapping a certain feeling), and the storyteller begins to channel feeling, to give feeling particularity, *form.*

FROM A NOTEBOOK

April 7, 1976. I write these notes near Mahlabatini. This trip to southern Africa consisted of two distinct activities: I worked in Nkanga, Gatyana, in the Transkei, mainly with Nongenile Masithathu Zenani and also with some of the neighboring storytellers in that area. A central purpose of this research trip was the work that I did with Masithathu Zenani. The second part of this research trip had to do with other parts of the Transkei, with the Ciskei, and with kwaZulu, where before, during, and after the work in Nkanga, I walked for miles, listening to stories and histories and private autobiographies, not taping or filming these. The purpose was to ensure that technological equipment was not interfering with the performances. But there was another reason, which flowed out of the apartheid history of South Africa. I wanted to hear stories, histories, poetry, and autobiography in circumstances in which people did not have to be concerned that a permanent record was being made of their words. And this was a frequently poignant, always revealing part of this research venture.

The work that I did with storytellers, in all of my research trips in southern Africa, has always been based on the conviction that these were collaborative efforts. Together, the storytellers, their audiences, and I were developing a record for posterity: these films and tapes would one day be placed in archives in a free South Africa, where future generations of scholars and others would have access to the thoughts and insights of storytellers, historians, and poets who were living through one of the most fearful historical experiences of the twentieth century.

SAN METAPHOR

"... and feel a story in the wind"

> ... one of the wonders of world literature, without
> which I would no longer like to live.
>
> *Elias Canetti, referring to Bleek and Lloyd's*
> Specimens of Bushman Folklore

The core of this study of metaphor has to do with nineteenth-century San oral traditions. However, these analyses must be placed within broader discussions of other southern African artistic materials, including the Xhosa, Zulu, Sotho, and English traditions.

This is what | | kábbo,[1] a San, said about storytelling: "I must first sit a little, cooling my arms, letting the fatigue go out of them. I just listen, watching for a story that I want to hear. I sit waiting for it, so that it may float into my ear."[2] Having been exiled from his home for some years, he savored the sensation: "I shall sit silent, listening with all my ears. I must wait, listening, behind me,[3] along the road; and I feel my name floating along the road. . . . I shall go and sit there, so that I may, listening, turn backwards with my ears to my feet's heels; and feel a story in the wind."[4]

To understand the complexities of San artistic thought, whether in myth, dance, or painting, one must appreciate the stark beauty of San metaphor.

Consider the mantis.[5]

| kággen is a San god, an ambiguous creature whose composition is complex: he is god, animal, and human. In San folklore,[6] Mantis is a culture hero and divine trickster, one of the oldest and most durable of the

characters of the oral tradition. In some of his stories, ||kábbo created mythic images of this deity, called |kággen by the San.[7] This deity creates, but he also has a destructive urge. He has godly knowledge, yet he is also capable of acts of mortal stupidity; he is sublime, yet he is also obscene. Mantis's involved make-up is suggested in several of the myths but nowhere more effectively than in one of the finest tales in a nineteenth-century collection of San stories and poems, in which ||kábbo tells the story of how Mantis took away the sheep of some ticks.[8] Part one of the myth establishes a theme of rejection or loss, while part two consists of a quest for wholeness. This is the loom for much of southern African oral tradition.

Mantis is involved in a foolish struggle, initiated by him, with ticks. The dispute establishes a necessary disjuncture in the mythical world that will lead to its dismantling and reconstruction in earthly terms. The ticks, who possess shelter, domestic animals, and clothing similar to those that characterized the San in the mid-nineteenth century when the myth was made, defeat Mantis but must then experience God's vengeance. What was the environment of the ticks in the world of myth is recast because of the divine wrath of the trickster/god in human terms: it is the origin of San civilization. God dreams, and his dream is fulfilled. It is an awesome dream, because it is a vision of genesis, of the first creation, fraught with the prophecy that orders all things. |kággen dreams "that all the ticks' homes arise and come. The sheep rise up, the sheep come and stand in front of his house, while the houses are at the sides of his houses. . . . [T]he karosses[9] are here, all the things are here, the knobkerries [clubs] with which those people beat him are here. Those people shall soon feel the cold. . . . Then they will miss the fire, early, for the fire will have gone with the houses, the pots will have entirely disappeared." The San world is coming into existence, with domesticated animals, clothing, utensils, and fire as symbols of civilization. But |kággen goes further and orders living beings as well: "[T]hose people [i.e., the ticks] will not cook, for their knives will have gone. . . . [T]hey will have to drink blood, because they no longer have a fire as they used to have. Real people will henceforth cook, while they walk entirely in the dark; they will have to stand biting things' bodies, they will have to drink things' blood and no longer eat cooked meat." The curse becomes an origin. When God's family of animals/humans/gods awaken, they find that what |kággen dreamed has become reality. "[L]ook at the sheep which are standing in the kraal which my grandfather the mantis has brought. They are here and the houses have come with them. Look at these pots which he has brought." |kággen then continues the process of first ordering.

In these pots here the [San] shall some day cook, because they shall have a fire. We who are here shall then also be as the ticks are. We shall eat different things, because we too shall lack fire. You, the ichneumon,[10] shall then go to dwell in the hills with your mother. She shall truly become a porcupine, she shall live in a hole, while Grandmother Dasse shall live in a mountain den, for her name is really "Dasse."[11] I shall have wings, I shall fly when I am green, I shall be a little green thing. You, the ichneumon, shall eat honey, because you will be living on the hill. Then you shall marry a she-ichneumon.

The creation is complete.

But it is then destroyed, swallowed by a swallowing monster, ||khwai-hemm, a fabulous mythical villain, fearful father of the porcupine. |kággen inexplicably and against the advice of the porcupine invites ||khwai-hemm to his home, and an awful pattern of destruction begins, as the monster swallows everything: plants, the things of the home, the domesticated animals, and finally the people—including God—themselves. Everything that |kággen has created goes into the monster's belly.

This second part of the story, a fantastic restatement of the things envisioned by |kággen in part one, ends with a second creation, as Young Mantis, |kággen's offspring, and Young |kwammań-a-⊙pwa, his grandchild, are taught to withstand the deadly heat of the fire-breathing ||khwai-hemm. This crucial pattern counters that of the destructiveness of the monster. When they are prepared to contain the great forces that |kággen has given them—the fire, symbol of civilization, but also, unchecked, symbol of returning chaos—re-creation can take place. Everything returns from the stomach of the swallowing monster, and the dream of God, culture hero and divine trickster, is fulfilled. As ambiguous god and man, |kággen bestrides the two worlds, leading early humans from the one to the other.[12]

Verbal superpositioning occurs in this tale. The story falls into two parts, the first having to do with |kággen's struggles with the ticks, the second with the San difficulties with ||khwai-hemm, the swallowing monster. There is a curious parallel between the two parts. It is, in mythic terms, a rite of passage for all humanity. God creates, but humans do not yet know how to make use of the forces that he has given them. This is shown by their destruction—|kággen as God and man symbolizes the relationship between gods and humans and also what happens to the flawed earth, as we see the ugly traits rather than the sublime manifest in humans. The forces that God has given humans, like God and the humans themselves, can be both creative and destructive. So the performer gives us Young Mantis and Young |kwammań-a-ꝏpwa, the new generation of humans. They are taught by the porcupine to withstand the great forces—represented here by fire in the untamed form of ||khwai-hemm. The humans bring about a second creation, man's re-creation of the original creation by God.

IN SAN SOCIETIES in southern Africa, images are carved into rocks, sculpted with human bodies, shaped by the words of the myth maker. The three art forms, though years apart in their practice among the San, nevertheless reveal significant relationships between the arts. Each—painting, dance, and tale—blends image and idea, the stuff of storytelling. San civilization has a venerable art tradition; its rock paintings and engravings, some of them over twenty-five thousand years old, reach deep into human history. A San artist blurred the gulf between the world of humans and that of animals: in a rock painting at Giant's Castle Game Reserve in the Natal Drakensberg, San hunters wear antelope head masks.[13] In another painting at the same site, two hunters wear antelope head masks; one of the hunters is carrying two small bucks. This painting is situated over paintings of hartebeest and a cloaked figure.[14] When J. M. Orpen asked a storyteller named 'Qing the meaning of paintings depicting men with rhebok heads, the San performer said, "They were men who had died and now lived in rivers, and were spoilt at the same time as the elands and by the dances of which you have seen paintings."[15] In rock art, the storytellers use superpositioning to achieve the same ends, with contemporary images of hunters, for example, painted over ancient images of the gods and fantasy creatures. In contemporary times, San rock painting and engraving have been discontinued, but there have been notable artistic achievements in dance along with a highly evolved myth and storytelling tradition—dances have been documented from the nineteenth century, and myths have been collected from both the nineteenth and twentieth centuries. In the dance, the dual imagery is especially graphic, because living people of the contemporary world don the masks, and so the present and the past are potently joined. During a dance accompanying a girl's initiation rite, for example, a man with a bird's beak on his head played a crucial role.[16] Said |háń‡kass'õ, a San myth maker of southern Africa, the divine trickster |kággen of the San people likewise masquerades to conceal his identity.[17]

Unexpected linkages between unlike images in oral tales and myths cause audiences to ponder the real world and their place in it. These images do not reproduce the real world. Rather, the oral and artistic experiences are meant to comment on the real world, as the artist plies images from the real world together with fantasy. The storyteller, whether raconteur, dancer, or painter, unites present and past with parallel imagery, a diversity of images connected in performance.

Fantasy imagery from the past becomes the masks worn in the dance, the masks worn by the strange figures in the rock paintings. The masks enable the forces of the past to move into and among the recognizable and realistic characters of the present. But the past is the means whereby the present is measured, and therefore the masking of the images of the past—giving those forces of the past the masks of gods and animals—becomes a means of summoning the mystical forces of the past that do not in themselves have form. Masking gives them form, and these forces, masked, thereby become recognizable gods, fantasy creatures, and the like. Those forces of the past are pure, and therefore they have none of the flaws of the present. These pure forces, in their fantasy and sometimes stark masks and forms, enable storytellers to make decisions about the present. The tale and the myth thereby come into contact. Myth consists of forces of the past given the form of the tale.

The various forms of the past, the masks, are brought into relationship with the present. The force of juxtaposition brings the pure forces into mask forms and joins them to realistic images, as in the dance and tale. From this comes metaphor, the linking of seeming unlike images, giving them a like force. Metaphor is thus born of masks, of the relationship between past and present, realistic and fantasy images, and humans and gods/ancestors.

THE DANCE OF FANTASY

"They told myths; and above all, they danced."[18] In dance, realistic images (images of the contemporary world) are immediately visible in the forms of the dancers: their mortal flesh engaged in pleasing movement. Fantasy occurs in various ways. The movement itself is fantastic: body movements are graceful, exaggerated, liquid. This is clearly not normal movement, routine behavior. Something has happened to the body: it is sublime in its grace, predictable at times and splendidly surprising at others, a grid developed that then admits of improvisation. In addition to the form of dance, fantasy in San dance occurs even more dramatically, in the form of mime and mask.

A San boy, seeing a herd of wildebeest, "got to his feet and gazed after them, unconsciously making a gesture with his hand representing the head and horns of a wildebeest. He moved his hand in time with their running, saying softly: 'Huh, huh, boo. Huh, huh, boo,' the sound of their breath and grunting as they ran."[19]

San hunters traditionally used bows and poisoned arrows with an effective range of about twenty-five yards.[20] They would stalk the herds, creeping up on them. They would shoot the arrow at the creature, then follow it as the poison took effect. When hunting particularly large animals (such as a hippopotamus, elephant, or rhinoceros), they would hunt with the bow and arrow, dig pitfalls, or construct harpoon traps—a poisoned blade attached to a large block of wood that would fall on the victim when its foot hit a line, the wood driving the blade into the flesh.[21] Sometimes they would disguise themselves as animals—wearing the head and hide of a hartebeest, the skin of a blesbok or zebra, the head and wings of a vulture, or ostrich feathers. As they approached their quarry, they would mimic its actions.[22]

While dancing, "the hunters regularly mimed animals: the courtship of the eland bull; the kudu; a gemsbok hunt; a hyena feeding off a carcass and keeping jackals at bay; vultures at the carcass of a zebra; ostriches. It seems as if the acute observation of animals, necessary to a hunter, had to find some expression in artistic form, whether it be painting, or dancing, or myth."[23] An observer remarked, "They appear to have had an almost passionate fondness for dressing up in masquerading fashion, in the guise of some animal or other, so that it was not only in hunting or war that they simulated wild animals by which they were surrounded, but even in their amusements, their games, and dances."[24] Fourie describes a San dance in which a hunt was depicted: a gemsbok bull, cow, and calf pursued by two men and their dogs. The hunters shot, and one of the gemsbok was wounded. The dance continued until all of the animals had been captured.[25]

A nineteenth-century observer wrote of "the fondness of the Bushmen for disguising themselves in masquerading dresses, representing various animals, birds, and imaginary monsters. . . . Beyond this, however, their powers of mimicry were wonderfully striking, and thus they were able not only to assume the appearance, but the action, manner, and cries of the animal they wished to personify, with extraordinary accuracy."[26] He discussed the "devices and disguises [that] were constantly employed by the old hunters to facilitate approach to the objects of their attack." Hunters and warriors wore heads and horns of animals and birds, and "they evidently prided themselves upon the correctness of the representation." The rock paintings would appear to the uninitiated, he went on, to be symbolic, depictions of supernatural deities "around which some ancient myth was embodied." Such disguises had their origins in early times, and the narration of the great hunting strategies and feats would be remembered in the oral tradition and so passed through the generations. As J. R. R. Tolkien wrote, "the animal form is only a mask upon a human face, a device of the satirist or the preacher."[27]

On certain occasions, the San held "a general masquerade, when each took the disguise or head-dress of some particular bird or animal, and upheld the character during the performance."[28] A simple pattern opens the tale: |kággen throws the honey of a wild bee out of a hole to the springbok child he is supposedly minding. But the child, taken away by an elephant, has been replaced with an elephant child who does not respond properly to the queries of |kággen. That is the pattern; it is broken when |kággen discovers that it is an elephant and not a springbok to whom he has been speaking, and he kills the beast. This is followed by a quest for the springbok, as |kággen, with the angry comments of the springbok's mother pursuing him, sets off after the elephant herd. The remainder of the narrative is a typical swallowing monster story. When the kidnapper-elephant sees the approaching |kággen, it swallows the springbok child. |kággen insists that he will go into the body of the elephant to bring the child out. Other elephants gather around and attempt to spear the intruder. But he enters the elephant through its navel, gets the springbok, and comes out through the trunk, thereby killing the swallower. The springbok has been reborn, with the help of a god. To emphasize his mystical nature, |kággen flies off with the child, taunting the pursuing elephants: "Can you equal me? I am the Mantis, from whom you tried to steal his child, whom you cannot rival; for he is an enchanter, from whom you tried to steal his child." This story, performed by Díä!kwăin, has to do with the child's movement from one state of being to another, in this case with the active intervention of God himself, which gives the ritual celestial sanction.

The loss of the springbok child and its movement away from its home to the fantastic never–never land of the out-there is the same as the struggle between |kággen and the ticks. The springbok's odyssey in "|kággen and the Elephants" is a puberty rite of passage in an individual's life.

Díä!kwăin created a powerful story, "A Young Man of the Ancient Race, Who Was Carried Off by a Lion, When Asleep in the Field,"[29] in which a "young man of the early race," while hunting, becomes sleepy: "What had happened to him? he wondered, as he stretched himself out on the ground, near a water hole. Never before had he been thus overcome by sleep." It is strange and perhaps mystical. Then a lion comes along and, thinking he is dead, seizes him. The lion fixes the young man's head in the lower branches of a tree so that it can safely go off and get some water (the lion is not going to take a chance: the young man may still be alive). It keeps returning, making certain the man's head is secured. The lion "licked away the tears from the man's eyes." When the lion finally departs, the youth escapes. He flees to his village and tells his people that he has "just been 'lifted up'—while the sun had stood high, he had been 'lifted up.' More he would not say." The people hide him in hartebeest skins. But "[i]t is the way of a lion, with anything [he] has killed, not to leave it until he has eaten it." This leads to the second pattern in the tale: the lion as a persistent pursuer. In their love for the youth, the people attempt to put the lion off. They shoot at it with arrows, "but [it] would not die." One of the men says, "Can you not see that this lion must be a sorcerer? It will not die despite our shooting at it, for it insists upon having the young man that it carried off." The pattern continues: the people throw children for the lion to eat, "but the lion merely looked at them and left them alone." "Again and again the people shot at the lion but all to no avail. The lion remained unharmed and kept looking for the young man." They attempt to spear it, yet still it "continued its search for the young man, for the young man whose tears it had licked. It wanted that man, none other." They give the lion a girl: "It wanted the young man it had carried off, none other." In the end, the people must give the young man up to the lion. The youth's mother says, "Give my child to the lion. In no wise, however, must you allow the lion to eat him, in no wise must you allow the lion to continue walking about here. You must kill him and lay him upon my child. Let the lion die and lie upon my son." So it is. The lion seizes the youth and bites him to death. Then the people stab the lion: "Finally the lion spoke and said that he was ready to die, for now he had secured the man he had all the time been seeking; now he had got hold of him." And so they both died. The story deals with inevitability, and the lion is linked to the python.

|háň‡kass'ō created the tale "The Son of the Wind."[30] "The son of the wind was once a man," we are told. Later, he became a bird "and flew, no longer walking as he used to do when he was a man." This tale deals with the creation of the wind: "when he was a man he had been quiet and still." And the storyteller takes the audience back to the time when the wind was a quiet, still man. A story is told of how the wind played ball with a boy, Nakati. When the child asks his mother the name of his playmate, his mother refuses to tell him this until his father has built a strong shelter. That is the pattern. The boy plays ball with his friend, not yet uttering his name. In the end, the shelter is built, and the boy is instructed that he must flee when he says the man's name. When he

states the man's name, he creates the force of the wind: "His companion thereupon began to lean over, and then fall down. As he lay there he kicked violently upon the vlei." And as he kicked, houses and bushes blew away, "and the people could not see because of the dust. Thus was the wind blowing." This is the flapping wings of the bird, the closest animal behavior to the unseen wind. The unseen force was once a man, then transformed into a bird, the physical manifestation of the violent behavior of the wind.

Kinship with Animals

|háñ‡kass'ō said, in 1875, "The Mantis assumes what people do also. . . . They change their faces, for they want us who do not know to think it is not a person. The Mantis also . . . cheats them that we may not know that it is he."[31]

The key to understanding the meanings of the myth (and the relationship between myth, dance, and rock painting) is masquerade: illusion, disguise, deception. This is why Mantis's role as divine trickster is so significant. There is a deliberate ambiguous rendering of Mantis and other myth characters by the performers, just as there is a blurring of humans into animals in the dances and a merging of humans, gods, and animals in the rock paintings.

In the myths, paintings, and dances, there is a feeling of kinship with animals. Human figures are sometimes partially animal, and in the juxtapositioning and superpositioning, animals and humans blend: in the paintings, humans wear animal masks, there is a half-human/half-antelope figure, and there is a man wearing an eland skin; the people mime animals in their dances; and the mantis in the myths is a complex combination of perfect god, flawed human, and future animal. Nature, gods, humans—the exquisite merging of these categories occurs in dance, painting, and myth alike. "The Naron say, in olden times the trees were people, and the animals were people, and one day [God] bade them be animals and trees."[32] Rock art scholar A. R. Willcox observes, "Their many tales of transformation of humans into beasts or birds and vice versa show how clearly they identified themselves with the animal kingdom.[33] Early ethnographer George W. Stow writes of the Gariep San that "[t]hey imagined that in the beginning of time all the animals, as well as the Bushmen themselves, were endowed with the attributes of men and the faculty of speech." Stow recounts the story of "a vicious and quarrelsome being" who attempted to injure every animal he met. Unaccountably, he disappeared, and when he did, "he committed, as a parting gift, a deed of vengeance; for immediately afterwards all the animals forsook the abodes of men, and were changed into their present condition, while the Bushmen alone retained the faculties of human beings and the power of speech."[34]

Stow repeats another Gariep San tale of origins regarding animals and the power of speech. In this story, the early San fathers came out of a hole in the ground, at the roots of an enormous tree, and "all kinds of animals came swarming out after them, some . . . by twos and threes and fours; others in great herds and flocks; and they crushed, and jostled, and pushed each other in their hurry, as if they could not get out fast enough; and they ever came out swarming thicker and thicker, and at last they came flocking out of the branches as well as the roots." At sundown, the emergence of the animals stopped. "The animals were endowed with the gift of speech, and remained quietly located under and around the big tree." When night fell, the men sat at the foot of the tree, having been told that they must not make a fire. The animals were sleeping peacefully around them. It grew so cold that night that "the men at last, not being able to withstand the extreme severity any longer, in spite of the warning that had been given to them, attempted, and at last succeeded in making a fire." The flames shot up, and "the startled animals sprang to their feet in terror, and rushed off panic-stricken to the mountains and the plains, losing in their fright all powers of speech, and fleeing ever afterwards from the presence of man. Only a few animals remained with the fire-makers, and these the men domesticated and kept about them for their service, but the great family of animals was broken up, and could never again be reunited."[35]

The majority of San myths that were copied down have to do with the origin of and differentiation between men and animals, with the ties with the gods remaining for the time intact. "Where is !Kaang?" asked Orpen, and a San hunter replied, "We don't know, but the elands do. Have you not hunted and heard his cry, when the elands suddenly started and ran to his call? Where he is the elands are in droves like cattle."[36] Monica Wilson comments, "It is as though Pan and the mantis held the poetic imagination in the south of Africa as on the Mediterranean shore." But she warns that "these ideas were not held by all the hunters, and from the scanty material it is not possible to formulate any general beliefs which have continued through time."[37]

The meanings of the rock paintings have preoccupied many scholars and observers, and numerous efforts have been made to link the paintings and engravings to San oral tradition and belief. Jalmar and Ione Rudner write, "There is a tendency to use the little which is known of

Bushman folklore to explain the rock art of Southern Africa. Arming himself with works on Bushman mythology and legends—no earlier than the 19th century and obtained from a small number of Bushman informants from a very limited number of areas—an individual will then proceed to relate the rock engravings and paintings to particular myths and legends, all too often without adequate first-hand knowledge of the paintings themselves."[38] |kággen's wife is a *dassie;* his daughter, a porcupine; his son, an insect. Rudner and Rudner documented that |kággen "could change his own shape or the shapes of other things, the moon was his sole which he threw up into the air. He had a pet eland, a pet springbok, etc. The Bushmen were formerly springbok which were changed into Bushmen by the mantis, and so on."[39] But rock paintings of the mantis are rare, as are pictures of the porcupine and *dassie.* And while the sun, moon, and stars are dominant images in the mythology, "[w]e know of no rock paintings which could be said to depict sun, moon and stars."[40] Rudner and Rudner conclude, "The Bushman folklore abounds with stories of people, animals and things changing into animals or other objects. You can pick out paintings in the Drakensberg and other areas which could, perhaps, depict such tales, but it is more probable that the artist was not thinking along those lines at all!"[41]

"Their modes of attack," writes Stow of the hunters, "the disguises they had worn, their appearance and their arms, the great achievements they had accomplished, and the mighty victories they had won, would be again and again recited." The narratives would, in the care of imaginative storytellers, become elaborated and intensified, "until the magnitude of their reported deeds would be considered something more than human." These heroic acts would, over time, come to be seen as the deeds of some supernatural power, and so a priestly caste would evolve. "In this progression from the natural to the supernatural, the Bushmen shew in their paintings the earliest stages of the process of exaltation."[42] It is, he argued further,

> not improbable that after the history of some of these paintings had been forgotten and the names of the heroes who were intended to be depicted had been lost, then it might have been . . . that some mythical description may have been occasionally connected with them; or some Bushman of the present day, deeply learned in the folk-lore of his tribe, may upon examining them imagine that he can detect a similarity between some myth with which he is acquainted and the pictorial representation before him, and he forthwith may cleverly join the

one with the other. He may probably belong to a tribe rich in myths, and now looks for the first time upon a painting by an artist of a distant tribe, of which previously he had not the slightest knowledge. Clever as they undoubtedly are, his natural shrewdness enables him to patch the myth and the scene represented in the painting together.

This is, Stow thought, a dangerous thing to do: "The knowledge of myths, which are passed from mouth to mouth, must naturally be far more widely spread than that of an individual painting, which can only be known to the inhabitants who once occupied the cave and those of the immediate surrounding country."[43] The myth, he insists, "was the afterthought, and never the intention of the artist who painted it."[44]

James David Lewis-Williams argues, "Myth serves to validate primitive society, its norms, hierarchy and customs. It brings us close to the heart of a people." Myth has three functions: "the elucidation of man's relationship with nature; the validation of social action; and the resolving of tensions and fears."[45] The myths and the paintings, he agrees, "perform similar functions; they arise from the same needs and drives. One does not, except in a few instances, illustrate the other." Myths and paintings "draw on a common store of symbols. The symbol antedates both myth and painting: it was not invented for the purpose of being used in either. The myths are a field in which the symbols are manipulated: in the same way, the art is another field in which symbols are manipulated, both media performing similar functions, but following syntactic rules peculiar to themselves."[46]

NARRATIVE MOVEMENT

The same capturing of a narrative moment occurs in both San paintings and myth—and in dance as well. In the paintings, especially evident in those that are superimposed one on top of the other, there is a dramatic—and narrative—merging of human, animal, and mythical figures, a blending of human, animal, and mythical identities. This is why disguise is such a crucial characteristic of all three art forms. Subjects of the rock paintings range from fairly realistic/naturalistic portraitures to more aggressively abstract renderings achieved through superimposition. The three categories—masked hunters and dancers, flying figures, and cloaked figures—are sufficiently ambiguous to become the devices that make the blending possible. The effect in the paintings is to trap the mythic moment in form, much as a tale does. The tale achieves this stopping of time by means of patterning of imagery and other aspects of performance; the painting does it in much the same way. The patterning is more palpable in the paintings that are superimposed—the artists obviously knew what they were doing. The same kind of superimposition is achieved in the tales through parallel patterns. In the paintings as in the myths, animals become effective images for suggesting the relations between humans and animals, among humans and animals and gods. The two great themes of the African oral tradition are much in evidence in San oral tradition as well, forming immediate connections between the San traditions and those of the Bantu speakers who became their neighbors—the relationship of harmony between humans and nature, and the relationship of harmony among humans—expressed most dramatically and tellingly in its rituals, especially its rites of passage.

WILHELM BLEEK AND LUCY LLOYD

In 1911, *Specimens of Bushman Folklore,* containing materials collected by W. H. I. Bleek and L. C. Lloyd, was published by George Allen of London.

The German philologist Wilhelm Heinrich Immanuel Bleek was born in Berlin on March 8, 1827. His father, Friedrich Bleek, was a professor of theology at Berlin University and, later, at the University of Bonn. His mother was Augusta Marianne Henriette Sethe. Bleek graduated from the University of Bonn in 1851 with a degree in linguistics. He studied Hebrew and also became interested in African languages. His thesis had at least partially to do with Khoikhoi languages. He edited vocabularies of East African languages, and in 1852 he began studying Egyptian. In 1854, he was the linguist to William Balfour Baikie's Niger Tshadda expedition. When he returned to England, he met George Grey and John William Colenso, the Anglican bishop of Natal. In 1855, Bleek was invited to join Colenso in Natal to work on a Zulu grammar. Then, in 1856, he went to Cape Town, where he became Grey's interpreter and catalogued Grey's library. Grey became governor of the Cape, and he developed a strong relationship with Bleek, who was becoming respected as a philologist.

Bleek continued to collect examples of African literature from missionaries and travelers. Bleek suffered from health problems: he had to return to Europe in 1854 while a member of Baikie's expedition because he contracted a tropical fever, and in 1859 he again returned to England because of health problems. He soon returned to the Cape. In Cape Town, he met Jemima Lloyd, and they married on November 22, 1862. Jemima's sister, Lucy Lloyd, joined them shortly after their wedding. Grey was then appointed governor of New Zealand, and his collection was given to the South African Public Library, with Bleek as its curator. Bleek retained that position from 1862 until his death in 1875. He wrote for *Het Volksblad* and published *A Comparative Grammar of African Languages* in 1862, the second part in 1869. Financial hardships made his research difficult. He worked with Lucy Lloyd, recording anthropological information. They interviewed many San, but much of the time was spent with six |xam. Bleek died on August 17, 1875, at the age of forty-eight. He was buried in Cape Town. His work on the |xam language and oral tradition was continued by Lucy Lloyd after his death.

In 1866, two prisoners provided him with the data on which his first paper on the San language ("The Bushman Language," in Roderick Noble, ed., *The Cape and Its People, and Other Essays* [Cape Town: J. C. Juta, 1869], 269–84) was based. "In 1870," Bleek wrote, "the presence of twenty-eight Bushmen at the Breakwater afforded an unprecedentedly rare opportunity of obtaining good instructors in the language. On the recommendation of the Rev. G. Fisk, the best-behaved Bushman boy was selected, and in August of that year, he was placed with me for this purpose by Her Majesty's Colonial Government" (Bleek, *Report of Dr. Bleek Concerning His Researches into the Bushman Language and Customs, Presented to the Assembly* [Cape Town: Printed by Order of the House of Assembly, May 1873]; reprinted in Bleek and Lloyd, *Specimens of Bushman Folklore*, 443). This was |a!kunta; he began working with Bleek in August 1870. "This experiment," Bleek continued, "was found to answer; but it was taken into consideration that one young Bushman alone, would soon lose a good deal of accuracy in speaking his mother-tongue, and, further, that the boy in question could relate hardly any of the numerous tales and fables which are met with in the traditionary literature of this nation. On these grounds His Excellency Sir Henry Barkly was pleased to direct that one of the most intelligent of the old Bushmen should join the other." This was ||kábbo, who began working with Bleek on February 16, 1871 (Bleek, *Report*; reprinted in Bleek and Lloyd, *Specimens of Bushman Folklore*, 443).

LUCY LLOYD WAS born on November 7, 1834, in Norbury, England. Her father, William Henry Cynric Lloyd, was rector of Norbury and vicar of Ranton in western England. Her mother was Lucy Anne Jeffreys, a minister's daughter; she died when Lucy Lloyd was eight years old. Her father remarried in 1844 and had thirteen children with his second wife. When Robert Gray established, in 1847, a diocese that included Natal,

William Lloyd was sent to Durban with his family. This was in April 1849; Lucy Lloyd was then fourteen. William Lloyd would later become the archdeacon of Durban. William Colenso was made bishop of the Anglican diocese in 1853, and he moved to Pietermaritzburg. His party included Wilhelm Bleek, who was to assist Colenso as an anthropologist and philologist. Lucy and her sister, Jemima, were very close. When Lucy had problems with her father, she was ejected from her home and moved to a farm. In 1858, she was engaged to George Woolley, the son of a minister. She later broke off the engagement. Jemima married Wilhelm Bleek in 1862; they had seven children, five of whom survived. Lucy went to Cape Town for her sister's wedding. The Natal mail steamer, the SS *Waldensian,* ran into a reef, and Lucy lost most of her possessions. She stayed with her sister and Wilhelm after their marriage.

In 1870, Lucy Lloyd began to work on oral histories of the |xam. She worked with Bleek until his death, then continued the work after his death, with the support of Jemima. Lucy Lloyd was appointed curator of the Grey Collection after Bleek's death, at the same time continuing her own research. She worked with George W. Stow on his *Native Races of South Africa* and was secretary of the South African Folklore Society. She also worked with the historian George McCall Theal on her manuscripts. Her last recorded work was in 1884. She went to Europe in 1887, having trained her niece, Dorothea Bleek, in San research. She moved about in Europe. She returned briefly to the Cape in 1905 and 1907, then returned to South Africa permanently in 1912. In 1911, she edited the texts that she and Bleek had assembled, and these were published as *Specimens of Bushman Folklore.* She received an honorary degree from the University of the Cape of Good Hope in 1911. Lucy Lloyd died in Cape Town on August 31, 1914, and is buried in Cape Town near the grave of Wilhelm Bleek. When Lucy Lloyd died, her niece Dorothea Bleek continued the work on the San research. Dorothea died in 1948. Her published works include *The Mantis and His Friends* (1923), *The Naron: A Bushman Tribe of the Central Kalahari* (1928), *Customs and Beliefs of the |xam Bushmen* (1931), and *A Survey of Our Present Knowledge of Rock-Paintings in South Africa* (1932).

SAN POEMS AND STORIES

A series of San poems and stories reveals the shield that the San people held against assault from without. The poets reveal the ease with which humans and their world interact, emphasizing that this interaction can be interfered with but not stopped.

A San Poem

THE ONE WHO DWELLED IN THE PAN

By !kwéiṭẹn ta | | kēn

The other one, who dwelled upon a pan, went to her.
She dwelled at the pan,
and the other one she said,
"Make a shelter for me,"
and he put down for the other one
a dassie's kaross.
. . . went to make a shelter for her
on the flat ground,
on account of it[47]
as the rain falling came.
And he made a shelter;
the rain falling came up,
as the other one sat.
And the other one sat there;
he sat,
he made a shelter there.
And the other one entered in,
on account of it,[48]
to the other one's house;
she shut down her lid,[49]
and the rain fell.
And . . . asked where the other one could be.
She was inside,
and . . . was dying of cold,
and he sought for her,
because he was dying of cold,
and he returned home,
ordered that the shoes
should go after him,[50]
and the kaross and the quiver,
that they should go after him,

Bleek Archive, http://lloydbleekcollection.cs.uct.ac.za/data/stories/386/index.html, Lucy Lloyd | xam notebooks, Book VI-2, 4034–42.

because he was returning home.
Therefore,
his shoes went after him,
because he returned home;
the quiver and the shoes
must go after him,
and the quiver,
and the kaross.
Because he felt
that the cold was killing him,
he returned.
The kaross
which he had gone and given to her,
and the shoes,
and the quiver, too;
they must go after him,
while they felt
that the other one had his things.[51]
He went away
to return home,
because he felt
that he was cold.
Thence it was
that his shoes went after him,
and the quiver,
and the kaross,
the quiver too.
And he returned to the home,
on account of it.
The rain fell;
he was dying from the cold;
therefore,
he returned home,
and he ordered
that his shoes should go to him,
and his quiver,
and his kaross as well.
And he returned home;
he ordered
that the things
which he had gone and given to her,

his shoes,
and the quiver,
the kaross too,
the kaross and the quiver
must go to him.

A San Poem

A MAN BECOMES A BIRD

By |háñ‡kass'ō

"I wish to talk with you while my thinking-strings still stand,"[52] *said the San story-teller* |háñ‡kass'ō *in 1879. A year earlier, in 1878, he had told a story:*

The wind was formerly a man.
He became a bird.
And he was flying,
while he no longer walked,
as he used to,
for he was flying,
and he dwelled in the mountain.
Therefore, he was flying.
He was formerly a man.
Therefore, he was formerly rolling a ball,
he was shooting, while he felt that he was a person.
He became a bird,
and he was flying,
and he dwelled in a mountain's hole.
And he was coming out of it,
he flew about,
and he returned to it.
And he came to sleep in it,
and, he early awaking goes out of it,
he flies away again,
he flies away.
And he again returns,
while he feels that he has sought food.
And he eats,

Bleek and Lloyd, *Specimens of Bushman Folklore*, 106–9.

about, about, about, about,
he again returns.
And he, again, comes to sleep in it.

A San Poem

PEOPLE BECOME FROGS

By | háñ‡kass'ō

A man once hunted the rain,
as the rain was biding there,
when the rain was an eland.
He hunted
approaching the rain,
and he came and lay down.
He shot the rain,
and the rain sprang aside,
the rain did this,
the rain ran away,
while he walked away.
He went to pick up the arrow,
he meant to go and put it back.
He went and picked up the bag,
the bag which he had,
hunting,
taken with him,
he had laid it down.
That bag was the one that he picked up;
he put in the arrow,
which he had shot at the rain,
he returned,
he lay down to sleep.
Early next morning,
he told the people

"The Rain, in the Form of an Eland, Shot by One of the Early Race of People, and the Disasters which Followed," by | háñ‡kass'ō, from ⊤xábbi-ah. He thinks she had it from her mother, ‡kạmmí. Bleek Archive, http://lloydbleekcollection.cs.uct.ac.za/data/ stories/746/index.html, Lucy Lloyd |xam notebooks, VIII-16 and VIII-17, 7461–72.

that he had shot the rain.
And they followed up the rain;
they went to trace the rain's footprints,
they were following them,
when a mist came up.
They followed up the rain's footprints,
they followed the rain's footprints up to the rain.
They caught sight of the rain lying
and went up to it,
and they cut up the rain.
They kept cutting off meat,
they kept putting it to roast,
the meat kept vanishing,
being burnt up in the fire.
They did this,
they went to take out the meat,
they went to turn over the ashes
looking for the meat,
at the place where it had been roasting,
it was burnt up.
Then they went on roasting,
and all the meat vanished from the fire.
Then they did this,
they meant to take out the flesh,
they went to turn over the ashes,
seeking to get the flesh,
while all the flesh
had been burnt up in the fire,
and the fire burnt out,
the fire died down.
Then this old man said,
"I did think,
I would walk
when this eland's meat was finished,
but I have not eaten it,
though I roasted it.
So now I will go,
while its flesh sits there."
And another answered,
"We will do so,

for we did not know
what sort of eland it was.
Therefore, let us go,
for it is an eland
whose meat we do not eat."
Therefore they walked away
while the rain shut them in,
when the rain saw
that they were making ready to go,
the rain shut them in.
And the rain's navel
shut them into the house
while they said
they feared the house,
the rain's navel
shut them into the house,
and they sat waiting for the rain's navel.
And they worked at a pond,
they worked,
they became frogs,
they hopped away
while the people of the house
became frogs,
they hopped at the houses,
jumped past the people
who had followed the spoor,
the old man made a pond,
he had been on the hunting ground,
he worked making a pond.

A Khoi Tale

The Lion Who Took a Woman's Shape

Some women, it is said, went out to seek roots and herbs
and other wild food. On their way home, they sat down and
said, "Let us taste the food of the field." Now they found that

---

Wilhelm Heinrich Immanuel Bleek, *Reineke Fuchs in Afrika: Fabeln und Märchen der Eingeborenen* (Weimar: Böhlau, 1870). Translated as *Reynard the Fox in South Africa; or, Hottentot Fables and Tales* (London: Trübner and Co., 1864), 50–56. "The original, in the Hottentot language, is in Sir G. Grey's Library, G. Krönlein's Manuscript, pp. 60, 65."

the food picked by one of them was sweet, while that of the others was bitter.

The latter said to each other, "Look here! this woman's herbs are sweet." Then they said to the owner of the sweet food, "Throw it away and seek other herbs."

So she threw away the food, and went to gather more. When she had collected a sufficient supply, she returned to join the other women, but could not find them. She therefore went down to the river where a hare sat lading water, and said to him, "Hare, give me some water that I may drink."

But he replied, "This is the cup out of which my uncle, the lion, and I alone may drink."

She asked again, "Hare, draw water for me that I may drink."

But the hare made the same reply.

Then she snatched the cup from him and drank, but he ran home to tell his uncle of the outrage which had been committed.

The woman meanwhile replaced the cup and went away. After she had departed, the lion came down, and, seeing her in the distance, pursued her on the road. When she turned around and saw him coming, she sang in the following manner:

> "My mother, she would not let me seek herbs,
> Herbs of the field, food from the field. Hoo!"

When the lion at last came up with the woman, they hunted each other around a shrub. She wore many beads and arm-rings, and the lion said, "Let me put them on!"

So she lent them to him, but he afterwards refused to return them to her.

They then hunted each other again around the shrub, until the lion fell down, and the woman jumped on him and kept him there.

The lion, uttering a form of conjuration, said,

> "My aunt! it is morning, and time to rise;
> Pray, rise from me!"

She then rose from him, and they hunted again after each other around the shrub, until the woman fell down, and the lion jumped on her.

She then addressed him:

"My uncle! it is morning, and time to rise;
  Pray, rise from me!"

He rose, of course, and they hunted each other again, until the lion fell a second time.

When she jumped on him, he said,

"My aunt! it is morning, and time to rise;
  Pray, rise from me!"

They rose again and hunted each other. The woman at last fell down.

But this time, when she repeated the conjuration, the lion said,

"*He kha!* Is it morning, and time to rise?"

He then ate her, taking care, however, to leave her skin whole, which he put on, together with her dress and ornaments, so that he looked quite like a woman, and then went home to her kraal.

When this counterfeit woman arrived, her little sister, crying, said, "My sister, pour some milk out for me."

She answered, "I shall not pour you out any."

Then the child addressed their mother: "Mama, do pour out some for me."

The mother of the kraal said, "Go to your sister, and let her give it to you."

The little child said again to her sister, "Please, pour out for me!"

She, however, repeated her refusal, saying, "I will not do it."

Then the mother of the kraal said to the little one, "I refused to let her[53] seek herbs in the field, and I do not know what may have happened. Go therefore to the hare, and ask him to pour out for you."

So the hare gave her some milk.

But her elder sister said, "Come and share it with me."

The little child then went to her sister with her bamboo cup, and they both sucked the milk out of it. While they were doing this, some milk was spilled on the little one's hand, and the elder sister licked it up with her tongue, the roughness of which drew blood. This, too, the woman licked up.

The little child complained to her mother: "Mama, Sister pricks holes in me and sucks the blood."

The mother said, "With what lion's nature your sister went the way that I forbade her and returned, I do not know."

Now the cows arrived, and the elder sister cleansed the pails in order to milk them. But when she approached the cows with a thong,[54] they all refused to be milked by her.

The hare said, "Why do you not stand before the cow?"

She replied, "Hare, call your brother, and the two of you stand before the cow."

Her husband said, "What has come over her that the cows refuse her? These are the same cows she always milks."

The mother of the kraal said, "What has happened this evening? These are cows that she always milks without assistance. What can have affected her that she comes home as a woman with a lion's nature?"

The elder daughter then said to her mother, "I shall not milk the cows." With these words, she sat down.

The mother therefore said to the hare, "Bring me the bamboos, that I may milk. I do not know what has come over the girl."

So the mother herself milked the cows, and when she had done so, the hare brought the bamboos to the young wife's house, where her husband was, but the wife did not give her husband anything to eat.

But when at night she fell asleep, they saw some of the lion's hair which was hanging out where he had slipped on the woman's skin, and they cried, "Truly, this is quite another being! It is for this reason that the cows refused to be milked."

Then the people of the kraal began to break up the house in which the lion lay asleep. When they took off the mats, they said, conjuring them,

> "If you are favorably inclined to me,
> Mat, give the sound sawa."[55]

To the poles on which the house rested, they said,

> "If you are favorably inclined to me,
> Pole, you must give the sound ǂgara."

They addressed the bamboos and the bed-skins in a similar manner.

Thus, gradually and noiselessly they removed the house and all its contents. Then they took bunches of grass, put them over the lion, and, lighting them, said,

> "If you are favorably inclined to me,
> Fire, you must flare up before you come to the heart."

So the fire flared up when it came towards the heart, and the heart of the woman jumped upon the ground. The mother of the kraal picked it up and put it into a calabash.

The lion, from his place in the fire, said to the mother of the kraal, "How nicely I have eaten your daughter."

The woman answered, "You now also have a comfortable place!"

Now the woman took the first milk of as many cows as calved, and put it into the calabash where her daughter's heart was. The calabash increased in size, and in proportion to this the girl grew again inside it.

One day, when the mother of the kraal went out to fetch wood, she said to the hare, "By the time I come back, you must have everything nice and clean."

But during her mother's absence, the girl crept out of the calabash and put the house in good order, as she had been used to do in former days. And she said to the hare, "When Mother comes back and asks, 'Who has done these things?' you must say, 'I, the hare, did them.'"

After she had done all, she hid herself on the stage.[56]

When the mother of the kraal came home, she said, "Hare, who has done these things? They look just as they used to when my daughter did them."

The hare said, "I did the things."[57]

But the mother would not believe it, and looked at the calabash. Seeing it was empty, she searched the stage and found her daughter. Then she embraced and kissed her, and from that day the girl stayed with her mother and did everything as she was wont in former times, but she now remained unmarried.

A San Tale

Tākkūmm Called by a Lion

By !kwéitẹn ta | | kēn

The lion questioned Tākkūmm, as she lay: "In what place are you, that you do not direct me?"

My elder sister thought the lion was seeking where she could be, wondering why she did not direct him to the place where she was.

The lion put its tail on its tongue, while it questioned, seeking the place at which Tākkūmm might be. It was lying down as it called its questions, seeking her. Because the lion was seeking her, she lay down, thinking that the lion had made itself into a man: when it holds[58] its tail on its tongue, it sounds like a man. Therefore, it continued to lie down[59] so that it could continue to call her, seeking her.

She awoke when the day was about to break. She saw the lion that had been here, seeking, calling for her. The lion sat upright, opposite to her, and she arose and walked away;[60] she returned home, feeling that a lion had called, seeking her. But she did not respond to the lion. It remained silent, while she lay listening, knowing that it was not a person who was calling to her, that it was a lion. She continued to lie down as the lion was calling there. Our mothers used to tell us that a lion was wont to resemble a person, its call sounding like that of a man, as it asks where Tākkūmm might be, why she did not direct it to the place where she was. It resembled a man; when it called, it sounded like a man. But we are not accustomed to answer when we hear a thing calling there in the darkness; we feel that a lion is wont to resemble a man to us, so that we think that it is a man who is calling us. We are not accustomed to answer if we are alone. This is what the old woman said, that is what they taught us, so that we who were children might understand.

And thus it was that my elder sister knew that it was a lion that was calling to her. Our mother had talked to us about this,

Bleek Archive, http://lloydbleekcollection.cs.uct.ac.za/data/stories/385/index.html, Lucy Lloyd |xam notebooks, Book VI-2, 4026–33. "Told to R. [Rachel] by her sister."

that the lion was wont to resemble a person: it called, sounding like a man, while it held its tail in its mouth.[61]

A San Poem

YOUNG GIRLS

By Díä!kwǎin

When a girl becomes a young woman, she must not
    look at people,
for when she looks at them, they stand immovable.
When a young woman looked at a young man, a
    long time ago,
he stood immovable.
When the young woman heard that he played so
    very nicely,
he became a stone.

This is why, when a girl becomes a young woman, San men tell her to stay in the house. The old women make a house for the young woman, then order the young woman to remain in the house, so that she may not look at the people,

for when she looks at them
the people will become just like the young man
    long ago,
when he was fixed immovable,
when he became a rock,
when he stood there on account of it.

That is why they hide the young woman in the house;

they remember that a young woman was the one
    who, formerly,
while looking at a young man,

Narrated in July 1874. Bleek Archive, http://lloydbleekcollection.cs.uct.ac.za/data/stories/126/index.html, William Bleek notebooks, Book XXVII, 2609–18, continued in Lucy Lloyd |xan notebooks, Book V-2, 3864–81.

fixed him so that he was immovable;
the young man became a rock.

This is why old San women are accustomed to take care of a
young woman, that she may not look at people, that she may
not also laugh at people. If she were to laugh at people, dropsy
would be the result, it would make the people ill. It would enter
the people, into their insides; the water would be inside the
people, and the people would become water.

The young woman's mother had given her orders about this,
but the young woman did not listen to her. When her mother
was unaware, she went out of the house which her mother had
put her into.

She went to the spring to wash herself,
she being a new young woman.
And when she had washed herself,
she became a frog,
and she went into the well.

The mud made a noise like the report of a cannon, on account of
it. Her elders listened, and wondered what the thing that sounded
like that might be, and they looked towards it, to the place from
which the thing arose, and they saw that the thing looked like a
mist, the mud sprang up into the air like a black mist, when the
girl fell down into the spring and the water was angry. They asked
what could have happened that the water did this.

The young woman's grandmother said to the girl's mother,
"Go look. It seems to be that daughters whom the water is angry
with are punished because the water does not like a new young
woman, because she has not done what you told her to do."

The young woman's mother looked, and she said, "She must
have gone to the water, she seems to be the one with whom the
water is angry and who is therefore being punished."

The children said, "That young woman is in the water spring."

The young woman's mother said that she had warned her
about it, that she should not go to the spring, because the
mother knew that it was a great pit which did not want young
girls, for it became angry with young girls, that is to say, with
new young women.

The water became angry with her because of her odor,
and she has become a frog.

This is why the people say that a frog was formerly a person,
a person who became a frog. The people say "frog," while
they remember that a young woman became a frog when
she went to wash herself at the spring; she became a frog
completely. This is why the people are customarily afraid, and
why the young woman does not walk about: it is because they
remember that a young woman had once fallen into the spring.
And this is why San women are to take care of their young
women, lest those young women have the same fate as the
young woman of the past.

   She had not been willing to listen to her mother, when her
mother regularly told her that she should not go to the spring
because she was a new young woman.

> She deceived her mother,
> she went to the spring;
> she went and washed herself,
> and she became a frog on account of it.

This is why old San women are afraid, lest their young woman
should also become a frog, if she also were to walk about.

> This is why they are accustomed to make a house
>   for her;
> they intend that she shall lie in the house,
> that she not walk about.

They also give her water and food, that she might eat while
lying inside her house. And they do not allow her to drink
herself; they give her to drink. And they remember that the
people would, if she ate greatly, also eat just as she ate. The
people wish that she might eat moderately, that the people
also might eat moderately.

> This is why the people themselves give her
>   moderately,
> why they wish that she not eat by herself;

the people take food to her,
cutting off little pieces of food, and giving them to her.
But they do not put them into her mouth for her.

The people also wish that she not drink much water; they want
her to drink moderately, so that the people might drink just as
she did. The people should drink moderately; if she did not drink
moderately, the people would also drink as she did.

This is why the people were accustomed
to give to her small pieces of meat,
very small pieces of meat;
the people wanted her to eat moderately,
so that they might eat like her.
This is why the people make a reed for her;
she must drink out of a reed,
placed in the mouth of the ostrich egg shell,
an egg shell with a small hole,
so that only a little water may come through,
so that she would not drink from large things.

If she drank from large things, she would not drink moderately,
and this is why the people made a reed for her, that she might
drink by means of that reed, that she might drink out from an
ostrich egg shell with a little mouth, a mouth that was very
small. The reed is what would enter her mouth; if the ostrich
egg shell's mouth were large, she would have got a great deal
of water.

A San Poem

THE RAIN'S STORY

By !kwéitẹn ta | | kēn

The girls sought food; they were digging about for rice. Then
they returned, because it seemed as if one round cloud would

Bleek Archive, http://lloydbleekcollection.cs.uct.ac.za/data/stories/374/index.html, Lucy
Lloyd |xam notebooks, Book VI-1, 3930–41.

come. San women tell the girls that when they hunt food, they must watch to see if a rain cloud comes, so that they may return home. As they were returning, the rain fell, and the girls sought great water holes.[62]

> The great water hole put a girl into the spring,
> and she became a frog on account of it.
> Frogs are people who have been put by the rain into
> water springs.

The rain fell, the water ran along the ground, and they crossed the water. The girls put buchu[63] between the water's horns. The girls put buchu between the horns of the rain, cross this, and go along on the back of the rain (an animal) and land safely on the ground beyond the water. This young woman also wanted to spring across, and this water put her into the great water hole when she attempted to spring through the water.

> This water drew her into the great water hole,
> and she became a frog.
> While she felt that she was not a person,
> she had become a frog.
> While she felt that she is not a person,
> for she was a frog.

The other girls then returned home.

> They went to tell their mothers
> that the great water hole had sat upon the
> other one.
> They returned when they concluded
> that the great water hole had sat upon the
> other one.
> The other one had gone into the great water hole;
> they returned home,
> because they knew that the great water hole had sat,
> and that the other one was a frog.

They returned to tell their mothers, that the other one had gone into the great water hole while they were dipping about for rice.

The clouds came, the rain's clouds, and they returned when they
felt the rain falling while they had not reached home.

> The water ran along the ground;
> the great water hole sat.
> And they returned,
> they went to tell their mothers
> that a great water hole was sitting upon the
>   other one.
> The other one was in a great water hole;
> she was now a frog.
> A great water hole was sitting on the other one.

That is why they had returned. The rain had fallen, the water
had run along the ground, and the great water hole sat, and
the rain fell while they were seeking about. They had not yet
returned home when the rain fell.

> While they were still returning,
> the rain fell,
> water ran along the ground,
> the great water hole sat,
> and the other one had gone in.

The great water hole sat while they were returning, while they
had not yet reached home. The great water hole had gone along,
it sat before them, and they had not returned home. The water's
pool, the girls who stood on the edge crossed over,

> while the other one,
> the stolen girl,
> was a new young woman.

The others were older girls, not new young women.

> The water took her,
> she went into the water hole,

and they returned home.

A San Poem

THE RESURRECTION OF THE OSTRICH

By |a!kunta

The San kills an ostrich at the ostrich's eggs. He carries
the ostrich to his house. His wife takes off the ostrich's short
feathers, which are inside the net, because they are bloody. She
places them on the bushes. They eat the ostrich meat.

> A little whirlwind comes to them,
> it blows up the ostrich feathers.
> It blows a little ostrich feather
> that has blood on it into the sky.
> The little feather falls down out of the sky;
> having whirled about,
> falls down.
> It goes into the water,
> becomes wet in the water.
> It is conscious,
> it lies in the water,
> it becomes ostrich flesh.
> It gets feathers,
> it puts on its wings,
> it gets its legs while it lies in the water.
> It walks out of the water,
> and basks in the sun on the water's edge,
> because it is still a young ostrich.
> Its feathers are young feathers,
> they are little feathers. They are black,
> for it is a little male ostrich.

He dries his feathers while lying on the water bank, so that he
may walk away afterwards, when his little feathers have dried, so
that he may walk unstiffening his legs. He has been in the water,
and must walk to strengthen his feet; he thinks that his feet must
be in ostrich's veldschoens,[64] his feet become strong.

Bleek and Lloyd, *Specimens of Bushman Folklore*, 136–45.

He walks,
strengthening his feet,
and then he lies down,
he hardens his breast,
so that his breastbone may become bone.
He walks away,
he eats young bushes
because he is a young ostrich.
He swallows young plants
that are small,
because he is a little ostrich.
It is his little feather that became the ostrich,
it was the feather that the wind blew up
while the wind was a little whirlwind.

He thinks of the place which he has scratched; he lets himself
grow, that he may first be grown before he, lying by the way,
goes to his old place where he died, lying there, so that he
may go to scratch in the old house, making the new house
on the old one, while he goes to fetch his wives. He will add
to the two previous wives another she-ostrich, he will marry
three ostrich wives. Because his breastbone is bone, he roars,
hardening his ribs, that his ribs may become bone. Then he
scratches out a house; he slept along the way and arrived at
the place of his house.

Roaring,
he calls the ostrich wives,
that they come to him.
Roaring,
he calls them,
that he may see the she-ostriches
coming to him.
And he meets them,
that he may run around the females,
for he had been dead;
he,
dying,
left his wives.

He will look at his wives' feathers, and his wives' feathers appear
to be fine. When he has strengthened his flesh, he feels heavy as
he moves, because his legs are big, his knees are large, he has
grown great feathers, the quills are great feathers, these feathers
become strong, they are now old feathers. He therefore roars
loudly, for the ribs are now big. And he is a grown-up ostrich, the
feathers on his wings are long. He decides to scratch, so that the
females may lay eggs. His claws are hard, they want to scratch,
and he brings the females to the place of the house. The females
stand there, eating. He goes back, he scratches, while the she-
ostriches eat there. He first goes to scratch, drying the house,
because it is damp, so that the inside of the house may dry. The
she-ostriches look at the house. One she-ostrich lies down to
try the house, she is seeing if the house seems to be nice. She
first sleeps opposite the house, because the inside of the house
is wet, as the rain has newly fallen. They first lie opposite the
house, they sleep opposite the house. She lies there, making the
ground inside the house soft, so that the inside of the house may
be dry, so that another female may come and lay an egg inside
the house which is now dry, for the earth of the house is wet.
She first goes to lie opposite the house. Another female comes,
she comes to lay another new egg. Then she flaps her wings in
the house for two small eggs now lie there, and she again goes
to sleep opposite the house. All the females now sleep in the
house. Galloping in the dark, he drives the females to the house.
Running, he takes the females to the house, they all arrive at the
house. And another female, a different one, lays another egg, and
again, flapping their wings, they peck at it. He drives the females
away, and he lies inside the house.

> These females,
> following each other,
> reach him at the house.
> These females send him off,
> they all lay eggs.
> He goes away to eat.
> Two wives lie in the house;
> another wife goes with him,
> they go to eat together.
> They sleep.

The two wives sleep in the house.
The two,
male and female,
return early;
they shall,
early,
send off the two wives
who had lain in the house.
The wife who had been with him
lays another egg.
Now all the wives go,
while he lies down,
that he may sleep in the house.
He will drive away the jackal
when he thinks that the jackal is coming
to push the eggs.
He takes care of the eggs,
because they are his children.
That is why he takes care of them,
why he drives the jackal away,
so that the jackal will not kill his children.
He will kick the jackal with his feet.

A San Tale

THE GIRL'S STORY, THE FROGS' STORY

By !kwéiṭen ta | | kēn

A girl once lay ill. She was lying down. She did not eat the food that her mother and other women gave her. She lay ill.

She killed the children of the water,[65] they were what she ate. She would not eat what her mother and other women were giving to her.

Her mother was there. They[66] went out to seek rice. They spoke, they ordered a child to remain at home. The girl did not know about the water-child. The old woman said that she must look at the things which her elder sister ate. And they left the

---

Narrated in December 1874. Bleek and Lloyd, *Specimens of Bushman Folklore*, 198–205.

child at home, and went out to seek food. They intended that
the child should look at the things that her elder sister ate.

The elder sister went out from the house of illness, and
descended to the spring, as she intended, again, to kill a water-
child. The San child was in her mother's house, she did not
know about the water-child.

And she went and killed a water-child, she carried the water-
child home. The San child was looking, as the girl boiled the
water-child's flesh and ate it. Then she lay down, she again went
to lie down while the San child watched her. And the elder sister
went to lie down, when she had finished eating. The San child
looked at her, and she lay down.

Her mother returned. The child told her mother about it, that
her elder sister had gone to kill a handsome thing at the water.

Her mother said, "It is a water-child!"

And her mother did not say anything more about it; she
again went out to seek rice.

While she was seeking food, clouds came up.

She said, "Something is not right at home, for a whirlwind is
bringing things to the spring. Something is not going well at home.
That is why the whirlwind is taking things away to the spring."

It was because her daughter had killed the water's children
that the whirlwind took them away to the spring. Something had
not gone well at home, her daughter had been killing the water's
children. That was why the whirlwind took the children away to
the spring. It was because her daughter had killed the water's
children that the whirlwind took them away to the spring. It was
because she had killed the water's children.

> The girl was the first one to go into the spring,
> and then she became a frog.
> Her mother and other women afterwards went into
>   the spring.
> The whirlwind brought them to it,
> when she was already in the spring,
> she was a frog.
> Her mother and the other women also became frogs.
> The whirlwind brought them
> when they were on the hunting ground.
> The whirlwind brought them to the spring

when the mother's daughter was already in the spring.
She was a frog.
Her mothers came afterwards,
the whirlwind brought them to the spring
when they were on the hunting ground.
Meanwhile, their daughter was in the spring,
she was a frog.

Her father also came to become a frog, for the whirlwind
brought her father, when he was on the hunting ground, to the
spring to the place where his daughter was. Her father's arrows[67]
grew out of the spring, for the great whirlwind had also brought
them to the spring. He became a frog, his wife also became a frog,
when the whirlwind brought them to the spring. Their things also
entered that spring in which they were. The things entered that
spring because the people were frogs. Their things went into the
spring because they were frogs. The mats grew out by the spring,
like the arrows, their things grew out[68] by the spring.

A San Poem
THE SCAPEGOAT

By Díä!kwăin

My mother used to do this when she intended to go out
to seek food. When she was about to start, she took a stone,
and, as she plunged the stone into the ashes of the fire, she
exclaimed, "Rider yonder!" while she wished that the evil things
about which she had been dreaming should remain in the fire
instead of going out with her.

That place to which she went
would not be nice
while she knew that she had dreamt of evil things
that were not nice.
Therefore, she acted in this manner,

Mode of Getting Rid of the Evil Influence of Bad Dreams. Narrated in August 1875.
Bleek and Lloyd, *Specimens of Bushman Folklore,* 364–65.

Figure 2. Díä!kwăin (San).
Bleek Archive. *Courtesy of
University of Cape Town
Libraries*

because she was aware that,
if she went out with the dream that she had dreamt,
her going out would not be fortunate.
The rice that she dug would not be favorable to her,
because it was aware that she had dreamt evil things.
Therefore, the rice would not be favorable to mama
while the rice was aware that mama had dreamt evil
    things.
Therefore, the rice would act in this manner about it.

A San Poem
CONCERNING TWO APPARITIONS
By Díä!kwăin

We buried my wife in the afternoon.
    When we had finished burying her, we returned to the home
of my sister, Whāī-ttū and the other people, whence they had

Narrated in January 1876. Bleek and Lloyd, *Specimens of Bushman Folklore,* 364–71.

come. They had come with me to bury my wife, and we then
went away, crossing over the salt pan.

> And we saw a little thing
> that looked like a little child
> as it sat on the salt pan,
> as if it sat with its legs crossed over each other.

And my sister, Whāī-ttū, spoke, she questioned us: "Look! What
thing is sitting over there on the salt pan? It is like a little child."

And !kwéiten̯ ta ||ēn, another sister, spoke. She asked us,
"Look! Why is it that this thing is really like a person? It seems to
be wearing the cap that Díä!kwǎin's wife used to wear."

And my sister, Whāī-ttū, answered, "Yes, my younger sister.
The thing truly resembles what my brother's wife was like."

> As we went along,
> it seemed as if it sat there,
> looking towards the place
> from which we came out.

And ||kū-ǎń spoke, "The old people used to tell me that the
angry people were wont to act in this way at the time when they
took a person away. They used to allow the person to be in front
of us, so that we might see it. You know that she really did have
a very little child. Therefore, you should allow us to look at the
thing that sits on this salt pan. It strongly resembles a person, its
head is there, like that of a person."

And I spoke, I said, "Wait! I will do this as I return to my
home. I will see whether I shall again perceive it, as it sits."

And we went to their home. We talked there for a little while.
Then I said to them that they must think that I did not want to
return home, for the sun was setting. So I returned. I thought that
I would go the same way as we had come, so that I might, as I go
along, look and see whether I will again see it, as it sits.

> Going along, I looked at the place
> where it had sat,
> because I thought
> that it might have been a bush.
> I looked and did not see it

at the place where it had sat.
And I agreed that it must have been a different kind
of thing.

My mothers used to tell me that, when the sorcerers who
take us away, when they intend to take us away, that is the time
when our friend is in front of us, while he desires that we may
see him because he still thinks of us. Therefore, his outer skin[69]
still looks at us, because he feels that he does not want to go
away and leave us, and he insists on coming to us. Therefore, we
still see him.

My sister's husband, Mănsse,[70] told us about it, that it had
happened to him when he was hunting about, as he was going
along, he saw a little child, peeping at him by the side of a bush.
And he thought, "Can it be my child who seems to have run
after me? It seems to have lost its way, while it seems to have
followed me." And Mănsse thought, "Allow me to walk nearer,
that I may look at this child to see what child it be."

> And Mănsse saw
> that the child acted in this manner:
> when the child saw
> that he was going up to it
> that he might see what child it was,
> he saw that the child appeared to fear him.
> The child sat behind the bush
> and looked from side to side;
> it seemed to want to run away.
> And he walked, going near to it,
> and the child therefore arose.
> It walked away,
> looking from side to side;
> it seemed to want to run away.

And Mănsse looked to see why it was that the child did not wish
him to come to it, that the child seemed to be afraid of him. He
examined the child,

> as the child stood looking at him.
> He saw that it was a little girl;

he saw that the child was like a person.
In other parts,[71] it was not like a person.
He thought that he would let this child alone,
a child who was afraid of him was here.
And he walked on,
while the child stood looking from side to side.
And as the child saw that he was going away from it,
it came forward, near the bush,
and it sat down.

A San Poem

GIRLS BECOME STARS

Mother and the others
used to tell us about it,
that girls are those whom the rain carries off.
The girls remain at that water
to which the rain has taken them,
girls with whom the rain is angry.
The rain lightens,
killing them,
and they become stars,
their appearance has been changed.
They become stars.

A San Poem

A MAN BECOMES CLOUDS

By Díä!kwäin

The wind does this when we die,
our own wind blows;
for we, who are human beings,

"Girls Become Stars" from "Death," in Bleek and Lloyd, *Specimens of Bushman Folklore*, 388–401.

"A Man Becomes Clouds" narrated in 1875. Bleek and Lloyd, *Specimens of Bushman Folklore*, 396–401.

we possess wind;
we make clouds when we die.
Therefore, the wind does this when we die:
the wind makes dust,
because it intends to blow,
taking away our footprints
with which we had walked about
while we still had nothing the matter with us,
and our footprints,
which the wind intends to blow away,
would otherwise still lie plainly visible.
For the thing would seem as if we still lived.
Therefore, the wind intends to blow,
taking away our footprints.
And our gall, when we die,
sits in the sky;
it sits green in the sky,
when we are dead. . . .
The hair of our head
will resemble clouds,
when we die,
when we in this manner make clouds.
These things are those
which resemble clouds;
and we think that they are clouds.
We, who do not know,
we are those who think in this manner,
that they are clouds.
We, who know,
when we see that they are like this,
we know that they are a person's clouds,
that they are the hair of his head.
We, who know,
we are those who think thus,
while we feel that we
seeing
recognize the clouds,
how the clouds do in this manner
form themselves.

A San Story

THE ‡NÈRRU AND HER HUSBAND

By |háñ‡kass'ō

The shift between worlds is revealed here. The husband, not understanding the world of his wife, removes her kaross, with the result that his wife loses a part of herself. The ‡nèrru, formerly a person, is now a bird. In this story, we see how the shift occurred, as a human transforms into a bird. The pattern of the story along with the admonitory words of the mother emphasize the change that is occurring, a change wrought by the man who has no understanding of the world of his wife. Two worlds are spoken of: the human world and that of birds. The nervous relationship between the worlds is revealed by the acts of the ignorant husband.

A man of the early race formerly married a ‡nèrru,[72] an ostrich. The ‡nèrru put dusty[73] rice into a bag when her husband had dug it out.[74] She went to wash the rice, and they returned home.

The next day, they went out early to seek food, she and her husband—for she was alone with her husband. He was the one who dug the rice out. That is why she was with her husband.

And the next day, too, she went out to seek food. Her husband dug out other rice. He put the rice that he had dug on the top of the morning's rice. Then he again arose, and sought other rice. He found other rice, he dug it out from the earth, he again dug out the rice. He put it on the top of the other rice. He put it on the top, and the bag became full.

Then he arose and sought other rice. He found other rice, he dug the earth out from it, and he dug it out.

He exclaimed, "Give me your little kaross, so that I may put the rice on it."

The wife said, "We are not accustomed to put San rice that has earth with it on the karosses that we wear on our backs, we who are of the house of ‡nèrru."

This tale, narrated in June 1879, is attributed to the storyteller's mother, ⊤xábbi-añ. Bleek and Lloyd, *Specimens of Bushman Folktales*, 206–13.

He exclaimed, "Give me, give me the little kaross, so that I may put the rice on it."

And the wife said, "You should put the rice on the ground, we are not accustomed to put rice that has earth with it on the karosses that we wear on our backs."

And he exclaimed, "Give it to me, give me the little kaross so that I may put the rice on it."

The wife exclaimed, "You should put the rice into the ground, so that you can cover over the rice."

He said, "Give me the kaross so that I may put the rice on it," and he snatched the kaross away from her.

His wife's entrails, which were on the kaross, poured out.[75]

And he cried, "Oh dear! Oh my wife! What shall I do?"

The wife arose, she said,[76]

> "We, who are of the house of ‡nèrru,
> We are not used to put earthy rice
> Into our back's kaross;
> We, who are of the house of ‡nèrru,
> We are not used to put earthy rice
> Into our back's kaross."

She walked on, replacing her entrails. She sang,

> "We, who are of the house of ‡nèrru,
> We are not used to put earthy rice
> Into our back's kaross."

Then her mother exclaimed, "Go and look at the place where your elder sister went to seek food. The noise of the wind sounds like a person,[77] your elder sister's husband did not act rightly. You see, the noise of the wind sounds like a person, singing from the side from which the wind is blowing."

Her daughter stood up and looked. She said, "Your daughter is the one who comes, she is falling."

Then her mother said, "You must see this. Your elder sister's husband does mad things, as if he does not understand. They marry among us as if they understood."

Then she ran to meet her daughter, she went to put the little kaross on her daughter. She put her daughter's entrails on the little kaross, and she bound up her daughter. She slowly conducted her daughter home, she went to take her into the mother's house.

The mother was angry about her daughter. When her daughter's husband wanted to come to his wife, she was angry. Her daughter's husband went back to his own people when the mother said that her daughter's husband should go back for he did not understand.

So her daughter's husband went back, while they continued to dwell there.

A San Story

QWANCIQUTSHAA—A LOVE STORY

By 'Qing

Qwanciqutshaa was one of three chiefs with great power; Qwanciqutshaa can take the form of a snake. As the bird and the man are the same in the poem, so too do Qwanciqutshaa and the snake remain the same. In this love story, the young woman is influential in effecting the movement from the one identity to the other.

Qwanciqutshaa, the chief, used to live alone.

He had no wife, for women would not have him.

A man sent a number of little boys to get sticks for the women to dig ants' eggs.

One of the women grumbled, saying the stick that she received was crooked and those of the others were straight. That night, this woman dreamed that a baboon came to take for his wife a young girl who had refused Qwanciqutshaa.

Next day, as she was digging alone, the baboon came to her in a rage—it had been present and heard her observation about the stick, and thought she was mocking the crookedness of its tail. It said, "Why did you curse me?" And it threw stones at her.

She ran home and told the girl of her dream, that it was coming true, and she told her to escape to Qwanciqutshaa. The

From J. M. Orpen, "A Glimpse into the Mythology of the Maluti Bushmen," *Cape Monthly Magazine* 9 (July 1874): 139–56.

girl sank into the ground and came up at another place, and
sank again. She sank three times, then came up and went to
Qwanciqutshaa's place.

Qwanciqutshaa had killed a red rhebok and was skinning
it when he saw his elands running about. Wondering what had
startled them, he left the meat, took the skin, and went home.

He asked her why she had come.

She said she was frightened of the baboon.

He told her to fetch water to wash the blood off his hand,
and she went. She came running back in a fright, and spilled
some on Qwanciqutshaa.

He said, "What's the reason for this?"

She said, "It's fright of the baboon."

He said, "Why are you frightened? He is your husband, he
comes from your place."

She said, "No, I have run to you for fear of him."

Then he put her up on his head and hid her in his hair.

The baboon had in the meantime come to the people she
had left, it asked for her.

They said they did not know where she was.

But it smelled where she had gone down into the ground,
and it pursued her, scenting her at each place.

When it came towards Qwanciqutshaa, the elands started,
ran about, and stared at it.

It came up to Qwanciqutshaa with his keeries,[78] saying, "Where
is my wife?" Qwanciqutshaa said, "I have no wife of yours."

It flew at Qwanciqutshaa and fought him, but
Qwanciqutshaa got it down and struck it with its own keerie.

Then Qwanciqutshaa banished it to the mountains, saying,
"Go, eat scorpions and roots as a baboon should."

And it went screaming away.

The screams were heard by the women at the place it came
from, and all the baboons were banished.

Qwanciqutshaa killed an eland, and he purified himself
because the baboon had defiled him.

He told the girl to go home and tell the people he was alive.

But the young men wanted to marry this girl, and she
said, "No, I love none but Qwanciqutshaa, who saved me
from the baboon."

So they hated Qwanciqutshaa, and when he had killed a
red rhebok and put meat on the fire to roast, those young men

took fat from a snake that they had killed and dropped it on the meat.

When Qwanciqutshaa cut a piece and put it in his mouth, it fell out.

He cut another piece, and it fell out.

The third time it fell out, blood gushed from his nose.

So he took all his things, his weapons, and clothes, and threw them into the sky.

And he threw himself into the river. There were villages down there and young women, and they wanted to catch Qwanciqutshaa. But he turned into a snake and said, "No, it is because of women that I was killed." And he eluded them and threatened them, and they all ran away.

The only girl who remained was the girl he had saved. She made a house, and went and picked things and made canna,[79] and put pieces in a row from the river bank to the house.

The snake came out and ate the charms, then went back into the water.

The next day she did the same, and that night he came out and went to the house. He took a mat and went up to the sky, got his kaross, then came down and slept on the mat.

When the girl saw that he had been there, she placed charms again and lay in wait.

The snake came out of the water and raised his head, looking warily and suspiciously around. Then he glided out of the snake's skin and walked to the house, picking up the charmed food. When he was asleep, she went in, seized him, and quickly forced more charms into his mouth. He struggled to escape, but she held him fast.

He was exhausted, he trembled and said, "Why do you hold me, you who caused my death?"

She said, "Though I was the cause, I was not the fault, for I love you and none but you!" And she smothered him in the kaross, she ran to the skin and sprinkled it with canna and burned it.

And they remained there three days.

Qwanciqutshaa killed an eland and purified himself and his wife, and told her to grind canna. She did so, and when he sprinkled it on the ground, all the elands that had died came to life again. Some came with assegais sticking in them, assegais[80] that had been thrown by those people who had wanted to kill him. He took out the assegais, a whole bundle of them, and they remained in his place.

It was a place enclosed in hills and precipices. There was one pass, and it was constantly filled with a freezingly cold mist, so that none could pass through it. Those men all remained outside, and they ate sticks, at last, and died of hunger.

But his brother[81] chased an eland he had wounded. He pursued it closely through that mist, and Qwanciqutshaa saw the elands running about, frightened at that wounded eland and the assegai that was sticking in it.

He came out and saw his brother, and he said, "Oh, my brother, I have been injured. You see now where I am."

The next morning, he killed an eland for his brother, and he told him to go back and call his mother and his friends.

He did so, and when they came they told him how the other people had died of hunger outside. They stayed with him, and the place smelled of meat.

A San Story

LYNX, WIFE OF THE DAWN'S-HEART STAR

by | háñ‡kass'ō

The major pattern, the pattern that holds the story together, is the repeated returns of the younger sister and her plea, "Oh Lynx! Will you not first allow the child to suck?" Flowing through the pattern are images of transformation, as the wife of Dawn's-Heart Star slowly becomes a lynx bewitched by the she-hyena. The story focuses on that transformation, with the mother's nursing of her child and her slow psychological distancing from that child the major narrative movement. In the end, Dawn's-Heart reverses this transformation, but Lynx instructs him to "leave the hair on the tips of my ears, for then I'll be able to hear." A transition has occurred, but the being experiencing that transition can never be the same.

This is a commentary by Bleek and Lloyd: "The Dawn's-Heart Star has a daughter, who is identified with some neighboring star. Her name is 'Dawn's-Heart Star-child,' and her relation to her father is somewhat mysterious. He calls her 'my heart,' he swallows her, then walks alone as the only Dawn's-Heart Star,

---

Bleek and Lloyd, *Specimens of Bushman Folklore*, 84–98. Words in italic are words that I have added.

and, when she is grown up, he spits her out again. She then herself becomes an-other female Dawn's-Heart Star, and spits out another Dawn's-Heart Star-child, which follows the male and female Dawn's-Heart Star. The mother of the latter, the first-mentioned Dawn's-Heart Star's wife, was the Lynx, who was then a beautiful woman, with a younger sister who carried her digging-stick after her. Dawn's-Heart Star hid his child under the leaves of an edible root (!kúissi), where he thought that his wife would come and find it. Other animals and birds arrived first, and each proposed herself to Dawn's-Heart Star-child as its mother; but they were mocked at by the child, until at last it recognized its own mother. Among the insulted animals were the jackal and the hyena, who, to revenge themselves, be-witched the mother (the lynx) with some poisoned 'Bushman rice' (so-called 'ants' eggs'), by which means she was transformed into a lioness. In the dark, the hyena tried to take her (the lynx's) place in the house, on the return of Dawn's-Heart Star; but the imposture was made known to him by his sister-in-law. Dawn's-Heart Star tried to stab the hyena with his assegai, but missed her. She fled, putting her foot into the fire, and burning it severely. The bewitched wife was enticed out of the reeds by her younger sister, and then caught by her brothers, who pulled off the lion skin, so that she became a fair woman again. But, in consequence of having been bewitched by 'Bushman rice,' she could no longer eat that, and was changed into a lynx who ate meat. This myth, which contains many minor, and some beautiful incidents, is partly given in the form of a narrative, and partly in discourses addressed by the Dawn's-Heart Star to his daughter, as well as in speeches made by the hyena and her parents, after her flight home."[82]

Dawn's-Heart Star was married to Lynx. While Dawn's-Heart was away hunting, the she-hyena bewitched Lynx with "Bushman rice" (grubs). The hyenas sought grubs,[83] they were digging out grubs. While they were digging them out, they went about, sifting the grubs. And, when the ants' larvae were moving into the earth, underneath the hillock, the hyenas collected together and they sifted the larvae of the ants on the hunting ground. Then the she-hyena took the blackened perspiration of the armpits and put it into the larvae. And they gave the larvae to Lynx.[84] In this way, the she-hyena took over Lynx.

Lynx exclaimed to her younger sister, "You shall leave these larvae alone. I will be the one who eats them, because the smell of this food is not nice, and you are the one who will take care of the child."

Now Lynx lost her identity to the hyena. As Lynx sat, eating the grubs, her ornaments, her earrings, bracelets, leglets, and anklets, of themselves came off. The kaross unloosened itself, and it also fell to the ground. The skin petticoat also unloosened itself, it too fell to the ground. And the shoes also unloosened themselves. Then she sprang up, and, in this manner, trotted away. *Now, naked, she went into the reeds.* Her younger sister, shrieking, followed her. But Lynx went, she went into the reeds. She went to sit in the reeds. *The younger sister now had difficulty getting Lynx to nurse her own child.*

Her younger sister exclaimed, "Oh Lynx! Will you not first allow the child to suck?"

And the elder sister said, "Bring it, that it may suck. I want to talk to you while my thinking-strings still stand." Therefore she spoke, she said to her younger sister, "You must quickly bring the child, while I am still conscious. Bring the child tomorrow morning." *And so the hyena's power over Lynx grew.*

Her younger sister returned home, as did the she-hyena. When the she-hyena had put on the ornaments, they returned home, while Dawn's-Heart and the rest were still out hunting.

Dawn's-Heart returned home, as the child cried there. His younger sister-in-law was the one who had the child. *And now, as she falls more deeply under the influence of the hyena, it becomes more and more difficult to lure the mother from the reeds to nurse her child.*

Dawn's-Heart came, he exclaimed: "Why is it that Lynx is not attending to the child, while the child is crying there?"

The she-hyena did not speak.

Her sister was soothing the child. She waited, and her elder sister's husband, Dawn's-Heart, went to hunt. Then she took the child on her back, and went to her elder sister; she walked there, and when she arrived at the reeds, she exclaimed: "Oh Lynx, let the child suck."

And her elder sister springing out of the reeds, came running and caught hold of her, turning her body on one side. She gave her elder sister the child. She said: "I am here."

And her elder sister allowed the child to suck. She said, "You must quickly bring the child again, while I am still conscious, for I feel as if my thinking-strings will fall down."

Her younger sister took the child upon her back. She returned home, while her elder sister went into the reeds.

Near sunset, she again went to her elder sister, feeling that her elder sister had told her to do so.

Her elder sister said: "You must quickly bring the child, for I feel as if I should forget you, I feel that I do not know."

Her younger sister took the child near sunset, she went to her elder sister. She stood there and exclaimed: "Oh Lynx, let the child suck."

Her elder sister sprang out of the reeds, she ran up to her younger sister and caught hold of her.

Her younger sister said: "I am here! I am here!"

She allowed the child to suck.

She said: "You must quickly come again, for I feel as if I will forget you, as if I will no longer think of you."

Her younger sister returned home, while she went into the reeds.

Her younger sister, on the next day, went to her elder sister; she walked to the reeds, coming, coming, coming, coming. She stood there and exclaimed: "Oh Lynx, let the child suck."

Her elder sister sprang out of the reeds, she ran up to her younger sister and caught hold of her.

Her younger sister, springing aside, gave her the child. She said, "I am here!"

Then the elder sister spoke, saying to her younger sister, "You must not continue to come to me, for I no longer feel that I know."

Her younger sister returned home. *And now, the hyena, having taken control of Lynx, moved into the house of Dawn's-Heart, pretending that she was Lynx.*

They went to make a *!kù*[85] there at the house. They played, the men played with them. The women clapped their hands, the men nodded their heads, and the women were those who clapped their hands for them. Then, Dawn's-Heart, nodding his head, went up to his younger sister-in-law, and laid his hand on her shoulder.

But his younger sister-in-law swerved aside, saying, "Leave me alone! Your wives, the old she-hyenas, may clap their hands for you." *And the sister of Lynx told Dawn's-Heart of the she-hyena's activities.*

Dawn's-Heart ran to the she-hyena; taking aim with his assegai, he pierced the place where the hyena had been sitting. The hyena sprang out, she trod, burning herself in the fire while she sprang away, while the ornaments remained at the place where she had been sitting, where she had been wearing them.

She sprang away, while the ornaments remained. *The hyena escaped, burning her feet in the fire outside the house.*

Dawn's-Heart scolded his younger sister-in-law. Why was it that his younger sister-in-law had not quickly told him about it? She had concealed from him the activities of the hyena, this was why he had seen that the woman had been sitting with her back towards him, she had not been sitting with her face towards him. She had been sitting with her back towards him, while his wife usually sat with her face towards him. The one who was here must be a different person, she had sat with her back towards him. And he said that his younger sister-in-law should quickly tell him where his wife was.

His younger sister-in-law said, "Wait until the place becomes light, for you seem to think that your wife is like she used to be. We will go to your wife when the sun has come out."

Therefore, the next day, he said that his younger sister-in-law must go with him.

His younger sister-in-law said, "We ought to drive some goats, we should take goats to your wife."

Therefore, they drove some goats. They drove along goats, drove along goats; they took the goats to the reeds. And they drove the goats to a stand.

The sister directed her elder sister's husband, she said that he should stand behind her, and the other people must stand behind her elder sister's husband's back, and she must be the one to stand beside the goats.

Then she exclaimed, "Lynx! Let the child suck."

Her elder sister sprang out of the reeds; she came running. When she had run to her younger sister, she saw the goats, she turned aside to the goats and caught hold of one.

Dawn's-Heart caught hold of his wife, while the wife caught hold of the goat, and his younger sister-in-law also took hold of the wife. All the people, altogether, caught hold of her. Other people caught hold of the goats. They cut the goats open, then took the contents out of the stomachs, anointing Lynx with the contents of the stomachs. And, taking hold, they rubbed the hair from her skin.

But when she sat down, she said: "While you're pulling, leave the hair on the tips of my ears, for then I'll be able to hear; otherwise, I do not feel that I should hear."

Therefore, her husband, pulling the hair off, left the hair on the tips of her ears, that hair which is thus on the tips of the ears, standing on the top of them.

Now Dawn's-Heart came home, arrow and spear ready in case the hyena tried again. When he was returning home, he put an arrow on the bow, and as he walked, he stuck the end of his assegai into the ground. His eyes were large, as he came walking along; they resembled fires. The people were afraid of him as he came on account of his eyes; they felt that his eyes resembled fires, as he came walking along. The jackals were afraid of him, as he returned.

COMMENTARY

> ... they sat waiting for the rain's navel.
> *"People Become Frogs," line 82*

The complexity of the relationship of the San with each other and with the world around them is revealed in the image of the rain as the navel that shuts people in a house. The rain is a natural phenomenon, and it is also an elandlike game animal. The people chase the rain, shooting it, but when they attempt to roast its meat, the flesh eludes them. In the end, they are captured by the rain and are transformed into frogs.

> And the rain's navel
> shut them into the house
> while they said
> they feared the house,
> the rain's navel
> shut them into the house. . . .

There is a fluid relationship among humans, animals, and nature: the result of this relationship is a sense of unity, of wholeness. It is an everlasting cycle, a situation that is never static, that is always in the process of change. The rain's navel is one image that is meant to suggest this rich linkage.

The image of

> ... a little thing
> that looked like a little child

> as it sat on the salt pan,
> as if it sat with its legs crossed over each other

suggests the cryptic nature of this relationship. It seemed to be

> . . . a little girl;
> he saw that the child was like a person.
> In other parts, it was not like a person.

And in the end, as the observer walked away from the child,

> . . . the child stood looking from side to side.
> And as the child saw that he was going away from it,
> it came forward, near the bush,
> and it sat down.

A phantasmagoric child, a variously dimensioned rain: an atmosphere is created within which humans have their being.

A man becomes the wind, then becomes a bird: he flies and lives in a mountain hole. The wind, a bird, a human: a unity of all living beings is emphasized. Girls remain at the water to which the rain has carried them; the rain lightens, killing them, and the girls become stars.

This connection between human and animal and nature emphasizes the transformations that humans undergo as they move through the biological and cultural changes in their lives. But note that when humans go through such changes as the puberty rite of passage, it is never done in isolation: it always occurs within the embrace of nature, with animals often as the intervening and secondary means whereby the change takes place. When girls hunt food, they have to be wary of a rain cloud. The rain falls; the girls seek water holes. A water hole puts the girl into a spring, and she becomes a frog: "Frogs are people who have been put by the rain into water springs." The other girls tell their mothers what has happened: "the stolen girl, / was a new young woman." During this difficult time of transition, certain restrictions are placed on the initiate's activities. When a girl becomes a young woman, for example, she must remain in a house. She must not look at people; if she does, those people will become immovable, stones. When one young woman went out of the house to a spring to wash herself, she became a frog.

The water became angry and created a mist. That is why people make certain that she stays in the house. During this period, she is set aside, and she moves into other shapes within the context of nature: the water and mist.

This ritual of change, or rebirth, is revealed when a girl is swallowed by a lion, which then takes her skin and masquerades as the girl—but in a negative way. In the end, the people burn the lion, and when the heart of the girl leaps out, they put it into a calabash, where the girl grows until she is reborn.

There is an aura of change: a lion resembles a man, so one must be careful when one hears "a thing calling there in the darkness." To help humans to navigate this apparently conflicting and menacing strait, certain precautions can be taken: when a mother intends to seek food, for example, she plunges a stone into the ashes of a fire, exclaiming a cryptic phrase, at the same time wishing that the evil things she dreams of will remain in the fire. If she does not do this, the rice that she digs will not be favorable.

It is a world in which inanimate objects become touched with life: when a woman takes a man's clothing because of the cold weather and he is consequently "dying of cold," his clothing and weapons follow him as he returns home. And it is a world in which humans live on the edge: a sick girl does not eat normal food; she kills the children of the water and eats them. A water-child, told to watch her, reports her forbidden acts to her mother. Clouds come up, and a whirlwind takes the children to the spring. The girl, the first to enter the spring, thereupon becomes a frog; her mother and father and the others also become frogs. Again, the movement is to the transitional phase, a regular metrical movement of humans in the context of animals and nature.

The seemingly ultimate rite of passage, death, is actually but one movement in a never-ending series of movements. After a San man kills an ostrich, a whirlwind blows the feathers into the sky. One feather falls into the water and becomes ostrich flesh. The ostrich, once regrown, goes to the she-ostriches, and they lay eggs, which he guards from the jackal. As for humans, when we die, the repetitive process continues. When we die, "our own wind blows," for humans possess wind: "we make clouds when we die." When we die, "the wind makes dust," intending to blow our footprints away, and "our gall . . . sits in the sky," while "the hair of our head / will resemble clouds."

The San Artist

Out of Two, One: The Metaphorical Process

In an oral performance, the audience (itself a participant in the process) can watch the performer as he deftly, with voice and body, brings one part of a story—often, but not always, realistic—into cohesion with another part of the story, which is frequently, but not inevitably, fantasy. This is the dancing metaphor: the storyteller is developing an illusion, giving the audience the sense that the two parts of the story are the same— not precisely the same, for they should never be precisely the same. The distinction between the two parts is what is crucial to this process, as important as the sensed similarity between those parts. The audience's emotions are worked, by means of the response to images evoked by the performer (images both verbal and nonverbal), into this process, so that the audience never remains outside the process of performance. And the emphasis is on process.[86]

Metaphor is always in the process of becoming, and when the performer has completed his story, metaphor, with the story's images, vanishes. The metaphor and the process are never tightly ordered: it is a shimmering process, it is a dancing metaphor. And that metaphorical process is the story's attraction, the definition that separates a storyteller performer from a mere rote storyteller.

The performer gives the spoken word a context both verbal and nonverbal. The music of the word along with the dancelike movement of the storyteller's body, sometimes shadowed by the bodies of the members of the audience, is the context for this metaphorical process. Sometimes the connections between the two parts of the metaphorical performance are purely nonverbal, the storyteller establishing a model with her body and then reproducing that model when the linkages are to be developed.

Whether the storyteller is an active performer or not, the body will play its role in the development of the metaphor. The music of the voice is also significant, sometimes actually evolving into song. Oral languages are frequently tonal; storytellers will exploit those tonal qualities, exploring the implicit poetry. The storyteller makes full use of the rhythmical qualities of the language, developing his own rhythms when necessary.

The performer creates a rhythmical environment in which the metaphorical process will be developed. He is simultaneously establishing that environment event and developing the dual metaphorical process. The environment and the process are inevitably a part of the story, of the dancing metaphor.

Poetry in the Oral Tradition: Une analogie réciproque

Poem and story[87] exhibit the same circling around a mythic center: the poem by metaphor, the story by narrative events. Begin with a poem and a story and create suspense about finding the mythic center: let that suspense last through the book. Create the book like a mystery, with the goal being to find the solution. Images in the poem and in the story alike are connected by the mythic center. The mythic center thus functions as the generator and repository of the images surrounding it. One should then organize the analyses in a precise, step-by-step way to define how the rhythm works to generate and reflect the emotions: cradled as the mythic center is approached.

In heroic poetry, or panegyric, the relationship among images seems obscure at times. Nevertheless, the images are indeed connected; a discourse is initiated by the poet, and the panegyric assumes lyrical form. As in the lyric poems, the rhythm of the poetic performance, its single subject, and the thematically designed boundaries bind the diverse images. Of all African art forms, heroic poetry is the closest to history in its choice of images. It frequently concentrates on historical figures. The creator of such poetry usually ignores repertories of fantasy, selecting instead images of animals and landforms to accompany the many historical allusions. Panegyric poetry examines heroic aspects of humans: positively, in the rush of pleasure in recounting the affairs in the lives of authentic culture heroes; negatively, in the comparison of the flawed contemporary leader with the great heroes of the past. While the raw material of this poetry is by and large realistic, it is history made discontinuous, then placed in novel frames. Within this new context, the hero is described, then judged. The metaphorical power of the work lies in the measurement of the poem's subject against the ideals of the society. Although such poetry is not a historical rendering, it nevertheless has no existence outside history. Images, selected at least partially for their power to elicit strong feelings from an audience, are first removed from their mainly historical contexts, as in the tales. Certain emotions associated with such subjects as heroism and the kingship are intensified and reordered. Because contemporary events are thus routinely measured against cultural values, history is constantly being revived and revised. The poems depend on this enhanced narrative—reproduced, atomized, and redefined. It is a subjective accounting, but the poet, using all his magic to convince his listeners otherwise, contains these as-yet-unchanneled bursts of energy and gives history a new gloss.

As with lyric poetry, panegyric builds on a diversity of images, tied to one another in intricate ways. This developing web reveals the character of the poem's subject, and at the center is the lyricism common to proverb and riddle, a regularly repeated pattern with alterations. The poem may have varied images, but the pattern organizes them. In many works, thematic parallelism, dominating other devices, unifies the poem. Into this unifying, steadying matrix, the bard places images that have somewhat ambiguous values, which adapt themselves fairly readily to whatever image environment they happen to be in. These lines take on the coloration of the dominant images around them and add to the illusion of unity. In this poem, the violent natural images are preponderant and act as the binding element, juxtaposing comparisons with deadly animals; both sets of imagery deal with violence in combat.

Fragmented history is also frequently a part of African epic, which treats the acts of both heroic characters who existed in fact and those who are fictional. It is not historical veracity in the linear sense that determines epic; it is the insight into history and culture provided by this confluence of oral genres. Within a pretext or setting that makes possible the merging of various frequently unrelated tales, the metaphorical apparatus—the controlling mechanism found in the riddle and lyric, the proverb, and heroic poetry—coordinates this set of tales to form a larger narrative. All of this centers on the character of the hero and a gradual revelation of his frailty, uncertainties, and torments: he often dies, falls, or is deeply troubled, in the process bringing the culture into a new dispensation often prefigured in his resurrection or coming into knowledge. The mythical transformation caused by the creator gods and culture heroes is reproduced precisely in the acts and cyclical, tortured movements of the hero.

While the tale is at the heart of epic, significant changes occur in this genre. The epic is a complex reshaping of the tale. Heroic poetry provides a grid, helping to organize the narratives and narrative fragments that are transported into the epic framework; it also supplies the specific historical and geographical data for certain epics. What African epics owe to the tale tradition is not difficult to discern. Less obvious is the role that heroic poetry plays in their construction. The simple tale weaves through the historical fragments trapped in images and given new context in the fictional activities. A strong sense of realism thus invests the imaginary character and his actions, even though they are taken directly from the imaginary tale tradition.

The significance of the panegyric influence on the epic is twofold. First, data about geography and history are injected into the narrative, tying the imaginative tales that compose the epic to the real world: to historical place, event, and time. Second, the emphasis on praise-names singles out the hero: his character, his ideals, and his struggles. This is not the case in the tale, where characters are not as important as the actions they perform; indeed, they are often not even given names. The stress in epic is on character, and the praise-names are evidence of this. Epic thus has a grander sweep than either the tale or heroic poetry. It enshrines the themes and emotional experiences of the tale on a broad scale; it embodies the details and historical and cultural specificity of panegyric poetry.

The combination of tale patterns and poetic rhythms in the epic transfers the images of those genres to historical figures and acts, endowing history with the cultural symbolism of the imaginative tradition. Heroes, whether or not they have existed in fact, become emblematic of change, and they are no less real for that. Epic is refracted history, revealing in telescoped, intensified images transitional periods in a culture's life. It is the shift from one kind of society to a new society envisioned by and imaged in the epic hero, who in some way typifies a cultural ethos. The epic carries with it images and experiences of the past (what the society has traditionally stood for) into the new world. The hero is a part of both realms; he would not be able to take his people with him if he were not identifiably a part of the cultural past. But he has a vision of the new world. If he dies in the process of realizing it, if his flaws are exposed, his vulnerability exploited, that is a part of change; and the atmosphere of yearning, regret, and loss are a part of the epic tradition, because it involves leaving a familiar world and making a transition into an uncertain one. Epic embraces both worlds. To make the change, the hero moves to the boundaries of his community, necessarily so; and as he escorts his society into the new world, he becomes its original insider.

As the epic form is built on the tale, so too does the epic character grow out of the tale characters. But the epic hero pulls at the sinews of the tale's cyclical pattern; that is the result of the emphasis on realism; in the end, he remains faithful to that periodicity. Still, the revolutionary zeal of the hero, his insistent posing on the borders of society, his vulnerability and mental struggles, and his agonizing battles with the traditions of his society and the teachings of the gods have emancipated him from the submissive tale character. The hero exists on both the outside and the inside of his society, as does another character from the oral tradition, the trickster, who pretends to be on the inside but whose tricks place him on the edge. He could not perform his tricks were he anywhere else; he needs dupes, and to dupe someone places him on the community's periphery. The trickster must be an insider to become an outsider; the hero is the opposite. The true insider, however, is the tale character. The tale deals with cultural activities and generally supports them; the epic allows anticultural actions because of the move from a view of the culture as it is to the culture as it will be; the shift from the one to the other places emphasis on the individual within that society who carries cultural and historical symbolism with him. Tales in their thousands regularly affirm the culture; characters rhythmically, routinely, and anonymously go through their rites of passage, helping others to do so and linking present culture to the timeless age of the beginning, in the process ensuring cultural continuity.

In the heroic epic, the etiological theme has to do with the birth of a society, as it does, albeit whimsically, in the trickster tales. In that respect, the trickster's illusions can be seen as the kernels of the heroic act of creation. The culture hero always leaves a residue; in his trickster activities, he transforms the earth or human society or the relations between humans and gods, between ruler and ruled. The trickster also recreates the world, through illusion and deception. The difference between the trickster and the culture hero lies here: the trickster's creations are evanescent; they die as quickly as he obtains fulfillment of his desires, though his dupe may never be the same. But the culture-hero's trickster-illusions are forever; they are the form of the mountains, the curbs on the rights of kings; they are the mediating force between gods and mortals. It is here, at the point at which the trickster and culture hero part, that the culture hero and epic hero merge. The latter, not a trickster in the same sense as the culture hero, is nevertheless cast in that role because his actions too have a permanent cultural imprint. The shift from the oral epic to the novel is accomplished because of the altered perception of the central character. If the novel is predisposed to the actions and mental processes of a changing individual locked in a struggle with his environment, then it has roots in the epic. Although epic heroes will always contain qualities of tale characters, the latter exist to fashion a model for human behavior. The trickster moves decisively against that model, as does the epic hero. This breaking of a cyclical pattern is what enables the trickster and hero to become outsiders, engaged in a struggle against the norms of their societies, changing those standards in the interest of immediate gratification or for a noble vision. In this way, the epic hero moves away from the tale character toward the historical figure. It is true that, though he breaks out of the cycle of the tale, his actions remain so under the influence of the tale tradition that he enters his own grand cycle. But the break is the thing, for it allows the introduction of realism into the oral narrative, making the transition to the novel possible. The hero's stand against his society, his reshaping of the values of his community, and his historical nature all argue for critical changes in the oral tradition. History and fiction have come into a tentative union in the epic, making possible the birth of the novel.

At the core of the heroic poem is the mortal being appraised. The efforts of the poet have the effect of giving that mortal being a mythic aura, moving the details of history and biography into a mythic center. This conversion is achieved largely by the introduction of one more set of images, in addition to those of history and biography: this set is usually composed of nature images but might also include fantasy material. Through the rhythmic interstitching of the materials of these three categories, the poet achieves a mythic transformation, converting a mortal, typically a leader, into a demigod. That mortal may suffer the consequences of this transformation when the poet does not allow the mortal to fuse with the mythic, and it is at that point that the poem becomes a fierce judgment on the mortal.

THE POET'S CANVAS is the imagination of the members of the audience, and his challenge is to unify those imaginations even as he appreciates the breadth of those imaginations. The art of the poet is to yoke those divergent and independent imaginations and memories for the moment of performance, thereafter to allow those imaginations and memories to go their own way, changed now perhaps, reshaped somewhat, and that is the experience of performance for the audience, its feelings evoked by the images and then shaped by the rhythm, given force and form by the voice and body of the poet. A poem lingers in the air, as it impetuously moves the audience members and then connects them. Movement and connection: these are the essential qualities of the effective poetic performer, the audience allowing that performer access to its innermost feelings and memories, confident that the performance currently being produced will fuel their feelings, move their memories. And weaving through the poems and the tales is the image of the uncoiling python. At the same time that the San people were being subjugated by the Europeans, to the point ultimately of being forced out of South Africa and into the Kalahari Desert, the San had built into the structure of their culture means for enduring and surviving the depredations of those who considered the San "Bushmen." Deep under the surface lurked the uncoiling python, the means of survival. It was only the word—a storyteller's verb, a poet's rhythm—that in the end enabled the San people to persist, as a people with a rich oral tradition, a tradition that provided the San with sustenance: " for he was a man," a man whose existence was interwoven with the world about him, "he is a tree, / he is a man."

ELIAS CANETTI AND FRANZ STEINER ON BLEEK AND LLOYD

From Elias Canetti, *Nachträge aus Hampstead: Aus Den Aufzeichnungen, 1954–1971* (Munich: Carl Hanser, 1994), 31–32.

Pavese war mein genauer Zeitgenosse. Aber er hat sich früher an die Arbeit gemacht und hat sich vor zehn Jahren das Leben genommen. Sein Tagebuch ist eine Art Zwilling zu meinem. Er hat sich mit Literatur befaßt, ich wenig. Aber ich bin [31/32] früher als er an die Mythen und an die Ethnologie geraten. Acht Monate vor seinem Tode, am 3. Dezember 1949, findet sich folgende Eintragung bei ihm:
"Ich muß finden:
W. H. I. Bleek and L. C. Lloyd: Specimens of Bushman Folklore. London 1911."
Dieses Buch befindet sich seit 1944, seit 16 Jahren, in meinem Besitz. Ich habe oft geglaubt, daß es das wichtigste Buch ist, das ich kenne. Wenn es auf die Konzentration von Unbekanntem in einem Buche ankommt, so its es mein wichtigstes Buch: ich habe am meisten daraus gelernt, und es ist noch immer nicht erschöpft. Dieses Buch, auf das Pavese knapp vor seinem Tode zuging, ist unser Gemeinsamstes, und ich möchte es ihm gerne geben.

From an entry, dated 1960, in *Notes from Hampstead: The Writer's Notes, 1954–1971*, translated from the German by John Hargreaves (New York: Farrar, Straus and Giroux, 1998), p. 30. The German edition was published shortly after Canetti's death in 1994. The translation reads as follows:

Pavese was my exact contemporary. But he started working earlier and took his life ten years ago. His journal is a kind of twin to mine. He cared mostly about literature, unlike me. But I happened onto myths and ethnology earlier. On December 3, 1949, eight months before his death, he wrote the following in his journal:
"I have to find W. H. I. Bleek and L. C. Lloyd, Specimens of Bushman Folklore, London, 1911."
This book has been in my possession for sixteen years, since 1944. I have often considered it the most important book

I know. The sheer quantity of new information about the un-known makes it my most important book. I have learned the most from it, and it is still not exhausted. This book, which Pavese turned to just before his death, is what we have most in common, and I wish I could give it to him."

FROM "FRANZ STEINER," in *From Prague Poet to Oxford Anthropolo-gist: Franz Baermann Steiner Celebrated; Essays and Translations*, ed. Jeremy Adler, Richard Fardon, and Carol Tully (Munich: Idicium, 2003), 256–57. The text was also included in Canetti's posthumous collection of notes, *Aufzeichnungen 1992–1993* (Munich: Carl Hanser, 1996), which I think has not yet been translated into English.

Both, he [Steiner] or I, liked to surprise the other with a book which he had been looking for for some time but did not yet know. It became a competition which we did not want to give up. The bookshops around the British Museum were inexhaust-ible and we spent as much time searching for antiquarian books as we did in our conversations. In the midst of all these days of searching, came the one when I was able to show him a copy of 'Specimens of Bushman Folklore,' by Bleek and Lloyd, one of the wonders of world literature, without which I would no lon-ger like to live. I had found it just before our meeting in the club [the Student Movement House in Gower Street], he could not believe it; I handed it to him, he leafed through it with—liter-ally—trembling hands and congratulated me—just as one would on the occasion of one of life's most important milestones.

3

THE NGUNI ARTIST

The Collapsing of Time

I wish to talk with you, while my thinking-strings
still stand.

The San storyteller | *háṅ̇ǂkass'ō*

*N*ongenile Masithathu Zenani, a Xhosa storyteller, told me, "The
art of composing imaginative narratives is something that was
undertaken by the first people—long ago, during the time of the ancestors.
When those of us in my generation awakened to earliest consciousness,
we were born into a tradition that was already flourishing. . . . Members
of every generation," she said, "have grown up under the influence of
these narratives."[1]

While I was collecting stories among the Xhosa, I was walking along
the lower reaches of the Drakensberg Mountains and arrived, one morning, at a homestead where some women were working. When they saw
me, they asked me what I wanted. I told them that I was hoping to col-
lect tales. The women were amused. They later told me that they would
have understood had I been interested in oral history, oral poetry . . .
but tales? They said that tales were as common and routine as washing
clothes, as working in the fields, as raising children. And I said that that
was precisely why I was interested in gathering tales.

Two observers wrote in 1920,

It is at evening around the fires that the tales are told, especially
on dark nights, when the people cannot dance so comfortably.
Many of the tales are known far and wide, others in lesser

areas. But, however often the people hear them, they never seem weary of the repetition. They never say, "Oh, that's an old tale," or make sarcastic references to chestnuts, but enter into the spirit of the thing all the more for knowing all that is to come. They heard the tales first as children from their mothers or grandmothers, but nevertheless they will, with no trace of boredom, come in with their ejaculations just at the right points, take, it may be, a sentence out of the narrator's mouth, or even keep up a running echo of his words.[2]

THE STORYTELLER

Time collapses, and we are in the presence of history: it is a time of masks. Reality, the present, is here, but with these explosive, emotional images giving it a context. This is the storyteller's art: to mask the past, making it mysterious, seeming inaccessible. But it is inaccessible only to our present intellect: it is always available to our hearts and souls, our emotions. The storyteller combines our present waking state and our past condition of semiconsciousness, and so we walk again in history, we join our forebears. And history, always more than an academic subject, becomes our collapsing of time, our memory and reliving of the past.

We never live wholly in the present, for much of our temperament, our nature, our character is rooted in the past: our emotional life has its origins in and its impetus from the experiences and images of history. The storyteller brings us unerringly into those spiritual centers of our lives, making us for the moment consciously aware of something that is a constant part of our unconscious lives. This emotional core is what largely dictates our actions and our thought, our decision making, our vision. Storytelling contains the humanism of the people, keeps them and their traditions alive despite life's daily vicissitudes. Time obliterates history. The storyteller arrests time and brings her audience into the presence of history, the heart and substance of the culture.

Storytelling is alive, ever in transition, never hardened in time. Stories are not meant to be temporally frozen: they are alive, always responding to contemporary realities, but in a timeless fashion. Storytelling is therefore not a memorized art. The necessity for this continual transformation of the story has to do with the regular fusing of fantasy and images of the real, contemporary world. Performers take images from the present and wed them to the past, and in that way the past regularly shapes our experience of the present. And the present can also influence the past. The storyteller deals with ancient images and mythic images and places these always into a contemporary, recognizable environment. And those ancient images are not themselves beyond reshaping by our experiences of the present. It is always a mutual and enriching relationship.

Storytellers reveal connections between humans, within the world, within a society, within a family, emphasizing our interdependence and the disaster that occurs when we forsake our obligations to our fellows. The artist makes the linkages, the storytellers forge the bonds, tying past and present, joining humans to their gods, to their leaders, to their families, to those they love, to their deepest fears and hopes, to the essential core of their societies and beliefs. "Much have I traveled in the realms of gold / And many goodly states and kingdoms seen," wrote the poet,[3] and he might have been speaking of the great Homers of all lands, of all times, the storytellers who remember all, forget nothing. The storyteller teaches us that we are as we have always been, from the beginning of time.

Storytelling never dies. It charts our course through history, from the most ancient of days to present times, and thrusts us into the future. The stories connect us to our ancestral past: in the tale are the echoing, reverberating, and overlapping sounds of storytellers through the generations. Too frequently, however, when people ponder stories and storytellers, they think of simple stories that point to facile morals. Narratives are not simply tales with obvious meanings.

Genres

In nonnarrative poetry, the lyric and the panegyric, the only relationship available to the bard is a metaphorical one; it binds images. In the tale, metaphorical union is not necessary to the sense of the story. But when it does occur, when both narrative and metaphor are present, the tale assumes the form of the lyric. In the African trickster tale, for example, the relationship is typically between the trickster and his dupe. All is illusion as the trickster creates a deceptive world to approximate the real. This linkage between the real world and an illusory realm contains the possibilities for a metaphorical relationship, a set of worlds controlled and manipulated by the trickster. While figurative movement is infrequently a consideration in such trickster tales, its structures and potential are evident. In the elaborated tale, metaphor becomes dominant. In fact, a reciprocal relationship exists: metaphor is a crucial compositional device that holds such tales together, at the same time that the unified narratives generate metaphor. In a Lamba story about two youths going through their puberty ritual, the storyteller moves the characters through three distinct worlds, as they journey toward the celestial realm. A model is established in the first of the worlds, and it is repeated with metaphorical depth in the second and the third, so that each experience in each of the worlds is at once the same yet more complex, as worlds two and three comment on the worlds that have come before, and so the audience is moved to an emotional understanding of the significance of the ritual.[4]

Storytelling is a sensory union of image and idea, a process of re-creating the past in terms of the present; the storyteller uses realistic images to describe the present and fantasy images to evoke and embody the substance of a culture's experience of the past. These ancient fantasy images are the culture's heritage and the storyteller's bounty: they contain the emotional history of the culture, its most deeply felt yearnings and fears, and they therefore have the capacity to elicit strong emotional responses from members of audiences. During a performance, these envelop contemporary images, the most unstable parts of the oral tradition, because they are by their nature always in a state of flux and thereby visit the past on the present.

Storytelling has to do with the emotions; artists typically take ancient emotion-evocative images, and they build contemporary stories around them, that is, they take images from the world that we know and build them around the venerable images. The two sets of imagery—ancient images and contemporary images—are brought into a close relationship by means of rhythmical patterns. In this way, the past exerts its influence on the present, and the present shapes our view of the past, a mutually nourishing and sustaining activity, in the process of which we once again learn through the storytelling process that we are not alone, and our emotional response to the images ties us to our fellows in the audience who are having similar emotional experiences, so that there is a sense of camaraderie not only with the past but also with our fellows in the present. Stories deal with the great changes that we encounter in our everyday lives, with the troubles that we encounter, and with the joys and nightmares of human existence. During a storytelling session, storytellers create space for encounters with ideas and experiences that are not the normal subject matter of discourse in our everyday lives.

The African oral tradition distills the essences of human experiences, shaping them into remembrable, readily retrievable images of broad applicability with an extraordinary potential for eliciting emotional responses. These are removed from their historical contexts so that performers may reorganize them in artistic forms. The oral arts, containing this sensory residue of past cultural life and the wisdom so engendered, constitute a medium for organizing, examining, and interpreting an audience's experiences of the images of the present. The tradition is a venerable one. Walter Benjamin, after having read an African tale, commented, "This story from ancient Egypt is still capable after thousands of years of arousing astonishment and thoughtfulness. It resembles the seeds of grain which have lain for centuries in the pyramids shut up air-tight and have retained their germinative power to this day." A story, he concluded, "does not expend itself the way information does. It preserves and concentrates its strength and is capable of releasing it even after a long time."[5] These images of the past, over the years honed into mythic images with the potential for metaphor, engage those of the present, which have not yet received figurative significance through the blending process. Contemporary images are still mere information. These oral performers, wrote the Xhosa novelist A. C. Jordan, "gave artistic utterance to their deepest thoughts and feelings about those abstract and concrete things that came within their experience."[6]

The imaginative tale carries images and themes that frequently dramatize social rituals. The heroic epic is the means of revealing the great shifts on a cultural level that are necessary to the securing of that passage for a whole people. Because it is dependent on the same metaphorical transformation as the tale, it is understandably constructed of tales stitched together; to further link fiction and history, the epic images are laced with those of heroic poetry. Central to these movements, if it is possible to generalize about so diverse a set of traditions, is a hero who is a composite of all elements of nature and society; these flow through him, and he comes to represent them in their interdependence, always with a temporal reach, involving past, present, and future.

The major oral genres—the riddle, the lyric poem, the proverb, the tale, heroic poetry, and the epic—are characterized by a metaphorical process, the product of pattern and image; they resolve themselves into models for human and cultural behavior, falling into a cyclical, not linear, mode. History, a part of heroic poetry and epic, appears in fragmentary form.

The oral categories are interwoven; a common internal structure characterizes them, each with a rhythmical ordering of image and mythic image that controls the ties between the art tradition and the real world. By means of this common structure—through the metaphor or its potential, the organizing factor in each of the genres—vital links are established with the visual arts, as well as with dance, mime, and music. Each of the forms in some way nourishes the other. The lyric poet partakes of the riddler's art, the tale operates according to the principles of the riddle and lyric poetry, and the tale contains the germ of the epic; in all cases, the metaphorical core controls expansion and development into more complex forms.

Many tales have a built-in capacity for linkage to other tales; several of them together, when placed in a narrative frame, produce a complex story. When two tales or more are thus joined and the parts harmonized by the metaphorical process, an epic matrix (if not an epic) is created, along, incidentally, with the roots of the literary novel. It is at this stage that organizing activities similar to those found in the proverb assume importance. In the shorter tales, a process like that of the riddle and poem is sufficient, but as organization and theme become more involved, the metaphorical movement found in the proverb becomes crucial because it supplies the structure necessary to carry a complex theme. The proverb-type activity establishes the ties between past and present; the type found in the riddle and lyric can then continue to supply the internal ordering of the larger forms. And panegyric poetry contributes the ties with history. When the number of tales develops to a complexity no longer supportable by the simple structure of the story, and when that set of tales is brought into a context that includes history and the hero, epic is the result.

The emotions of the audience are evoked by the key mythic images, intensely familiar to its members: the wretched treatment, the mythic aura produced by the mother and her supernatural acts, the splendid transformation from rags to riches. These emotions, by means of the rhythmical ordering of the story, are woven into the character and actions of that main character.

The storyteller begins with the mythic images, crucial to his story because they not only provide the controlling knot of the tale but also critically involve the emotions of the members of the audience. Rhythm, or patterning, follows: the repeated bad fortune of the central character, the repeated visits to the ball, disguise and transformation, the quest for the foot that will fit the shoe. These patterns have the effect of moving the linear melody of the story at the same time that they disrupt and subvert that linearity. This is the poetic center, and it depends on the linearity at the same time that it exists outside that linearity. The meaning of the story is ultimately bound up with the way the storyteller links the varied emotional responses of the audience—pity and sorrow and fear at the plight and treatment of the girl, delight and joy at her transformation, suspense involved in the quest, and, at the end, death and regeneration: a reborn adult. These emotions, evoked by the mythic images, are worked by the performer into the pattern of the story. And it is this rhythmical union of the images and emotions that constitutes the meaning, the theme, the message of the tale. The mythic center is this churning cauldron of diverse emotions: in the hands of a lesser storyteller, these might get out of hand. But the accomplished performer is able to work these emotions into form and thereby unite the members of the audience, for the duration of the performance, into a single entity. That sense of commonality is a part of the joy and the myth of performance. So the poem in the story is not the linear movement of the tale, although the storyteller uses the linear images to create that poem. At the heart of the story, throbbing, bristling with potential, is the set of mythic images, the emotions evoked, the patterns that give the emotions form and the story its meaning.

The independent genres interact primarily by means of their identical metaphorical construction. As oral forms become longer and more complex, this same process animates them, as if the riddle and lyric poem formed their core with the proverb adding a somewhat didactic bridge between the worlds of the real (that is, the present) and the fantastic (that is, the past).

The single most important characteristic of African oral performances is the patterning of images. Children learn to organize like images, establishing a model for the comprehension of forms that are more sophisticated, in which unlike images are meant to be aligned. In the simple tale, patterns are built on the actions of a single character, as fantasy and reality are linked in a linear movement from conflict to resolution; at the same time, the metaphorical structure, not unlike that which governs the movement in lyric poetry, controls the patterning, providing the possibilities for complexity, for meaning, and for the revelation of the mimetic relationship. That lyrical core ensures that the potential for expansion and development is not lost. Out of a triangular relationship that includes a central character, a helper, and a villain, the basic movement is developed. The tale at this stage will not necessarily be metaphorical; it may simply bring like image sets into contact with one another for no purpose other than to move the tale effectively to its resolution. But the possibilities for metaphor are a part of the form because of the existence of patterning.

Fantasy

Themes that are common to stories typically concern transformation, change, as humans move from one state of being to another. Hence, rites of passage, and especially those having to do with puberty and marriage, are emphasized. The language of storytelling involves most significantly patterns, repetition, the rhythm of storytelling. The ancient fantasy images are wedded to contemporary real-life images by patterning.

Fantasy is the creation of parallel worlds with their own rules and laws. We have to understand those rules and laws. The raw material of stories is fantasy mythic images and real-life images. The storyteller links these through patterning, bringing unlike images into relationship with each other. Other images, image-sets, and minor patterns weave these larger patterns together. The tools of fantasy, therefore, include fantasy images, realistic images, patterns that connect fantasy and realistic images, minor and supporting image-sequences, image-sets, patterns, and so forth that link the larger patterns—and the metaphorical result.

The crucial thing is two worlds: one world that echoes, in prismatic ways, another. In understanding the prism, we come to a deeper understanding of that world that is under investigation. The parallel world is the storyteller's tool whereby he analyzes the world that we inhabit. The argument is that such investigation can take place in no other way. So it is that a congeries of characters may come to represent a single real-life character and a complexity of events may explain a single real-life event. But there is more to it than the two worlds. The thing to remember is that the parallel world is not a contemporary world: it is apparently ancient, and it encapsulates images that are ancient and have the capacity to elicit strong emotional responses from members of audiences. The sense in storytelling is that these ancient images contain the wisdom of the ages, that when they come into contact with the real, our experience of the real world is given a new shape. Sometimes these ancient images, called mythic images, are fantastic, but they do not have to be: their behavior is what is important. So if we get caught up in debating whether or not an image is fantastic on its face, we miss the point of storytelling. Fantasy is the combining of two worlds: one thought of as real and the other thought of as fictional. It is the metaphorical sparks that fly when those two worlds come into contact. What we have to do, then, is understand the limits of the two worlds and how they intersect. That is the excitement of analysis, because the two worlds are not neatly separated: they fold into each other, so that the one seems at times an intrusion into the other. Fantasy is the joining of fiction and history.

Fantasy always occurs within the shadow of the real, but it frequently subverts the real and always provides the real with new dimensions and layers of experience and meaning. Fantasy is a world of rhythmical order, a world of connections, of transformations, of metaphorical relationships often between the real and the marvelous. These relationships and other encoded meanings are apprehended by an understanding of the form that establishes these parallel worlds. Without an understanding of form, there can be no understanding of the poetry of fantasy. Fantasy contains history, fragmented history, reconstituted history, the marvelous, and myth.

Images that we may characterize as fantasy are joined in rich meta-phorical linkages, so that the images blur and shimmer and blend, and in the end what is reality and what is fantasy? To get caught up in the question of whether a given image is fantasy is to mistake the elephant's tail for the rest of the beast. A study of fantasy takes us to the very foundations of art, because fantasy is in the end rhythm, the very heartbeat of narrative production. When we move into the world of the storyteller, we are in the realm of fantasy, whether there is a monstrous dragon or not.

Part of the problem is that we tend to view fantasy as an end in itself, as a part of the completed material of story. In actual fact, it is a part of the animating elements of story: the fantasy images are marvelous, uncanny, supernatural, and the like. Or we may believe that they are simply poetic or allegorical representations of the real. And they are doubtless both of these. There are indeed fantasy images in stories: they are fantastic, surreal, supernatural, uncanny, disguised versions of the real. But fantasy is also a part of the form of story: it is, in fact, the activator of the imagery, moving the several images into metaphorical arrangements. Those metaphors are not always easily "read." They may be primarily emotional.

How does one experience the image that seems to be unreal? The movement toward metaphor is the essence of the story, and that explains fantasy. As we move closer to metaphor, fantasy (which is our lack of understanding, for the images seem not to fit, not to be real) slowly forms into poetic ordering. In the end, fantasy is no longer present: its residue is, but it has been replaced by metaphor. The movement of story is to metaphor. The material of metaphor is that with which we are familiar and, more important, that with which we are unfamiliar. This is why scholars see fantasy in various categories: the supernatural, the marvelous, and the uncanny. But the really important thing is that fantasy is a poetic device that evokes emotion of one kind of another. Fantasy takes us to the boundaries of our experience: out there, we are not so sure. Then fantasy moves us back to the familiar, but with a significant change: the familiar can never be the same. It has been leavened, given new dimension, by an experience in fantasy. In the end, fantasy becomes metaphor, a part of the activity that we go through intellectually and imaginatively and emotionally as we sort out items in the wondrous puzzle given to us by the storyteller. Fantasy, then, is never an end in itself. It is the engine of change, the activity in the betwixt and between area as the parts of the metaphor form themselves and slowly begin to coalesce. What begins as fantasy ends as an understanding, and fantasy, having done its work, fades or, newly disguised, simply becomes a part of the completed poetic puzzle.

The storyteller creates a view of reality that depends heavily on images of reality. But from time to time, fantasy images move across the scene, or reality finds itself within a fantasy context; this is startling, causing emotion, uncertainty, and sudden unpredictability in a scene that up until now has been totally predictable. But the fantastic object, act, or creature does something else as well: it alerts the audience to latent meanings, to arcane meanings lurking behind familiar realistic images. We are not, after all, living in a world that we know. Strange truths are behind every hill, every structure. Fantasy leads us to something else about the tales, to their structures, revealing to us certain unrealities: this is not the real world after all. Something weird and wonderful is happening here, and if we can just understand that, we shall get a penetrating insight into that reality. The reality is there, but the disturbing thought is that it is not just reality, it points to something else. Fantasy exposes a culture's definitions of that which can be.

Transformation

Stories are ambiguous in the sense that they are metaphorical. The meaning of stories is not to be found on their obvious surfaces. Meaning is the product of all aspects of the story, including those surface images but also involving the rhythmical linking of imagery, relationships between characters that transcend the clearly evident.

The self is constantly in a process of becoming the other. This is the promise of the oral tale. It is what accounts for all the emphasis on change, transformation, the character in the princess of becoming. It is what accounts for the emphasis on patterns. Patterning is obvious, but what is not so obvious is why patterning is used. Some observers see patterns as mnemonic devices, but patterns are the means whereby the secrets are enfolded within the images of the story and by which the secrets can be disclosed. Participating in oral narrative performances is a constant process of rediscovery, looking behind the realities we know so intimately to the eternal cultural truths lying behind.

Transformation is the crucial activity of the story: the movement of the story, the betwixt and between space and dynamism of the story. The storyteller is examining the relationship of the audience with its world, that is, with history. To do this, the storyteller invents characters and events that correspond to history but are not history. At the center of the story is myth, the fantasy element, a character or event that moves beyond reality, though it is always rooted in the real. In the oral tale, this is clearly the fantasy character; so it is in literature as well. Myth, which has to do with the gods and creation, also serves as the essence of a belief system, the imaged embodiment of a philosophical system, the giving of form to thought and emotion. Myth is deeply, intensely, emotional. It is the driving force of a people and is that emotional force that defines a people; it is the everlasting form of us and our culture; hence its link to the gods, to the heavens, to the forever. In mythic imagery is the embodiment of those emotions—the hopes, fears, dreams, nightmares—of a people. Myth is always emotional. History is the story of a people, their institutions, and their community. History is the way we like to think things happened, in the real world.

The hero is everyperson, who moves through a change, a transformation, and so moves into the myth, the essence, of his or her history and thereby becomes a part of it, representative of it, embodying the culture. The hero is everyperson with myth inside him or her. He or she has been mythicized: art does that. Metaphor is the transformational process, the movement from the real to the mythic and back again to the real: changed forever, because one has become mythicized, one has moved into history and returned with its prize. There are the ambiguous, the charismatic shapers, those with connections to the essence of history. In each case, a real-life character moves into a relationship with that mythic character, and that movement is the movement of the hero, as he or she becomes a part of history, of culture. The hero is the person in the process of being created. Myth is the stuff of which the hero is being created. History is the real, the past, the world against which this transformation is occurring and within which the hero will move. The real contemporary world is the place whence the hero comes, to which he or she returns. In the story, we see characters in the process of becoming, characters being transformed. That is the movement of the stories, with the betwixt and between stage the key. The shaping forces are history and myth.

Myth is fantasy, the strange. Characters who are charismatic death dealers and life givers are the essence of storytelling. The access point, the common human point, is the character (often not especially interesting) being formed. The common humans are often timid, uncertain; they are the ones being formed. The forming force itself is the exciting element, that which most effectively claims our emotions. Those emotions of ours become the raw materials around which the new character is formed, shaped. His or her formation is our formation. This is the metaphor of fiction: we become a part of what is happening. What is occurring in story is like what is happening in our own lives. This is the language of storytelling: history is here, but these works are not history. They are stories, with all the manipulation of storytelling. The fantasy character is our access to the history, to the essence of history. It is the explanation of the historical background of the novels. The hero is the person who is being brought into a new relationship to that history, be it the history of a certain area (Kenya or South Africa or Algeria, for example) or of a wider history (such as Africa generally).

These are the keys, then: the hero who is being shaped; the fantasy character who is the ideological and spiritual material, both material of shaping and the artist or shaper; and the larger issues, that is, the historical panorama. The fantasy character is the key: more than the shaper or artist, he is the stuff of the artist even as he is also the mythic element of the story. This character is the heart, the spiritual essence of history, right or wrong. Here is where reality and fantasy, history and fiction blend, the confluence at which they meet. The real-life character, the hero (who is us, members of the audience) comes into a relationship with that mythic figure, and so the transformation begins, as the hero moves through a betwixt and between period into history. The hero's relationship with history, actual identification with history, is what enables us to speak of him or her as a hero. This movement of a realistic character into myth is metaphor, the blending of two seemingly unlike images. It is the power of the story, the center of the story. The image of Africa, then, is that rich combination of myth and history, with the hero embodying the essence of the history, or battling it, or somehow having a relationship with it, by means of the fantasy mythic character.

All stories have messages, but it is an error to think that such messages are of the obvious Aesop's fable–type messages. Instead, they are encrypted in the stories. Stories do two things: they provide insight into African societies, but they also reveal the connections among the world's societies. Humans across the world tell the same stories. The way stories are put together, the images that appear in the stories, and the themes that are revealed through the meshing and organizing of the images do reveal a certain similarity in stories across African societies.

Behind the diversity of human societies, then, is a unity that makes brothers and sisters of us all. This is the great lesson of the world's storytellers, a lesson that is craftily kept hidden in the parliaments of the world. The human image in folklore is an image of unity. This common element in human experience, which binds us irrevocably as members of the family of man, is nowhere more obvious than in evocations of the life cycle in the folklore traditions of the people of the world. Storytellers have always dabbled in astral matters, have ever been at home in the celestial realms. Storytelling contains the essence of a people, takes them to the core of what they are.

Creation of Stories

The difficulties of taking tales from the oral tradition and making these available to wider audiences are considerable. Those African oral narratives with which most of us are familiar are but shadowy blurs of the original productions, mere scenarios written down in the nineteenth and twentieth centuries by missionaries, by colonial administrators, and later by anthropologists. Even in the fragmented and often badly transcribed narratives taken down by foreign observers, the underlying structures and, therefore, the themes are evident. There is an order to all aspects of the narrative images, from their transmission to the movement of the story, from conflict to resolution. This order, and the various structures that exist below the surface of the performance, must be discovered if the dynamics of this elaborate and complex system of memory and communication are to be appreciated.

The problems for the translator of oral materials into a written form are enormous, some of them insurmountable except by extensive multimedia productions,[7] and even then the impact of the original performance is diminished. Edwin W. Smith and Andrew Murray Dale wrote in 1920,

> We have to reconcile ourselves to the fact that for us, at least, it is impossible to do justice to these tales, and we doubt if the most skillful hand could reproduce in a translation the quaintness, the liveliness, and humor of the original. For one thing, fully to appreciate them one must be familiar, as only those who have always lived in the country can be familiar, with the characteristics of the animals spoken of; and then they gradually lose flavor as they pass from the African's telling, first into writing and then into a foreign idiom. It would need a combination of phonograph and kinematograph to reproduce a tale as it is told. One listens to a clever story-teller, as was our old friend Mungalo, from whom we derived many of these tales. Speak of eloquence! Here was no lip mumbling, but every muscle of face and body spoke, a swift gesture often supply[ing] the place of a whole sentence. He would have made a fortune as a raconteur upon the English stage. The animals spoke each in its own tone: the deep rumbling voice of Momba, the ground hornbill, for example, contrasting vividly with the piping accents of Sulwe, the hare. It was all good to listen to—impossible to put on paper. Ask him now to repeat the story slowly so that you may write it. You will, with patience, get the gist of it, but the unnaturalness of the

circumstance disconcerts him, your repeated request for the repetition of a phrase, the absence of the encouragement of his friends, and, above all, the hampering slowness of your pen, all combine to kill the spirit of story-telling. Hence we have to be content with far less than the tales as they are told. And the tales need effort of imagination to place readers in the stead of the original listeners.[8]

The problems of developing literary correspondences for oral non-verbal artistic techniques are staggering, for the translation of a single narrative performance involves profound transformations that defy equivalence. The major problem centers on the translation from the oral form to the written word, not merely from one language into another. And the translation of a narrative performance freezes in the written word the creation of a tradition that is fluid and flexible, thereby suggesting a permanence that is not characteristic of the oral system that produced it. The artist obviously has no script; his materials include ancient images, his body and voice, his imagination, and an audience. Within a broad thematic framework, he is free to deal with the images as he chooses, and he is praised by the audience for the originality with which he objectifies them. Little is memorized, so that the artist must depend on her imagination and on the controlled cooperation of the members of the audience to develop the skeletal core image that she has drawn from a repertory of remembered images, inherited from a venerable artistic tradition. The development of a plot is not always the most important achievement in a performance. The performers are storytellers; they are intellectuals as well as artists, a role that has been defined for them for generations. They are craftspeople who can use the narrative surface as a tool, as a language to be utilized to generate a theme, to create an argument, and to elicit some emotional or intellectual response from an audience. The image that is externalized has never before been produced in just that fashion and will never again be created that way. The narrative surface can be manipulated by the artist and made to project a certain idea at one time, a special emotion when it is produced the next time, a solution to a problem currently plaguing the society, the communication of the artist's own preoccupation.

In the creation, combination, and management of images will emerge ideas, values, arguments, affirmation of social institutions, and most important, the eliciting and organizing of emotions. The surfaces of the stories are constructed of the core images, that part of the special language of the tradition that is transmitted through the generations. These core images are readily recalled and implicitly contain within themselves the conflict and resolution, which will become evident only when the artist develops them in a performance, giving the ancient image renewed life with his words, his body, and the rhythm of the language. As the artist urges the plotting of images forward in a linear development, underlying structures and organizational devices are simultaneously guiding the imaginations of the members of the audience in nonlinear fashion, enabling the surface narrative to turn in upon itself, and this becomes a nonverbal commentary on the imagery. What is often dismissed as a simple fascination with a world of fantasy is really a metaphorical language, sophisticated and useful and communicated through the ages.

As the storyteller projects the remembered images, she is constantly in need of the active participation of the audience, and if she is talented and confident, she makes use of the many potentially disruptive tensions that might exist between her and the members of that audience, which has the same repertory of core images as the artist. The translator must not only be aware of the images developed on the surface of the story but also be sensitive to their poetic use, to the deeply metaphorical nature of the oral narratives. She must also be sensitive to the aesthetic principles that guide the creation of the work, for what might appear on the written page as an awkwardly conceived-of fragmented story may not be so regarded during its actual performance. Problems of artistic proportion are indeed considerations in African oral societies, but these frequently go beyond the plotting of images, becoming involved in the complex logic and interworkings of the imaged language itself. What initially appears as simply a matter of verbal equivalence is actually that unique metaphorical language which the unwary translator may hopelessly bungle.

This relationship between artist and audience becomes further complicated for the translator when one considers its nonverbal quality. The performer expects that the members of the audience will actively participate in the development of his images. It is necessary to the success of his story production that he wholly involve the audience in the unfolding work of art, and to do this he utilizes several devices. These devices are used most obviously to externalize the images, to clarify their plotting, and to take the images to a climax. At the same time that the audience, always under the control of the artist, is helping to create and sustain the images, it is simultaneously being integrated into the images. It is a part of the work of art in two ways: it helps to build the images, and it is emotionally caught up in the images.

The linear plotting of images is the most apparent of these narrative devices; it has its own appeal, as the conflict develops and is slowly moved toward a resolution, with a deft alteration of core images the artist can change to suit her own designs. The opening images of the performance are often filled with realistic details drawn from the immediate environment of the audience, the artist seeking to make the transition into her world of metaphor smooth. The demand for realism goes beyond this; in fact, the entire performance is in a sense realistic, the fantastic and magical elements being the metaphorical extensions of reality. The artist will exploit the rhythmic possibilities of an oral language. She will move her body, arms, face, and shoulders rhythmically, at times becoming a dancing in place. These musical characteristics of the performance have their own beauty and bring the members of the audience into a fuller emotional participation in the developing images. They move their bodies in harmony with the performer's; they clap, sing, express their approval, and are in physical and emotional accord with the artist and her creation. The audience knows the hackneyed plots, for its members have witnessed their production numerous times. But there is a freshness about the work that is not evident on the surface; moreover, the artistic delight in the performance goes deep, and the rhythms set in motion by the performer sustain images that are intricate. The society is somehow affirmed every time the core images are objictified with serious intent, and the members of the audience are wholly caught up in that narrative. They are totally involved in the ideals being metaphorically crafted in the performance. At the moment of creation, the entire society is woven into the artistic image, and the audience's experience is deepened by its emotional involvement in the artistic logic of image structures that the audience is manipulating. During the performance, the members of the audience are immersed in their culture as it is ideally visualized by the artist; they are involved in its structure and are emotionally caught up in its values and aspirations. Fragments of social history and myth are at the heart of the images.

The word persists. A world is created that provides a sanctuary against hostile forces. That sanctuary, as is evident in the stories that follow, is constructed against the peril that would penetrate and subvert it. Stories are deceptive: apparently not illuminating these forces that would overwhelm the society; seemingly insufficient weaponry against those potent external powers. Yet these stories (those that follow and many like them) in southern Africa became the means whereby a people became an uncoiling python, seemingly without threat yet with an enduring force of its own. The word poetically evokes the image of the uncoiling python, symbol of rebirth, as is evident in a series of stories performed by Nguni people of southern Africa. The commentaries on the stories are summaries of my discussions with the storytellers and their audiences following the performances.

NGUNI STORIES

A Zulu Tale
THE GRAVE-ROBBER

By Sikhwelesine Ngcobo

At a wedding, the bride hears the sounds of mourning as a person is being buried. The bride wants to join the mourners, to which her husband finally reluctantly agrees. She digs up the corpse and carries it away. A pattern is developed as she does so: she repetitively sings a song. She hides the corpse, then returns home. The groom, who has followed her and seen all this, concludes that he has married a witch; he will not sleep with her.

A young woman, who had become betrothed, went to dance the wedding dance. When she arrived at the wedding dance, it happened that mourning was heard in a neighboring homestead because the man of the house had died. The mourning was loud: there was wailing, there was crying.

Early in the morning, people came to offer condolences, and there was more lamentation.

The young woman observed all of this.

This person who had died was buried, this person was buried.

That night, when this person had been buried, the young woman said, "We people are close. I feel that I should go and join the mourners in that homestead."

The bridegroom said, "Why would you mourn?"

"Well, I shall go for only a short time and cry a tear or two. Won't you agree to this?"

The groom remained silent for a time.

The *inganekwane* (2S-1105) was performed by Sikhwelesine Ngcobo, a Zulu woman, about forty years old, on Sunday, September 24, 1972, in the home of Asilita Philisiwe Khumalo, at 8 am, in Nongoma, kwaZulu, under heavy clouds and thunder, some rain in the morning. The audience consisted of three Zulu women.

Figure 3. Sikhwelesine Ngcobo (Zulu). *Photo by the author*

"If I had my way," she said, "I would go and mourn at
that homestead."

The groom then said, "Go then."

So the woman went to mourn at that homestead. When she
got there, she did not go to the place where the mourning was
taking place. Instead, she went to the grave, and she dug it up,
she dug it, she dug it up. Then she took the corpse out of the
grave and placed it outside. There was a blanket that acted as
a shroud; she rolled that blanket into a head cushion, and she
carried the corpse on her head. As she went along, she sang:

"My father will sing my praises,
My father will sing my praises.
He will say that his daughter
Has brought him a man of Nokhenke![9]
Ye ye, Skenke! Ye ye, Skenke!"

Unknown to the bride, the groom had got up after she had left,
and he had followed her. The bride went on and on, singing,

"My father will sing my praises,
My father will sing my praises.
He will say that his daughter
Has brought him a man of Nokhenke!
Ye ye, Skenke! Ye ye, Skenke!"

So the young woman went on, and when she was near to her
homestead, she put the corpse down in a cluster of palm trees.
When she had put it down, she plucked palms and covered it
with them. Then the bride returned.

The groom ran, he returned to the house first. He crawled
into bed and pretended to snore. Soon, the bride arrived.
She came in and closed the door. The man began to quake.
He thought, "It turns out that I have courted a witch!" He
was agitated.

When the bride prepared to sleep with the groom, the
groom said, "Oh no! It is inappropriate for a person who has
gone to a mourning vigil to sleep with another person, they
do not sleep together. You sleep over there, there's a mat over
there," and he took down a mat and gave it to her. Then he took

an old blanket and gave it to her. "After all, she is coming from a wake. She ought not to sleep on a mat with me."

So they went to bed.

Early in the morning, the bride woke up.

The groom said to the people, "Hee, cook quickly! Cook quickly! Surely you know that this person is leaving."

The people said, "Is she going today?"

The groom said, "This person is definitely leaving. She told me that she is departing."

Hesitantly, the older people demurred vaguely, saying, "No!"

But the groom said, "This person is in a hurry, she is going."

The bride said, "Actually, I am in a hurry, I am indeed going."

The older people let her alone. Food was prepared for her.

Her younger brother said, "Heee, you! Cook quickly, prepare the food at once so that it is ready to eat soon. The place this person is going to is far away."

So they hurriedly prepared food for the young woman. She ate and ate. They went out to accompany her part of the way, then they turned back. The groom, however, accompanied her farther. He was carrying two spears and a club. They went on and on.

When the bride got to the place where she thought he would turn back, she sat down.

"Why do you sit down?"

She said, "I thought you would turn around here."

"Why?"

"Because, surely, you will turn back here."

He said, "Well, I thought I'd go farther. I'll go with you to that point over there."

They went on once more.

Again, the bride sat down.

"Why do you sit down?"

"I thought you would turn around here."

"But did I say that I was turning around here?"

She said, "Well, I thought that you would be turning back here."

"No, I shall turn back when I choose."

On and on and on they went.

When they were close to where she had put away this thing of hers, well, the bride again sat down.

"What's the matter now?"

"I thought you would turn back here."

"Did I say that I was turning back here?"

She said, "Well, actually, I said it because you usually do not come as far as this, you usually turn back there."

The groom said, "I told you that I would turn wherever I chose."

So the bride went on, and she passed by the place where she had put away this thing of hers. She went right past that place.

It was under those circumstances that the groom said, "Have you forgotten your thing?"

"My thing? What thing?"

"What I meant was *your* thing that you put over there in that brake."

"You tell me: what did I put there?"

"Hee! Turn back, go and take your thing that you brought here. For what purpose did you bring it here?"

"But what was it?"

"Well, just go and see where you will find your thing!"

"Yehee! What ominous thing has befallen me that I should have to go into shady places!"

He said, "I shall hit you! Go and pick up that thing of yours!"

"I have no such thing, I own nothing like that!"

Then she turned and went into that marshy place.

"Uncover it."

So the bride uncovered it.

"Take it; that is your thing."

"*I* can never take it! I don't know this person. Why would this person impress me into a dark deed concerning a dead person?"

"Well, it is the one you said you were going to mourn for that night. Now lift him up and raise him, take him out by yourself. You've got to take him to your home."

The bride said, "*I* don't know this person!"

So the groom hit her, he hit her again and again.

"Pick him up!"

The young woman picked him up.

"Roll up this blanket of yours that has been used as a cushion."

So she unwrapped it and rolled it into a coil. Then the bride raised the load to her head. And she walked on, on and on, crying all the time.

"Look here! Don't cry, you were not crying when it was night."
She traveled on.
"Sing out in the way you were singing."
The bride sang,

> "My father will sing my praises,
> My father will sing my praises!
> He will say that his daughter
> Has brought him a man of Nokhenke!
> Ye ye, Skenke! Ye ye, Skenke!"

The girl ran.
"Run harder!"

> "My father will sing my praises,
> My father will sing my praises!
> He will say that his daughter
> Has brought him—"

By now, toward sunset, the bride was reaching the place where
she was going, but it was still a long way off. It was sunset,
about dusk. And so she arrived.

> "My father will sing my praises,
> My father will sing my praises!
> He will say that his daughter
> Has brought him a man of Nokhenke!
> Ye ye, Skenke! Ye ye, Skenke!"

Her mother came out of the house. Her mother came
out of the house, and said, "My daughter!" She saw that her
daughter was accompanied by someone, so she kept quiet.
She saw something falling in the doorway. "What's this that
you're carrying?"
"I don't know! It was this one, the one with whom I'm
walking, who said that I should pick up this thing!"
The people of this place from all the neighboring
homesteads were summoned. They were called together.
The man then said, "This young woman is mine! She
accepted me as a suitor, you of the assembly, your child has

accepted me. I have been hiding this. But today, no more! *I did
not know that she is a witch!* This father who died over there—
she said that she was going to mourn him. But when she got
there, this young woman dug him up from the grave. What she
said to me was, 'If you would only allow me to do so, I would
go over there and mourn the dead person.' When I was about to
refuse, she said that I should please let her go to the wake. She
would not be long, she would only drop a tear or two. When I
allowed her to go, I accompanied her, but she did not see me.
I followed her at a distance. Then I saw her dig up this person,
I saw her dig up this person and carry him to a cluster of palm
trees in a certain place, all the time saying,

> 'My father will sing my praises,
> My father will sing my praises!
> He will say that his daughter
> Has brought him a man of Nokhenke!
> Ye ye, Skenke . . . '

"This dead man's regiment was Nokhenke. Now then, as I
appeared in her company right here, her mother says, 'My
daughter has really helped me!' and when she saw me, she
changed her tune, and said, 'Who is this person you are traveling
with? What are you carrying?' The mother was pretending to be
startled. Now, I don't want to have anything to do with her."[10]

The man got up to go, leaving the bride behind there.

The men were saying, "How can you remain quiet when
someone has come and smelled you out?[11] Do you know this
person at all?"

The man said, "I don't know him."

Her mother also said, "I don't know him."

And the bride, too, said, "*I* do not know this person. All that
happened is that I saw him there and I thought maybe I should
pick him up."

The man departed, as he said, "I want to have nothing to do
with you, absolutely, absolutely, absolutely."

COMMENTARY

To comprehend how Africans in South Africa dealt with the sustained European invasion of their land, one must understand

how the stories and poems in their oral traditions worked. If one remains on the surface of those stories, one concludes, as did many Europeans, that these are the harmless products of a not very complex oral tradition. What the whites did not see was that beneath the surfaces of these stories was the uncoiling python.

A woman longs for the past, a past that is now apparently dead. Her present world will not accept her past. The corpse is the mythic center in this story, occurring within the context of the real world of the groom. The bride is an ambiguous being: she is married to the real-life groom but is also attached to the mythic corpse, and she moves between the two, at the same time that she is attempting to keep her husband ignorant of her strange movements between the worlds of the living and the dead. A change has occurred, and the past is past. But the woman cannot give up the past, cannot accept its loss. Her mother, too, is reluctant to give that up. Two forces are operating here.

A Swati Story

KABETANA AT THE OCHRE PIT

By Nokwazi Gaulana

Three girls had been instructed to go and dig ochre at an ochre pit. Among them was a girl who had menstruated, who was older. The others were to go and dig red ochre so that this girl might be anointed the next morning on the occasion of her puberty initiation celebration.

So, friends, the girls went, they went to dig red ochre.

With them was a girl whose name was Kabetana; she was a twin who had been instructed at home not even to try to go into the pit, not under any circumstances, because the pit would cave in and fall on her.

So the others dug, friends, and this girl, Kabetana, refused to go in. She said, "I dare not! I was instructed at home not to enter the pit."

The storyteller was Nokwazi Gaulana, a Bhaca woman, about forty-five years old. She performed this *intsomi* (1S-1702) on November 4, 1967, at about 4 pm, in a home in Mpoza Location, Mount Frere District, the Transkei. In her audience were ten women and fifteen children, all Bhaca.

"In that case, sit over there as long as you want. *We're* going in now!"

These girls filled their buckets, and the other girl just sat there. When they were ready to leave, she said, "You might as well go." So the others departed, leaving Kabetana behind.

But when she went into the pit, it fell in on her and closed in. She screamed until her voice became hoarse, but nobody heard her.

Back at home, people inquired about where the girl was.

"Well, she has married. She—she was abducted by some rogues."

"She has been married!"

"Wait for the cattle for the dowry."

"As we recall, it was said that the groom's party is to arrive this very week."

"Is that so?"

"Yes."

Meanwhile, back to Kabetana, this girl in the cave: a bird passed near her. The bird heard her cry, it heard that a human being was in there. It hurriedly returned to the forest and told another bird that there was a person over there.

"Her crying is heart-rending. She is crying piteously."

That bird told other birds, "I went over there, I took her on my back, and flew off with her. When I got to the forest, I put her high up on a tree. She is there now."

Meanwhile, preparations were going on for this other girl's celebration over there; it was to take place the next day. Some boys yoked oxen and went to the forest to the place where the girls had been sent out to dig ochre. When they got there, they cut wood.

While they were cutting wood, they heard a song, the song of a person who was singing sadly.

They looked up, but they saw nothing. They looked up but did not see her.

And again, they heard the song: she spoke now and said, "You are my people! I am Kabetana. I was left behind by Khabelungu and her friends at the ochre pit. Please go to my mother and father; they should come and fetch me. I am dying of hunger. Do not tell anyone else."

The boys ran; they told no one until they arrived at the royal residence. They called the old man to one side and gradually, bit by bit, they discussed the matter with him.

That night, they went to steal her away. They made a little ladder, putting bushes together in a certain way, sewing them, until they made a ladder that would reach the girl over there in the forest. They lowered her successfully, they lowered her successfully.

She was emaciated, skinny as bark. They carried her on their backs, they carried her home.

The king said, "Tomorrow morning, at dawn, there will be a confrontation!"

He summoned from the village all of those girls who had gone to the ochre pit: they must come to the royal residence the following morning.

Well, friends, the girls dressed up, thinking that there was to be a dance. But when they filled the courtyard at the royal residence, men who were the scouts of the royal residence emerged, bearing lethal weapons. They surrounded the girls, who were startled.

"What's happening here?"

It was not at all pleasant. The old man went and fetched his child over there in the house. These girls who had left her in the ochre pit were surprised when they saw her. And they died there, they departed for good.

The king then told the people everything that had happened, how those girls had left her at the ochre pit. "That is why you have seen these girls die."

That's the story.

COMMENTARY

Typical of rite-of-passage stories is the scene of transformation, when the real-life girl or boy undergoes a change. That transformation is traditionally the realm of such fantasy villains as ogres. It did not take long before Europeans were firmly fitted into the roles of these ogres.

The story details Kabetana's puberty ritual: her childhood past is indicated by Khabelungu and her friends, who are in the end destroyed. The community participates in the destruction of her past. Nature is appropriately involved in this identity transformation, with the birds saving her and placing her in a tree. A girl undergoes a transformation, a transition from childhood to adulthood. Here is the uncoiling python, in the form of the girl herself, of nature, and of sympathetic members of her community. Those forces that would restrain her, that would not allow the transition, are in the end overcome. The traditional rite of passage becomes, in Nokwazi Gaulana's tale, a means of coping with those forces that would interfere, that would prevent this transformation: forces that are alien even though they bear faces that are familiar.

A Swati Story

A Boy Goes after a *Nyanyabulembu*

By Sarah Dlamini

There was once a monster that lived in a deep pool, a water monster that was widely known as Nyanyabulembu.

The king of that land, Mavumabi,[12] said, "In these deep pools lives Nyanyabulembu!" So he summoned all the regiments. He wanted to obtain the skin of the water monster so that he could make a cape for his child, because that child would in time become the king.

The people gathered, and he spoke to them: "Who is bold enough to go to the deep pool and entice this monster that is called Nyanyabulembu?" It was no easy matter to bring that monster out from under the water.

Not a single person agreed to go.

The king pleaded with his people.

Then one boy stepped forward.

"But how can this be? He is so young!"

He said, "*I* can try to catch that monster, my lord!"

They regarded him in disbelief; they had sympathy for this child and refused to take him seriously.

"How can this child catch such a fearful monster?"

He was resolute, however, and said, "Even if the monster seizes me and kills me while I'm luring it from the pool, I am ready to go!"

So all sorts of preparations were made, and the child received many injunctions. He was told how he should proceed.

The performer was Sarah Dlamini, a Swati woman, thirty-five to forty years old. The performance (2S-1312) took place in her home in Mliba in Manzini District, Swaziland, on October 6, 1972, about 10 am. The audience consisted of five women and three children.

Figure 4. Sarah Dlamini (Swati). *Photo by the author*

The boy set out alone; no one accompanied him, because this monster evoked genuine fear. He walked a long way, until he reached the first deep pool. He stood over the body of water and called out.

He said, "Nyanyabulembu! Nyanyabulembu! You've not responded, Nyanyabulembu!" Then he said, "Everything is yours, Nyanyabulembu!"

The deep pool churned.

Again, the boy called out in a loud voice.

After a while, the water monster surfaced. This monster, an old one, said, "Look at me! I have no teeth with which to eat you!" Then it went back into the pool.

The boy just stood there, then looked around for another pool. He came to a second one. When he got to this pool, he looked at it intently—it was deep and very blue.

He called out, "Nyanyabulembu! Nyanyabulembu! I was sent by Mavumabi, Nyanyabulembu! He said that everything is yours, Nyanyabulembu!"

A water monster surfaced, but it too was old. This one said, "Look at me, I have no teeth! How can I eat you?"

So the boy set out once again, still hungry because it had been several days since he had started out on this adventure.

He continued his quest, and when he had gone a considerable distance and was tired, he came to another deep pool. This one was big, extremely deep, and it was very green, like grass.

Again, the boy called out, and he saw the waters churn. He was convinced, "This must be where it is!" and felt that he would surely confront it here.

He called out once more, and before he finished, he saw the monster coming to the surface. This water monster asked no questions: as soon as it had come to the surface, it began to chase the boy, attempting to seize him, to kill him, to eat him up at once.

The boy saw the monster come to the top of the pool, and he turned his face away. It followed him, and he ran, he ran really hard. It was a breathtaking chase. The stakes were high, he might be killed. This was a chase to the death; it was no child's game. The monster was in furious pursuit. The boy ran and ran.

When he was exhausted and about to be captured, he put into effect the plan that the others had given him, which would save him when it became necessary for him to rest momentarily along the way. He turned a little from the road, then threw an object to the ground.

Suddenly, it became dark, and the water monster had to stop.

The boy ran, while the monster stood there.

The boy ran and ran. Then, when he had run a great distance, he was surprised to find that the monster was close to him again. It was a monster that had as many tricks as he himself had. They were on the open prairie now, and the boy realized that it was almost upon him, very very near to him! He looked back, wondering what he could do. Then he quickly stepped aside, he stepped behind a rock—this was a very rocky place. And the water monster was pricked by a thorn. It was delayed while it attempted to pull the thorn out. As the monster was doing that, the boy continued to run. The others had told him that when the monster encountered an obstacle of some kind, the boy should run really hard. And the boy did just that; he did not look back.

But when he did glance back, he was amazed to find that the monster was again close behind him. Then, suddenly, there was a solid rock in the path of the monster, a real obstacle. The monster just moved about aimlessly now, because it was unable to climb over the rock. It moved about slowly. Meanwhile, the boy ran on.

But the water monster overcame this obstacle too, and again it was in fierce pursuit, and again it was closing in on the boy. And the boy was running very very hard.

When he was close to his home, he called out to the people there, telling them to take pots out to the road, to stand them up on the sides of the road. The pots were brought out, and they were placed on both sides of the road. When the boy got to that place, he went straight to these pots, and hid behind them. The monster arrived, and it was trapped. The prominent people of the village, already there, seized the monster and killed it. Then they prepared the skin, they tanned it well.

And they took this boy and put him into a house. He sprawled out there because he was exhausted.

The next day, the boy's father took the cape over to the king, and said, "The boy returned with the skin, it's here now!"

There was a great celebration throughout the land, because there was just no person who could go out and contend with such a monster over there in the river. It had become clear that this boy was a hero who surpassed other heroes. The king then promised the boy that, when he grew up, he could take a man and claim him as his own. In addition, he would be given a large territory over which to rule; he would become the ruler of the people in that region, he would become the great man of that place.

They made the preparations for this boy, then. The king gave him the large tract of land, and he gave the boy his daughter.

And this person ruled over people because he was an incomparable hero, because he had drawn this awesome monster from the river.

The skin of the water monster was prepared and properly tanned by experienced men. Step by step, they prepared it. When they had finished, it was time that the chieftainship should fall to the king's son, because this king was now very old. When the king died, this cape fashioned of the skin of the water monster was draped upon him. It was a garment that distinguished him: whenever a great assembly gathered, he wore it as a kind of insignia for a governor.

COMMENTARY

Storytellers take the traditional imagery of the tales (the deadly ogre, for example) and transform that imagery into a means whereby the contemporary world is considered. What stands in the way of the boy as he comes of age? A youth, typically a least likely hero, leaves home and moves into the separation phase of his rite of passage. That separation is marked by a pattern: various water monsters are encountered by the youth, but they are all too old, and the boy moves deeper and deeper into fantasy, which is the place where the ordeal or initiation stage of his ritual occurs. This ordeal stage is dramatized by a chase, with Nyanyabulembu pursuing the boy. "The stakes were high, he might be killed. This was a chase to the death; it was no child's game." The boy is moving into manhood, with the swallowing monster representing the betwixt and between stage, as the boy leaves his childhood behind. The pattern in this part of the narrative has to do with slowing the water monster: by darkness, by a thorn, a huge rock. Then the boy arrives at home, the return segment of his rite of passage, and orders that pots be put out to line the road, thereby trapping the monster. The audience understands the language of storytelling, notes the forces that would interfere with cultural transformations. Those negative forces are ancient, cast in the form of traditional villainous beings. It is up to the storyteller and the audience to transform those traditional beings into contemporary counterparts. Once the monster is killed and a cape is created from its skin, the passage is complete: "The king gave him the large tract of land, and he gave the boy his daughter. And this person ruled over people because he was an incomparable hero, because he had drawn this awesome monster from the river."

A Xhosa Story

THE MAGICIAN'S DAUGHTER

A Hlubi Tale

This performance by a Hlubi woman was highly rhythmic, with much body movement and gesturing to develop the images, particularly in the vivid use of body and vocal dramatics during the evocation of Dolosikuhlumba's evil activities. She was a very engaging performer, close to the members of the audience. As she calmly developed her story, she was constantly seeking the participation of the members of the audience, anxious to keep all of them totally involved in her images.

Now for a story . . .

There was a man who was called Dolosikuhlumba.[13] One of his knees was as big as the knee of a gelding. This knee of his had a stopper, and he stored his deadly medicines there. This man was feared in the village because of his powerful magic. He had a daughter who was amazingly beautiful. But the young men who saw her were afraid of her father's potent magic.

On a certain day, a young man from a far-off land was journeying, and he met that girl as she was drawing water at a river. The young man asked the girl whose daughter she was.

She said, "My father is Dolosikuhlumba; he lives up there in that great homestead—over there."

This youth said, "I want to ask him if he'll allow you to become my wife."

The girl said, "But aren't you afraid of my father? After all, he has such powerful magic."

This performance (1S-2050) took place on November 16, 1967, at about 9 am, in a home in Bubesi Location, Matatiele District, the Transkei. The narrative was performed by a Hlubi woman, about forty years old. Her audience consisted of fifteen children, fifteen women, and about fifteen teenaged boys and girls, all Hlubi.

The young man said, "Even if I did fear him, that would make no difference at all. There's nothing that can stand in the way of my love, because your beauty is so pure. I cannot give you up!"

The girl agreed that the young man should go and ask her father for her.

When he arrived at Dolosikuhlumba's homestead, the young man greeted him and said, "Well, sir!"

The great man admitted him. He sat there with his wife.

When the young man arrived, he said, "I ask for your daughter, that she might become my wife. Please allow us to be married."

Dolosikuhlumba said, "Will you endure the task that I set for you?"

The young man answered, "Whatever task you give me, father, I will persevere, because of the beauty of this daughter of yours. I'm unable to give her up, because she is so pure."

Dolosikuhlumba was an eminent man, a very rich man. He had one hundred cattle, and he gave that son-in-law some of those cattle to herd out on a mountain. The son-in-law went out with those cattle in the morning.

Dolosikuhlumba opened his knee and brought out his bottle of magic medicine. With it, he caused hailstorms to occur, storms that would kill that young person who wanted to marry his daughter—because Dolosikuhlumba also valued her, he too loved her very much. The weather was created then, a rain- and hailstorm came up, and it raged on and on and on and on. When the young man felt the fury of this storm, he was not able to endure it. He was in trouble—what could help him?

Then, there in the grass, a mouse came along. It said, "Young man, do you know what can save you?"

That young man, Dolosikuhlumba's son-in-law, said, "I know of nothing that can help me."

The mouse said, "Kill me and take my skin! It'll help you a lot! It'll give you advice about the many things that Dolosikuhlumba will seek to harm you with, so that you'll not be able to get his daughter."

The youth then killed the mouse, and he took the skin of the mouse and put it into a sack.

Then the mouse said, "So that you'll be safe now, hide yourself beneath the legs of the cattle so that this hailstorm will not be able to harm you."

Dolosikuhlumba's son-in-law did just that, he disappeared among the legs of the cattle. The hailstorm went on and on and on and on, and finally it passed over.

Dolosikuhlumba thought that his son-in-law was dead, but after the storm had passed, he saw that son-in-law returning with the hundred cattle—and he was not at all harmed!

When he got home, the youth was asked, "Son-in-law, what saved you in such a storm?"

The son-in-law said, "I disappeared among the legs of the cattle and was saved."

Dolosikuhlumba said, "I can see, young man, that you have great wisdom. All right, then, I'll arrange for you to marry my daughter, whom I love very much, who has a pure kind of beauty!"

A month had gone by since the young man had departed from his home, and his parents were worried. They wondered what had befallen the young man at the homestead of Dolosikuhlumba because of Dolosikuhlumba's notorious magic, renowned throughout the land.

The following week, a marriage was made with the daughter of Dolosikuhlumba—she married that fellow from the far-off country. When they were married, they were given goods— clothing, such things as mats for making a bed, and many other things that Dolosikuhlumba gave to his child to take as bridal gifts when she went to the far-off country. The girl and her bridegroom carried these goods then, going to the homestead at the groom's kraal. When they arrived, they were welcomed at home with great kindness, the parents rejoicing that their son had wedded the daughter of that fellow whose magical powers were so well known throughout the land, the same daughter having been despaired of by the many men who had wanted her.

When they arrived at home, it appeared that this girl could have no child.

Many years passed.

Then one day, she went to hoe in the fields, crying along the way because of the grief of the heart, which she suffered because she had no children, while those who had married at the same time she did had children. As she was cultivating in the field, some doves suddenly appeared.

They said, "*Hobe hobe!* You seem to be crying, little woman. Why?"[14]

She answered, "I'm crying because I haven't been able to have any children during the many years that I've been in this homestead."

The doves said, "If we enable you to have a child, what can you do for us?"

She said, "I can give you some maize."

The doves answered, "We don't have throats wide enough to swallow maize."

She said, "I can give you corn."

The doves answered, "But we don't have throats wide enough to swallow corn." And again the doves asked, "What can you give us?"

That little woman said then, "I don't know what you eat. Tell me, and I'll give you anything you want."

The doves said, "We want some wheat."

It happened that she carried a few kernels of wheat here in her handkerchief. She gave these to the doves, and the doves said, "We'll enable you to have two children, a girl and a boy, so that you'll be loved over there in your homestead. Because a wife who has no children is not loved at home."

They made that young woman sit down, and they took some water in their beaks. They scraped her thighs and washed off her dirt—one of them put some of the dirt into one calabash, the other put some of it into another. Then they said to the young woman, "Now when you get home, hide these calabashes so that no one sees them. Hide them for five days. After five days, look inside and see if there's anything in the calabashes."

The young woman took the calabashes, and she put them into a storehouse so that they might not be seen by any person. Then, after five days, she went into that storehouse and was surprised by sounds of loud laughter, children speaking baby-talk sweetly, in cool voices, voices that kept saying, "There's mama! There's mama!"

She opened the calabashes and was surprised to find a girl in one of the calabashes, and in the other she found a boy! Both of these children were astonishingly beautiful. She feared to tell her husband and her father-in-law and her mother-in-law, so she continued to take milk to the children there in the storehouse.

On a certain day, her husband enviously asked, "Why do you go into this storehouse alone? What are you doing?"

The young woman said, "I'm afraid to tell. But even I have children, I found twin children! Some doves gave them to me!"

When he got there, the man found the children crying. It was clear that these children would soon be able to go out and bring home the sheep and the goats and the cattle. He had unsurpassed joy. He would dress them in beautiful blankets: the boy would herd the livestock, the girl would play with a doll here at home.

It happened after two years that the wife did not again have any children. The man's heart was filled with discontent.

He said, "I shall take another wife, so that she might bear other children for me."

His wife said, "All right. When your heart allows you to, take another wife, because it's clear to me that I'll never again have children."

That man then climbed a mountain and came to the homestead of some ring-necked ravens. There was a raven there who had five daughters. He arrived and took the raven's junior daughter and went off with her. The raven returned with him to his home, and she gave birth to four children—girls. But their ugliness was shocking, indescribably dreadful!

After a certain number of years, the daughter of the raven was betrothed. She was betrothed, and so was that twin daughter of the great wife. When they had both been betrothed, the daughter of the raven received a dowry: cattle that were emaciated, indescribably so. That one who was a twin, the daughter of the great wife, was betrothed with a dowry of fat cattle.

The day arrived, then, the day on which the young women would be married. Marriage ceremonies were conducted on the same day for both of them. That daughter of the great wife had a pure beauty; the daughter of the raven had an astonishing ugliness, a fearful leanness!

When the marriages were completed, and each young woman had to go to her respective homestead, it was seen that the one who was lean would not be able to reach her homestead because of her leanness. When they were getting close to the house, she died on the road.

Her father was then no longer able to value his junior wife. He killed that raven, and this great wife came then and stayed well in happiness. Her husband now showed her a love which was steadfast.

The story has ended, it has ended.

COMMENTARY

The story opens with the mythic center, the realm of Dolosikuhlumba, his fantasy make-up suggested by one of his knees, "as big as the knee of a gelding," where deadly medicines are stored. Then we see the move of a real-life young man to that mythic center; this is the separation stage of his identity transformation. At this mythic center, the youth is given a task: he must herd Dolosikuhlumba's cattle if he is to wed the daughter, whom other young men are afraid to court. With his medicine, Dolosikuhlumba causes storms that will destroy this youth. At his nadir, the youth is aided by a mouse, a representation of harmony with nature and the youth's developing inner wisdom. The mouse then instructs the youth, and in the end the youth triumphs and gets Dolosikuhlumba's daughter as a wife. Once the youth has become a man, his ordeal ends, and he returns, is reincorporated, to his home. Dolosikuhlumba's is the elixir wrested from the deadly father: together, father and daughter represent the dualism within the youth as he passes from childhood (Dolosikuhlumba) to adulthood (Dolosikuhlumba's daughter). The young man now having completed his ritual, Dolosikuhlumba's daughter undertakes her own transformation. She cannot give birth, and doves, again manifestations of harmony with nature while simultaneously representations of the wife's inner change, make it possible, after a pattern that links them and the woman, for her to give birth. This delights her husband, but he again becomes unhappy when she bears no other children. He takes another wife, a raven-wife, and so it is that the dove-wife and the raven-wife become oppositions. A daughter of the dove-wife and a daughter of the raven-wife are each to be married. But the distinction between them is shown by the disparity in the dowries, and the raven-wife dies on the way to her home of marriage. Then the father, "no longer able to value his junior wife," kills the raven, and he and his dove-wife live in happiness. The dualism in this second part of the story is significant. It is revealed twice: once in terms of doves and ravens; and again when the daughter of Dolosikuhlumba undergoes a transformation that parallels the transformation of her husband.

Dolosikuhlumba is the external threatening power that would interfere with the movement of the youth to manhood. The uncoiling python is the tradition of the youth, a tradition that, with the allied force of nature, deals with that intrusive force.

A Xhosa Story
A DAUGHTER SOLD

By Noplani Gxavu

This story was told at the celebration that accompanied the coming-out from the usuthu *(the place where the circumcision ceremony was performed) of two* abakhwetha *(boys undergoing the circumcision ceremony) youth. Noplani Gxavu heard this story from her grandmother.*

Now for a story . . .

There was a country in which there was a drought. And there was a huge monster that dwelled in a lake where no human dared to venture, because it devoured people, the thing that was there.

There was also an old man, still alive. He lived with his daughter, and he had no wife. He was in the habit of sending this daughter, because he was aged, to go and beg water for him, to procure water on account from this monster.

Well, then, the daughter would go. She reached the age of sixteen years. Then, on a certain day, the monster went to the home of the young woman to demand what was due to it, to pay for the water that had repeatedly been obtained on credit.

Well, then, friends, the monster arrived while the young woman was at the millstone in the house. While the young

---

The *intsomi* (1S-642) was performed by Noplani Gxavu, a Gcaleka woman, on September 14, 1967, at about 3:30 pm, at a party in a kraal overlooking a steep valley in Mboxo (Nkanga) Location, in Gatyana District, Transkei. The audience consisted of about forty women, six men, and twenty children, all Gcaleka.

Figure 5. Noplani Gxavu (Xhosa). *Photo by the author*

woman was grinding at the millstone, that monster greeted her
father at the cattle kraal.

Her father asked, "Where do you come from, sir?"

The monster said, "I came from home. I have come to seek
my payment."

Said this man, "I have nothing, I am just as you see me, I am an old man who lives with this child of mine. I shall offer her as payment. There she is, grinding in the house. Let her be your wife."

Meantime, while grinding, the young woman was listening. She went out and fled from the monster. She journeyed through the land, traveling about all over, and she came upon a homestead where there was a Saturday night gathering of boys. When she came upon this homestead where the boys' party was taking place, she reported this matter, she came in running.

The boys said, "*We* shall beat that thing. Go and join the music-making up there."

So this young woman went and joined the music and dancing at the upper part of the homestead. But she clapped her hands hardly two times before the monster appeared at the upper side of the homestead.

When the boys saw it, they said, "Well, go out, young woman. We are not in a position to contend with that thing. We have never encountered such a big thing."

So the young woman went out, running, and she went farther ahead. Then she saw a crowd of men who were riding horses. Well, the men could see that the young woman was sweating.

The men asked, "What is the matter, young woman?"

She told men, "I have been sold at home to pay for water."

The men said, "Well, young woman, come in here among the horses even though you are on foot. After all, we are twelve men. That thing cannot be more than we can handle, all of us, that animal."

Then the monster appeared while they were thus talking and before they proceeded on their journey.

When the monster had appeared, it was the horses that made the men aware of the presence of the monster by becoming restless. They were bucking and would not respond to the pulling of the reins. And when the men looked ahead, they saw that monster.

They said, "Young woman, we're going to take another route. We're not adequately armed to fight that monster."

So the young woman ran ahead as before, and she reached another land, a land which she did not know. By now, it was sunset, dusk, early dusk now. She heard chanting coming from some homestead. It was a Xhosa young men's party.[15]

When she arrived there, she threw herself to the farther side of the house and fainted. The young men grasped her, produced the medicines that they had, and made her sniff them.

When she came to, they questioned her, and that young woman explained, "Well, my father at home is selling me off for water. He owns nothing, so he offers me as payment, that I should become the monster's wife. Perhaps you too will see the monster when it appears. That is why I am in flight. And I am tired. I have run all over the land and can find no redeemer."

The young men then said, "Well, there is no chance that a full house like this could be unable to cope with that thing, all of us. Just join the chanting a little up there with the other women."

So this young woman went up there. She clapped her hands maybe twice, then she opened her mouth to sing.

Suddenly, a young man who happened to be outside was heard to say—I am about to use gross language—he was pissing, he was heard to say, "Fellows, don't take a chance and dance much farther. Just observe what thing is approaching from the upper side of the homestead. It could well lay waste to this homestead!"

So all the young men went out, leaving the young women inside the house.

When the young men came back in, they lifted the young woman by the arms to throw her out, to the upper side of the homestead, saying, "Well, be off, because we do not own the house here where this party is being held; we realize that the whole of this homestead could well be destroyed."

So the young woman ran, and by now it was dark. Then she saw a fire that glowed in a land that seemed safe, a certain village. She saw a fire that glimmered, and she went there. As it turned out, it was one of the local white farmers who owned a homestead. He resided there with his servants, who lived in servants' quarters in the back. It turned out that she went straight for the white folks' house. The door was opened, and the dogs harassed this person who came in in such an unusual manner, by jumping over the gate.

The white man asked, "What is the matter, young woman?"

The young woman explained, "I am running away from a monster to whom my father offers me as wife."

The white man asked, "How far away was the monster at the time you arrived here at this homestead?"

The young woman said, "Oh! Well, I may get a chance to sleep, perhaps it will arrive at dawn."

He sent out six "boys" to dig a pit in front of that gate so that as soon as the monster entered it should fall into the pit. He made the servants work very hard and instructed that water be boiled in two large pots. All that was done quickly. A pit was dug in front of the gate.

The monster arrived, loud and agitated, calling to its wife. As it tried to go through the gateway, it fell into the pit. Then those two pots of boiling water were taken and poured into the pit into which that monster had fallen.

So the monster died.

The son of the owner of this homestead was much pleased by this young woman, and he desired to take her as a wife and marry her. The father of that "little boss" was also pleased with her. So the fortunes of that young woman began to change for the better.

After some time had lapsed and the future had come, and after she had had two children, the young woman asked for permission to visit her father, to see if he still lived.

Permission was granted by the "little boss," because he too wanted to go and see the person who had sired this person and had then given her away gratuitously.

Well, then, friends, they packed many things, because the young woman had explained her father's hardship, the poverty of her father. All sorts of foodstuffs were loaded on a lorry, all kinds of food as well as two gelded sheep and expensive blankets. There was bedding for that old man, and money, too, so that if he should die the people who bury him would be rewarded with money. Then they set out for that homestead.

When they reached that home, the old man could not see clearly now. He asked where these people came from.

The young woman explained, "I am yours. I am the one you gave away to a monster as payment for water."

The old man broke into tears.

As he cried, the "little boss" and his "boys" comforted him, to stop him from crying anymore: she had not died, and the monster had been killed. All people now had freedom to use the dam in that land and could dip water freely. "The monster is no more, it cannot rise from death."

So they left all the good things they had brought as gifts to that old man, and they made a request to the headman, asking if they might take the old man with them to the home into which his daughter had married. Clearly he was old and had no one to look after him.

The headman agreed and pleaded with the old man, and the old man also agreed freely.

They loaded him, then, onto the lorry on the appointed day for departure. The "little boss" did not want to spend one night here; he wanted to set out immediately, that very night.

All of them set out; they departed with that old man, having clothed him in all the garments that they had brought, along with the provisions.

They returned to the home of the "little boss," having come to the conclusion that they should not leave the old man behind.

The story is over.

COMMENTARY

Noplani Gxavu's Xhosa story, "A Daughter Sold," has to do with a monster that devours people. A man's daughter begs for water from the monster; this develops into a pattern in which water is begged from the monster. The people thereby go into debt to the monster, and it demands what is due. The man, in a Faustian bargain, offers his child in payment. She flees. There is a pattern of flight: (1) she comes to a boys' party; they offer but cannot help. (2) She comes to men with horses; they cannot help. (3) She comes to a young men's party; they offer to help but in the end cannot. (4) She comes to a white farmer, who has his servants dig a pit and boil water; the monster falls into the pit and is killed with boiling water, thereby saving her. The son of the owner marries her. They return to visit her old father, and he weeps. She assures him that the monster is dead. The old man is repentant for the bargain that he had made with the monster, and they take him home with them.

As always, a pattern identifies the mythic center: in this story, a monster who demands humans as payment for life-sustaining water. The pattern, the flight of the girl from the monster, emphasizes the helplessness of those encountered by the girl: the boys, the men, and the young men. None is able to help her. Only a white farmer is able to destroy the monster, and his son marries the girl. The movement into the mythic realm, then, has to do with both the monster and (given the history of apartheid, at its depths at the time this tale was told, 1967) the white family as well. Ironically, the white man is not cast as parallel to the monster; on the contrary, he destroys the monster, and the elixir achieved by the girl as she endures this ordeal is the son of the white man. So it is, Gxavu argues, that the Africans become subsumed by the whites . . . and the shadow of the traditional ogre places the whites in their historical roles.

A Xhosa Story

The Errant Woman

By Mahlombe Nxesi

Mahlombe Nxesi's technique was very animated. She fairly shouted and was in a sweat, with her entire body involved in the telling: although she sat, her legs did much work. In presenting the dialogue she leaned to the right when one person spoke and to the left when another spoke, to indicate different speakers. Nxesi, although normally a very quiet person, made an excellent storyteller, being wholly involved in the story and exhibiting great concentration.

Here begins a story . . .[16]
In a certain big forest lived a very large and terrible animal. Three women set out to go to that forest to gather wood. They arrived there, and as they gathered wood, one of them, whose name was Mabani, said to another, "Mh! What smells so foul here?"

One of the others said, "Careful! Don't talk like that when you're inside the forest! Such subjects are not spoken of!"

They remained quiet for a time and gathered wood. They gathered wood, then one of them said, "Oh no!"

"What's the matter with you? Have you at last taken note of what I was saying, that there's a strange stench in this forest?"

Mahlombe Nxesi, a Bhaca woman about fifty years old, told this story on November 5, 1967, about 2:30 pm, in a home in the Rwantsana part of Mhlotsheni Location, Mount Frere District, the Transkei. The audience consisted of fifty women, four men, and sixty children, all Bhaca (1S-1715).

The other said, "Oh, my god! Why do you behave like such a fool of a woman? Haven't you heard that when a person enters the forest, one does not talk about what one sees? The usual thing is to sneak away when one sees that there is something bad here."

Oh! They became agitated!

She said, "You know, this talking of yours has caused my bones to knock together against each other! This idle talking of yours is like the babbling of a child—but you're not a child, you're an adult! Let's just gather our wood. We'll just tie up what we have here and go home."

That was the situation, and they put the pieces of wood together.

One of the women said, "Here's a cat. I picked it up."

"Oh, what a fool you are! What kind of talk is this? I just got through telling you that no one mentions what one sees here!"

But she just went on: "How beautiful my cat is! It has many colors!"

The other one said, "Oh, well! Take—pile up the wood on your side. I'll arrange the wood here on my side, because I can see that your idiosyncrasies are amazing! Now you say *this*! I restrain you from saying one thing, and you say another! And I must restrain you in that as well!"

Then they started running. As they were running, she said, "Just go and look. It's a goat now!"

The other said, "Take it then. After all, that goat is yours! I don't have a goat here. I told you, I said that the things in the forest should not be talked about! Any of them!" So saying, this one ran very hard, because she knew that this thing in this forest was a crocodile.

At this point, a leopard woke up and began to roar.

Then she said, "Say! Listen, people! Is it not possible that this leopard is roaring in the forest?"

Repeatedly she said, "Umh! umh! I wonder where these groans of labor pains are coming from?"

When she looked, she discovered that the others were no longer there.

She cried out, "Where are you?"

No answer.

They were not there anymore, because they were running away from the foolishness she had been engaging in despite their warning: "Sensible people don't mention everything in the forest!"

They hurried off.

Suddenly, in an instant, the leopard threw itself at this woman! Not a bone was left behind!

When the others reached home, they reported the strange occurrence over there in the forest: "While we were gathering wood, the fool of a woman, despite the fact that we warned her about everything—still, she told us all these things, whereas we ourselves knew that in that forest was a lion which devours people who talk about everything. When one notices that there is a smell, one goes to another area of the forest, because we know that in the side where one has entered there is a terrible thing, a dangerous thing—"

The men went out, saying, "Let's go and investigate at the place where wood is gathered!"

So they went. They entered the forest, the ominously thick, black forest. When they had arrogantly entered, these women said, "If we may tell you, we repeatedly jump at nothing because we're so afraid. In this forest are things that are usually seen, and things that behave in strange ways."

At this point, they reached the spot where the firewood was. They said, "She was here! Here's her rope."

It was clear that the thing had devoured her completely.

The men came out of the forest and went home, going to report at home that "Well, it has devoured that one altogether," because it had been in the custom of devouring people and not leaving even a bone behind.

They came to a tree, and pressed on—this tree was large. People were called, and it was announced that, at home here, a strange thing had happened to the woman who had gone out with other women, to go and gather wood in the forest. The monster of the forest had altogether devoured her. Not even a bone remained behind. At this point, there was nothing else to do. Time passed; they just sat there.

The thought came that maybe other wood-gatherers should go into that forest.

As these wood-gatherers were still entering the forest, one of them said, "What's happened? It is as if in this forest there is a thing that stinks!"

Another said, "This is the second time this has happened. It has happened before, this is the second time. Excuse me, let's go home; this is too much for us."

They reached home. Time passed, time passed.

Earlier, a man had said, "I need firewood, to make fire and cook, because at home here, as you know, there is no wife, there is just me, because as for you, you are not bothered with cooking, you cook at night. You are secretive. *I* do not want food that has been cooked in secret, food that has been cooked in darkness. My mother used to cook for me while the sun was still shining, while it was broad daylight!"

This man then got up and began to cook.

The very foolish woman, whose name was Mabani, stretched her legs, sitting there. She did not do what her husband wanted her to do. She listened to the man say, "Sit down while I cook. My mother never used to cook when it was already dark!"

This woman just sat there; she stretched her legs, and the man cooked.

When the man had finished cooking, he began to dish the food out. He casually placed food in front of the children, but he ignored the woman.

She said, "Say, Father of Bani, why are you not serving me also?"

The man said, "Mabani, is it a fact that

> I am the woman in this homestead?
> You, on the other hand,
> must be the man!
> Here, take my penis cover,
> and put it on,
> become a man,
> because I will walk about
> in woman's dress,
> I will wear a skin skirt.
> As of today,
> you will be the man.
> And I will be the woman."

These were harsh words. She took them to heart, realizing that she had said a strange thing, saying to the man that he

should squat and serve food to her while she sat flat on the
ground, completely relaxed.

At bedtime, the bedding was prepared at this home. There
were many children in this home, there were very many of them.
That is how it was in this homestead.

Nighttime came to this homestead. The sleeping mats
were brought in and beds were prepared. When the bedding
was prepared—the name given to the flat things was *ududayi*,
because everybody would then be covered with karosses. A
beast had been slaughtered. And when the cow had been
flayed, the skin was tanned, the skin was tanned and made
into a kaross, so that all the people of this home would be
covered snugly with this skin. Even a child and everybody,
including the man, all slept under the same kaross. The kaross
was made of a cow's hide—one skin or more, from which
this blanket was made—a very good blanket indeed. Nobody
would shiver from the cold, even a cold-blooded person,
because there was not even a small hole in it. It was a blanket
which was extremely warm.

And so there would be sleep.

However, this woman who had never properly learned the
customs, proceeded to stray from the kaross. And she went
outside to her paramours.

The husband, who had been asleep, woke up and said,
"Mabani! Where is she?"

Mabani was nowhere to be found. She was with her lovers.

So the man got up and left the children comfortably
snuggled under the kaross, comfortably tucked in under the
kaross. When these children slept, they slept soundly, they went
into a deep sleep. It would happen that, as a child slept, she
would imagine herself here or there—in Mpondoland, at sea—
because wherever she imagined herself, she would sleep soundly,
really sleep soundly, because this kaross was a thing that kept
the children very warm.

Then the man left the bed; he departed, leaving the children
in their sound sleep, to go and look for Mabani. He went off
and searched and searched, but he could not find her. He
looked in all sorts of places, but he could not find her.

The very naughty woman was over there in the cattle kraal,
where she had a rendezvous with her lover.

The husband returned to the house, and as he looked for her, he saw her dashing from the cattle kraal.

He said, "Mabani! I have been looking for you for so long! Where have you been all this time?"

For her part, she said, "Well, I went to inspect the cattle! I heard something; they seemed to be restive."

The man said, "I have been saying it for a long time, I have been saying that

> you are the man!
> Why don't you tell me to give you
> my penis cover,
> and you give me your skirts,
> so that I may gird myself
> like a woman,
> because you are the man in this home!"

So saying, the man gave it over to her. He used what was in his hand, a thick short stick, quite a big one, and he hit her hard on the loins. She fell down and skidded. He struck her again on the waist, and she skidded.

This man said, "I am doing this so that she should stop this immorality, this rampant promiscuity, because she is married!"

In the meantime, the children—lying beneath that warm and secure kaross—were asleep. They did not see that their mother was being killed here in the house. When they woke up in the morning, they found their mother lying there.

She was repeatedly saying, "Ohh!"[17]

The children asked, "What is it you are giving to us, Mother?" She kept on saying, "Ohh! Ohh!"

"Oh, Mother! What could it be that you are giving to us?"[18]

Their mother said, "I am not giving you anything! What I am giving you is my waist. I cannot walk, I can only slide along the ground!"

Tshitshilili-i! Tshitshilili-i! Tshitshilili-i! Tshitshilili-i![19]

She slid toward the doorway to go to urinate. She had difficulty standing up, because of her promiscuity.

And even today, a person who is promiscuous usually gets what is coming, some kind of retribution meted out for promiscuity.

Tshitshilili-i![20]

Tshitshilili-i! Tshitshilili-i!

That is how the story ends.

COMMENTARY

In the first part of Mahlombe Nxesi's Xhosa story "The Errant Woman," a woman breaks a taboo and is ultimately destroyed because of it. In part two, a man exchanges positions with a woman: he does all the work of the home, while his wife does nothing. They change gender roles, with him saying, "*I* am the woman, *you're* the man." He dresses in women's clothes and gives her a penis cover. The link between parts one and two is that in each, a woman breaks tradition, and when she does so, she is destroyed. Part one is thus the mythic version of part two.

As is the case in many oral tales, tradition is necessary for the survival of the people. When tradition is broken, the society is broken. The mythic forces in part one of the story are those that weaken society. Those forces are given everyday significance in the second part, when a woman forsakes her traditional role.

The coming of the whites is not an obvious part of this story. But those forces that would alter traditions of society are the crux here: the uncoiling python is once again those traditions, and any interference with traditions is dealt with.

A Xhosa Story
A BOY GROWS UP

By Nontsomi Langa

Now for a story . . .
There was a boy, the son of a king. His parents died while he was still small. His uncles,[21] as well as his aunt, brought him up.
This child grew up, he grew up until he became a big boy.
This child did not speak, except to his aunt, except to his aunt.
Even his relatives would send his aunt when they wished to communicate with him.[22]
When he became a big boy, it was said, "All right now, Sister, please speak to your brother's child. We want him to

---

Nontsomi Langa, a Gcaleka woman about fifty-five years old, performed this narrative (1S-618) on September 13, 1967, about 2:30 pm, outside, in the kraal of Nontsomi Langa, in Mboxo (Nkanga) Location, Gatyana District, before an audience of about twenty women, six or seven men, fifteen teenagers, and thirty children, all Gcaleka.

Figure 6.
Nontsomi Langa
(Xhosa). *Photo by
the author*

be circumcised and become a man, so that we may hand
over to him the reins of his father's kingdom. The regency, the
interregnum, has gone on long enough."

So his aunt went to him and said, "Now, my brother's child,
the grey-heads, the elders, of your home have sent me. They
have told me to suggest to you that it is time to get circumcised;
you're old enough now. Then your father's kingship can be
handed over to you."

"Oh!" He said, "Well, that is all right, I agree. However,
before I get circumcised, I want a cape made of the skin of a
water monster. A water monster must be killed."

"Go and explain that we have no way of doing that. There is no way for us to confront the water monster."

He said, "It is all right, Aunt. Prepare a lot of loaves of bread. I myself will bring the water monster. Let the members of the entire community gather, bringing their guns with them. Others should bring spears. I shall lure the water monster, that it might be killed here at home."

So his aunt prepared the loaves of bread and filled a corn-basket with them.

The boy went to the river. He came to the first pool in that river, and said,

> "Water-monster! Water-monster,
> Come out and eat me!
> Come out and eat me!"

From the pool came a response: "Pass on to the pool ahead. I cannot see anymore."

So he passed on. He came to the next pool:

> "Water-monster! Water-monster,
> Come out and eat me!
> Come out and eat me!"

A water-monster emerged then, and the entire pool churned, the entire pool churned.

Then the chase began: the boy would throw a loaf of bread, and the monster would be delayed, spending some time eating it. Meanwhile, the boy would gain ground, running, throwing a loaf of bread, and again running ahead, until, at length, he reached home.

When he arrived at home, the water monster was shot. It was flayed; its skin was tanned.

The boys were circumcised then, and when they had been circumcised, after some time, it was said, "Go again, you, his aunt, and say that it is time for the boys to go through the graduation exercises[23] now. It has been long enough."

He agreed. But he added, "Before I graduate, I shall emerge from the circumcision lodge, but after the rituals, it is necessary to get for me a daughter of Ngangazulu."[24]

It was said, "All right. However, he will have to see that *we* know of no one who could possibly go to Ngangazulu's home."

The boys came out; they graduated then. The men of the community gathered, and they set out to go to Ngangazulu's homestead, to ask for her daughter in marriage, to be married to the king's child.

So they went, they traveled and traveled. When they were a long way off, they rested. Ngangazulu's homestead was now in sight, over there and across.

Then two doves flew by.

Someone said, "Kill them! Hit these birds!"

One of the birds said, "*Vukuthu!*"

The other said, "*Vukuthu!* Nonsense! Why don't you, instead, tell these people that we have come to tell them what they should say when they get to Ngangazulu's place."

"*Vukuthu!*"

"*Vukuthu!* Nonsense! Why not say, instead, to these people that they should sit in the courtyard when they arrive."

"*Vukuthu!*"

"*Vukuthu!* Nonsense! Why not, instead, tell these people that, when they are interrogated, they should merely sigh and not open their lips—just sigh."

"*Vukuthu!*"

"*Vukuthu!* Nonsense! Why not, instead, tell these people that they should decline to stay in a new house, accept to stay in a shack."

"*Vukuthu!*"

"*Vukuthu!* Nonsense! And when a beast has been slaughtered for them, they should refuse to eat the meat that they have touched with their hands; instead, they should eat the meat touched by the hosts."

"*Vukuthu!*"

"*Vukuthu!* Nonsense! Why not, instead, tell these people that they should not eat from new vessels, they should not eat with new spoons. They should eat from old vessels, they should use old spoons."

"*Vukuthu!*"

"*Vukuthu!* Nonsense! Why not, instead, tell these people that, when they are enjoined to go out to herd the cattle, a thunderous rain cloud will come upon them; they should then lean against the homestead's dun-colored ox, all of them."

So they went on ahead. They traveled until they reached the place of Ngangazulu. When they arrived, they took the appropriate positions in the courtyard.

Ngangazulu came out. She flung her breasts, one at a time, over her shoulders, and said,

> [sings:] "I don't quite understand these people of
> Chengeletya,
> The people of Ndlel' ethusini,[25]
> The people of Gabadul' imilibo.[26]
> *Mh mh, mh mh.*
> What kind of misers are these?"[27]

She turned away then and went into the house, where she picked up one of her magic charms. She crushed the charm open; it was in calabashes. She crushed it open, then again picked it up. She picked it up and poured it into other calabashes.

Then they were told to go into a new *rondavel.*[28]

"We sleep in a shack."

So they were offered a shack, and they slept in it.

On the next day, they were told to go out and herd the cattle. When they had gone out with the cattle, clouds gathered, becoming thicker and thicker. It began to thunder, and lightning crisscrossed the sky. Yes, lightning crisscrossed the sky. So they went to lean against the dun-colored ox.

The storm passed, it passed, and they went back to Ngangazulu's homestead. They arrived and slept in the shack.

An ox was slaughtered for them. They assisted in this slaughtering, and when the beast had been cut up, they leapt for the other side of the carcass, protesting, "*We* don't eat this side!" Magic had been administered to that side, so it was thrown away.

The next day came, and they went to sit in the courtyard. Ngangazulu came out, and said,

> [sings:] "Why don't the people of Chengeletye
> respond?
> The people of Ndlel' ethusini's place?
> The people of Gabadul' imilibo's place?
> *Mh mh! Mh mh!*
> What kind of miserly people are these?"

However, their wife was handed over to them, and they took her away.

This young woman did not work in the daytime; she worked at night only. They were informed of that.

After a while, they departed with her. And when the sun rose, because she did not work in the daytime, they sat under a tree and covered her. And when the sun set, they traveled on with her.

They reached home, and this bride was placed behind a partition so that she would go out and work at night, she would go out and work at night.

One day, while the people were away at a beer party, a man who was a stranger to her came into the house, quite an elderly man. He came into that house and said, "Daughter-in-law, Daughter-in-law, give me some water."

Her sister got up and dipped some water for him.

He took the water and threw it out.

"Daughter-in-law, Daughter-in-law, give me some water."

Her sister got up and decanted whey from the calabash and gave it to him.

He took the whey and threw it out.

"Daughter-in-law, Daughter-in-law, give me water."

Then the bride herself went out, leaving her infant behind, and she went to the river. She got there and disappeared into the river. Then her grave appeared; it was like this.

That stranger departed.

The people returned from the beer party. The child, the sister of the bride, reported that a stranger had come there. "Then my older sister went to the river to get water. The stranger declined the water that was offered to him. So she went to the river to dip water, and she has not returned."

It was decided to go and report the matter at her home, that some harm had befallen her.

A fowl was sent, a rooster, to carry this message. It flew to Ngangazulu's homestead. It got there and perched on the cattle kraal post. It said, "I have been sent to report that Ngangazulu's daughter has drowned in the river."

Ngangazulu chased the rooster away, pelting it with those calabashes containing these herbs of hers, this magic charm of hers.

The rooster fled and eventually reached home.

In the meantime, Ngangazulu flung her breasts over her shoulders and eventually reached her daughter's home of marriage. Then she pressed on, moving to that river.

She got there, dug up her daughter from her grave, and returned with her.

She left her there, dear friends. And from that time on, she could work during the daytime, this young woman of this homestead.

So ends the story.

COMMENTARY

In Nontsomi Langa's Xhosa story "A Boy Grows Up," the parents of a son of a king are dead, and the son does not speak except to his aunt. The first part of the story deals with the growth of the boy, when the time has come for him to be king. The second part of the tale has to do with marriage: the boys come out, they graduate from their circumcision ritual, and the youth goes to Ngangazulu's place to marry her daughter. In part three, there is a shift from the king's son to the son's wife: she works at night only but an old man sends her to fetch water in the daytime. The mythic center in this first part involves the water monster. The move of the prince to the water monster's lair is the separation stage of the youth's puberty ritual, which culminates in the boys' circumcision ritual. The separation stage also involves the prince's ordeal: the struggle with the water monster. That ordeal deepens when he moves to Ngangazulu's place, and the mythic center is further developed. Here, doves become the youth's tie to nature, representative of his deepening maturity and wisdom, which are revealed in the way he struggles with and eventually overcomes Ngangazulu. He wrests life, in the form of Ngangazulu's daughter, from death, personified by Ngangazulu herself. There comes a shift as that elixir representation, Ngangazulu's daughter, undergoes a change at her place of marriage. For her, in this reversal of settings, the prince's home is a mythic center, and it is there that she undergoes a transformation, represented by her shift from working only at night to working during the day. The transformation of the mythic daughter becomes a mirror of the real-life transformation of the prince. A series of transformations reveals the uncoiling python.

A Xhosa Story

MBENGU-SONYANGAZA

By Nontsomi Langa

Now for a story . . .

There was a man who had two wives, a senior wife and a junior. The senior wife became pregnant, and she bore a child.

The junior wife also bore a child: she did so while blindfolded with a turban—here, over the eyes.

The senior wife took a splinter of a sneezewood tree and killed that baby. Then she said, "Remove the turban; yours has been a stillbirth."[29]

She uncovered her eyes, and that child was buried.

Both became pregnant again. The senior wife gave birth, and again the junior wife bore a child. Again, she was blindfolded, and once again the senior wife took a splinter of the sneezewood tree, and the throat of the child was severed just at the time the sorghum crops were being watched over to keep them from being ravaged by birds.

This young wife went over to the sorghum, mourning all the while over her children who repeatedly died.

Two doves came along.[30]

The doves said, "Woman, why are you crying?"

She said, "I am weeping over the misfortune that all my births are stillbirths.[31] I mourn over the fact of repeated stillbirths."[32]

These doves said, "Suppose we enable you to have a child— What will you give us?"

She said, "I shall give you maize."

"Do you imagine that our throats can swallow maize? We use it as decoration for our garments."

"Well, then, I shall give you sorghum."

"Do you imagine that our throats can swallow sorghum? We use it to adorn our heads."[33]

The *intsomi* (1S-617) was performed by Nontsomi Langa, a fifty-year-old Gcaleka woman, on September 13, 1967, at about 2:30 pm, outside, in the kraal of Nontsomi Langa, in Mboxo (Nkanga) Location, Gatyana District, the Transkei, before an audience consisting of about twenty women, six or seven men, fifteen teenagers, and thirty children, all Gcaleka.

"Then I can give you very fine grain."

The doves said, "Show us."

So she scattered fine grain before them, and the doves pecked it, they pecked and pecked.

When they had finished, they said, "Go to the river now, and bring water."

She brought it.

The doves said, "Now soak your body."

She soaked her body.

They said, "Now then, this dirt from your body, all of it, all of it, all of the dirt from your body—pour it onto the lid of some container. Then, when you get home, put it under a large pot, placing the pot upside down over it. And do not open that pot for four days, then uncover it."

Well, friends, she got home and put the pot over the lid containing the dirt from her body. When four days had gone by, she uncovered it.

She found two infants there—twins, a girl and a boy.

These children grew up underneath that big pot, these children grew up under that pot.

Then she went to report to the doves: "These children are growing up fast; they are crowded in that vessel."

The doves said, "Get up early and stealthily bring the children here to the fields."

So indeed she got up, friends, and surreptitiously took her children, very early, and went down to the fields with them. And when she had gone down to the fields with her children, when she had arrived there, and the doves said, "Now, erect for them a beautiful lodge here in which they can grow up. They must be seen at their home only when they are already old, to avoid the slitting of their throats."

The children grew up then,[34] the children grew up, they being twins. The boy was Mbengu, the girl was Nqunuse. Mbengu had a moon on his chest along with a cloud. Nqunuse had three beads here.

The children grew and grew.

The boy was circumcised in the wilderness, he was circumcised right here on the veld.

They went to bathe. They regularly went secretly to young people's parties and would then return to the wilderness. One

day while they were bathing, they were surprised by ogres. They
fled that day.

But the ogres laid an ambush for them.[35] And on that day
they seized the twin who was a girl. The other twin, the boy,
eluded their grasp.

Then there was thunder, thunder and lightning.

And the ogres ran off in the midst of all that lightning.

The twin who was a boy gave up and returned home. He
went to that home and reported this matter: "I had a sister,
Nqunuse. The ogres took her and fled with her."

When the ogres had taken her to their land, they did not
harm her. She became the wife of the king of the ogres. She
became pregnant and bore a daughter who resembled her. Then
she again gave birth, bearing a boy-ogre: he was actually an ogre.

In the meantime,[36] Mbengu had set out from his home, and
he arrived in the land of these ogres on the day that an ox had
been slaughtered and was being feasted upon.

Just after sunset, the children were sent to the river because
the adults had become thirsty. When they reached the river,
Nqunuse's daughter's billycan began to leak. Those who were
with her would not seal the billycan for her. What they did was
pluck off thorns and punch holes in her repeatedly. Then, when
her blood flowed, they sucked it off.

It was soon dusk. And the other children left Nqunuse's
daughter there.

As it became dark, a person suddenly appeared.

"Child, come here."

She went to him.

He asked, "Whose child are you?"

She said, "I am Nqunuse's child."

He asked, "What does Nqunuse say when she swears an oath?"

She said, "'Mbengu-Sonyangaza.'"

He said, "I am Mbengu-Sonyangaza."

He plucked a reed for her, and he sealed her billycan. He
also dipped water for her. Then he said, "This reed, then, when
you get home, drop it across the doorway. Then call to your
mother. Ask her to come and help you to put down the water.
When she tramples on and breaks this reed, you should break
out crying, insisting that she come and replace it at once."

The child departed.

She arrived at her home and put the reed in the doorway.

She said, "Come, mother, come and help me to take the water from my head."

Her mother came to her, and as she approached she stepped on the reed.

The child screamed and said, "I want my reed back!" She cried in a heartrending way, "I want my reed back!"

Her father said, "Go, woman, replace that reed!"

So both of them, mother and daughter, went down to the river.

And they suddenly came upon this person.

"Oh! Mbengu! What brought you here? Do you not realize that you will be devoured by the ogres? You know that they are seeking you, they have been seeking you ever since the thunderstorm."

"Well, I am seeking you. I want you to find a way for me so that I can go home with you."

"Go, then, ask for a place to sleep far away from here. Then, when the sun has gone this far, arrive here. You should dress in ragged clothes—everything, strange tins, wear filthy rags. And pretend to limp: you should be a cripple."

The next day came.

Then there came into view a spectacle. As the woman was tanning her leather skirt in front of the house, tanning her leather skirt in front of the house, that thing suddenly came into view, limping along as it approached.

Nqunuse said,[37] "Everyone come out, see the queen's wretch! There he comes, the queen's wretch! That wretch is mine!"

So that wretch approached.

The ogres came out to see. They said, "Bee hee hee hee! There is the queen's own wretch! The queen's wretch has appeared, that one![38] It is the queen's wretch, that one!"

Eventually, the wretch reached the place.

Well, then, friends, everyone fussed over the queen's wretch; they fussed and fussed over him.

Then it was said, "Tomorrow, we shall go hunting."

Mbengu said, "Well, I am still limping. I am tired, I am tired, I am limping. I shall join you in the hunt the day after tomorrow."

"Oh."

And everybody went to sleep.

Mbengu had covered the moon as well as the clouds with mud, because these clouds tended to clear away at night.

He went to that house. He was put into a house with Mlenzana-mnye, One-Legged-One.

But unknown to Mbengu, the mud had fallen off the clouds and the moon. The clouds cleared away, and the moon shone brightly in the house while he slept in the same room with Mlenzana-mnye.

When the clouds cleared and the moon shone, Mlenzana-mnye saw Mbengu, and said, "Oh! All this time, you are Mbengu! You are Mbengu-Sonyangaza!"

Mbengu woke up and pleaded with him, saying, "Please don't identify me!"

Well, then, friends, Mlenzana-mnye did not reveal Mbengu's true identity.

The ogres departed, going to hunt.

When they had departed, Mbengu remained behind, busy with his sister as well as that child who was a girl. Mbengu and Nqunuse took the child who was a boy and shoved him under a rock.

Then they departed, they traveled.

But Mlenzana-mnye, One-Legged-One, got to the top of a mountain and shouted, "The cattle are departing with Mbengu-Sonyangaza!"

The ogres asked, "What is he saying?"

"Well, he says, 'There's a buck going over and down this side!'"

So the ogres gave chase in that direction.

Mlenzana-mnye said, "The cattle are departing with Mbengu-Sonyangaza!"

The ogres asked, "What does he say?"

"He says, 'There's a human being over the hill, right here!'"[39]

They chased that person but did not find him.

"What is he saying?"

"He says, 'The cattle are departing with Mbengu-Sonyangaza!'"

The ogres went in dogged pursuit[40] belatedly.

When Mbengu got over to the other side of the hill, he found the river in full flood. He struck the water with his staff, and the river went dry. Then he crossed with all that horde of the ogres' cattle, as well as his sister. When he got to the other side of the river, he rested, and the river was in flood again.

After he had rested, the ogres arrived.

They shouted, across the river, "Yho! How did you manage to cross the river?"

Mbengu shouted, "Use tall grass and plait a rope; make it long! Keep most of it on your side of the river, then throw enough of it to our side for us to get a firm hold of it!"

The ogres became busy. They plaited, they plaited and plaited, then threw a lasso across. Mbengu seized the rope.

Now, all of the ogres held on to the rope firmly—all of the ogres, except for two.

When they were in the middle of the river, Mbengu let go of the rope, and the ogres were swept away.

The other two ogres gave up; they went home.

Mbengu went to his home with those cattle and with that sister of his. He got home, and the cattle poured in. That daughter of his sister was with them as well.

So ends the story.

COMMENTARY

Nontsomi Langa's "Mbengu-Sonyangaza"[41] is the story of Mbengu's rite of passage. His separation occurs when he moves to the land of the ogres to rescue his sister. The ordeal has to do with wresting life, in the form of the sister, from death, represented by the ogres. Typical of the ordeal stage of the puberty ritual, identity is significant: Mbengu reveals his identity to the daughter of his sister by means of the leaky billycan. Mbengu's identity plan has to do with stepping on a reed. The plan works, and Mbengu and Nqunuse, his sister, are reunited. Now the problem for Mbengu is how to get to the ogres so that he can rescue Nqunuse. He devises a plan: he will disguise himself as the queen's wretch, and the result is a pattern of identity. He disguises himself, and his identity is revealed to One-Legged-One when the clouds on Mbengu's chest clear away at night. But One-Legged-One does not reveal Mbengu's identity at this time. Mbengu escapes with his sister and her daughter (her son is shoved under a rock). Then One-Legged-One alerts the other ogres about the escape. There is a pattern built around the alarm, which is misunderstood by the ogres. A chase results, and the death of the ogres occurs by means of a rope ruse.

The story shifts from the real world of Mbengu to the mythic world of the doves and later to the mythic center that is the realm of the ogres, with those two mythic centers, that of the doves and that of the ogres, representing the struggle between the positive and negative sides of this youth who is undergoing his puberty ritual. His sister, Nqunuse, is another representation of his positive side, and he moves to her as he destroys the ogres. How does the society survive against external onslaughts? Again, tradition is the only viable shield.

A Xhosa Story

The House with Seven Heads

By Nontsomi Langa

Nontsomi Langa's performance of this Xhosa tale illustrates narrative, mythic, and poetic qualities of the imaginative oral tradition. She describes a conflict between Sathana and a young man. The initial relationship between them seems friendly but in actuality, Sathana means to lure the youth to his home with the promise of work. The rhythmic patterning of the narrative involves a series of tasks set by him. The youth is unequal to Sathana's challenge; he can function only with the assistance of the villain's daughter. The tasks comprise the narrative substance of the performance.

Now for a story . . .
A certain young man was thirsty one night, just before dawn, so he took a billycan and went down to the river. At the river, he found[42] a man crouching on a rock
He greeted him. "Hello."
"Yes, hello!"
They conversed, and at daybreak they parted. The young man dipped his water and went home.
The next night, again just before dawn, he again became thirsty. He again awakened at the same time, in the middle of the night, just before the dawn, and he again went to the river. And that same man was there.
They chatted once more; they talked and talked.

This narrative (1S-615) was performed by Nontsomi Langa, a Gcaleka, about fifty-five years old, on September 13, 1967, at about 2:00 pm, outside, in Nontsomi Langa's kraal in Mboxo (Nkanga) Location, Gatyana District, Transkei, in front of an audience of twenty women, six men, fifteen teenagers, and thirty children.

As they were parting, that man asked, "Say, my friend, where do you come from?"

He said, "My home's right over there."

The other man said, "I'm asking you this because even though we're on quite friendly terms, we haven't discussed our personal lives."

"Where do *you* come from?"

He said, "There's my home, over there on the horizon. You can just see it above the trees. There are jobs available at my home. You must come over there if you're looking for work."

"Oh, well, it's all right. I'll be there right away. Tomorrow. When I go there to your home, what'll I say? Whose homestead will I say I am seeking?"

"You should say that you want Sathana's homestead!"

He woke up, then, in the morning and set out to go to that homestead of Sathana. When he got there, when he had gone this far, he found the daughter of Sathana, the only person at home. However, that person with whom he had chatted was not there.

"Hello!"

"Yes!"

"How dreadful that you should be coming to this homestead! Nobody ever comes here!"

"Well, I had met a man of this homestead, and he said this was his home, and there was work. I have come to seek a job."

"Oh. Well, you will die today! No one ever comes at home here. Come here and I'll show you. There's our house."

And so they entered the house. She said, "Look up there! Do you see those seven heads? That seventh head is my mother's head! Because my father wants to have *eight* heads, he wants yours now!"

Then that man sat down and wept. "What shall I do?" The man just sat, and cried and cried and cried.

The man noticed the arrival of Sathana. When he arrived, he was no longer a young man. There arrived an elderly man now.

He said, "Hello!"

"Yes!"

"Go into that house, and go to sleep."

So he entered that house with seven heads. The girl came during the night, having stolen food for him.

She said, "Don't you tell on me to my father! If you tell on me, I too will die!"

"I thank you for this food."

And so he did not tell on her.

On the next morning—he came, that man came, and said, "Say, fellow!"

The other said, "*Hiii.*"

"Come out!"

He came out.

"Do you see that small forest?"

He said, "I see it!"

"I want that today it all be cut down! All of it, completely! You should level even a tree this small!"

"Well, that's all right." So saying, he thrust a huge axe into his hands and departed, riding away on his gelding, a horse powered by fire.

And so the young man got there—but no matter how hard he struck at a mimosa tree, it would not fall down. No matter how hard he struck it, it would not fall down.

Then, at midday, the girl arrived, having stolen some food for him. She took up that axe and swung out and cut down a mimosa tree. And all the mimosa trees were leveled.[43]

Then the girl went home. She said, "Don't you tell on me however, to my father, because I too will die!"

Well, then, the young man returned some time later.

Sathana arrived, coming from his trip, searching for those heads.

"Say, fellow, did you cut down that mimosa forest?"

He said, "Completely! I went *tshece! mminmm tshece! tshece!*"

"Oh, well, it's all right."

Then it was bedtime.

In the morning, it was time to get up. Sathana came.

"Say, fellow!"

"*Hii?*"

"Come out!"

And he came out. And when he had come out, he saw that in that place where there had been a small forest, by morning there was a huge lake—there was a huge plain, more than before, full of crows.

He said, "Do you see those crows?"

He said, "I see them."

He then said, "Take this, then. Do you know how to shoot?"

"I do know."

"By the time I come, there should not even be one of them alive! You should have killed them all. You should shoot down even the young ones."

And so he gave him bullets—two rounds. And he loaded the guns. No matter what he did, the crows just scattered and immediately came down again.

Not even one was dead! No matter how he shot, the crows just scattered and came down again, not even one being dead.

At length, the girl came up once again. She loaded the gun. The girl loaded and loaded and shot one crow down. And they all died at once.[44]

Then this girl said, "Don't you tell on me to my father! All you should say is that you defeated them!"

And so she went home. And when the girl had gone home, her father arrived.

This fellow too arrived afterwards, and Sathana asked, "Did you shoot them?"

He said, "Well, they are all dead. I routed them. Even now, I came back with a lot of bullets!"

It was night, and all went to sleep.

Then they got up. That man got up and went to the other one, and said, "Say, fellow!"

"*Hii?*"

"Come out!"

And he came out.

In that flat land where the crows were, by morning there was now a big pool that glimmered.

"Do you see that pool?"

He said, "I see it!"

"It contains my daughter's needle, over there! By the time I return, you should have retrieved it and brought it here!"

And so the young man went and disrobed and jumped around in the pool, scooping up mud, scooping up mud, but he could not recover the needle.

Once again, the girl came at midday. She disrobed and went in and came out with the needle. She gave it to him, and the girl went home. The fellow followed behind.

Sathana came, having returned from his journey. Sathana then said, "Well, then, I must admit that you are a very skillful worker."

He was not given his wages for each day that he had worked. He had earned thirty shillings. He did not get them; Sathana kept them.

Well, then, bedtime came. Then rising time.

Sathana went over to him: "Say, fellow!"

"*Hii?*"

"Come out!"

And he came out.

Where the pool had been the day before, this morning there was a dam—not a pool now, but a dam.

He asked, "Do you see that dam over there?"

He said, "I see it!"

"Go and find my daughter's engagement ring in that dam. Have it here when I return!"

He saddled his horse and departed.

At the dam, the young man sifted through the mud, he sifted, sifted, working outside the dam.

At length, the girl came, and when she had come, she drew out this engagement ring, and she gave it to him, and the girl then went home. The fellow also went home.

He found Sathana already at home.

"Well, I came up with it!"

"Well, that's good."

It was night; they slept. Sathana woke up and went to that house once again.

"Say, fellow!"

"*Hii?*"

"Come out!"

And he came out. In the place where there had been a dam, by morning there was a meadow, a big meadow, and there was a lot of undergrowth.

He said, "Take this bag full of millet, and sow it over there! You should sow it all and not leave even one grain in the bag! Then you must pick up every grain until the bag is full!"

And so the young man scattered it around, he scattered and scattered it. Then he began to pick grains by twos and put them into the bag. Then he would sit down and cry, and he would pick up two grains and throw them into the bag, and then sit down and cry, pick up two grains and put them into the bag, then sit down and cry, pick up two grains and put them into this bag, sit down and cry, pick up two grains, put them into this bag, sit down and cry.

Then the girl came. She picked up one grain and cast it into the bag. Right away, the bag filled, and the girl went home.

This fellow lifted the bag up to his shoulders and carried it home. He reached home at the same time as Sathana.

"Did you gather the grain?"

"Well, I did gather it, my lord. I am quite accustomed to filling a bag from an undergrowth. I have done it before, and I picked it up again!"

"Oh. Well, you're quite a worker, young man! Come to think of it, what have you been eating all this time?"

"Well, I live on water. At home, I never ate food. Even as you yourself saw me over there in the river. That is all I eat—water."

"Oh."

Time passed; it was dusk. There was sleep. When they had slept, they woke up in the morning. Once again Sathana came.

"Say, fellow!"

"*Hii?*"

"I am going off again. This time I will rest you a bit from the hard work, so that you may take a rest here at home. You should go and change that horse.[45] And when you go to untie it over there and take it to drink water at that dam, you should then tether it on another ridge."[46]

Well, then, friends, he went over there to the horse; it gave him a lot of trouble. No matter how he tried to get hold of it, it obstructed him. No matter how hard he tried, it obstructed him.

Then the girl came and managed to take it to drink. And when she had watered it, she went on to tether it on some other ridge, then she went home. The fellow went home too.

Sathana came.

"Have you changed it?"

"Well, I have changed it, lord."

"Oh! You're quite strong! Did it not burn you up?"

"Well, it gave me a lot of trouble at certain intervals. However, I persevered."

"Oh, it's all right. You're a good worker!"

Then it was night, and there was sleep. And when they had gone to sleep and risen in the morning, once again Sathana woke up.

"Say, fellow!"

"*Hii?*"

"Come out!"

He came out.

"Today also, I will let you rest! Pass the time at home here. But before you rest, do you see that willow tree?"

"I see it."

"Go and bring down my life secret from up there! My life secret is over there, right up on the willow tree, over there at that ridge which you see swaying this way. That place you see going like this!"

"Oh, well, all right."

Now this willow tree had been barked; it had been made smooth, smoothed, smoothed, and then it had been greased with pig fat.

So the young man went to the tree but could not find a foothold at all.

Then that girl came. Then that girl came. At first, it looked as if it would be an easy climb for her. But when she was halfway up, she slipped and landed on the ground on her buttocks. Again, she was set on darting up the tree, but when she was midway, she slipped and landed on the ground.

The young man wept. The girl ran and entered that same room of her home and came out with a cat. And she put the cat on the tree. Up went the cat—*krwempe krwempe krwempe krwempe krwempe krwempe krwempe*—and reached the very top, and laid hands on that life secret: two eggs.[47] And the cat brought them down in its mouth; it came and put them down.

Then the young man said, "Girl, I am courting you. You have preserved my life! I want us to go now while your father is absent. Devise a plan. You have been devising plans for me consistently. Soon I might die at home here; my luck will soon run out here at this home. What I want—what I want is that you become my wife!"

The girl agreed. And so they packed and packed and packed some provisions on top of that horse of the wind. And they mounted, carrying these two eggs.

Sathana, wherever he was, suddenly knew that there had been a departure from his home. So he went and arrived to find the place deserted. Nothing remained, not even his money. Everything had been taken away. So he gave chase.

As it turned out, he had already stopped their progress. They imagined that they were running away; they were only marking time. He had used his magic to slow them down: while they thought that they were galloping at full speed, the horse was actually standing still; it was not gaining ground!

Well! The girl took that egg, and she dropped it behind her. It broke—and suddenly cliffs and stony hills appeared, great rivers appeared. It was not possible for Sathana to go on, so he turned around and went back home. There, he took an axe and a spade; he also brought a knife along and, to decant the river, a dish. He returned, and he splashed the water out of the rivers, he splashed it, he splashed and splashed it. Then he knocked the hills and cliffs down with his axe, and so everything became level again. Then he mounted his horse and gave chase.

The girl allowed Sathana to move to the front of them. Then she took the other egg and threw it at him. The egg struck him right in the forehead, and he fell. He died, along with that gelding on which he was mounted—a gelding hog.

The young woman thereby gained freedom and departed with her husband. On and on and on and on and on and on and on they went. And when they were close to his home, near that river from which water is dipped, this young woman said, "We just can't, the two of us, just strut into town this way, mounted on those horses! Why don't you just go ahead and unload the things at your home? When you've done that, inspan a yoke of oxen to come and fetch me here with those oxen from your home. But you must not greet anyone during this period! If you do that, you will forget about me! You must not even allow your dog to welcome you! You might even have to strike it to keep it away from you. You can stroke it when I arrive at your home."

He agreed. When the young man reached home, he proceeded to lay out the yokes, remaining quiet the whole time. He spread them out over there at his home and instructed the boys to bring up the oxen.

His mother remonstrated with him: "Why? Why? My child, I missed you so much! Why? why? why?"

And now he greeted his mother.

His dog also came now and fussed over him.

And now the young man forgot that he had left someone over the hill.

And that was the end of that.

In the meantime, this girl was being exposed to hot rays of the sun. There was a mimosa tree that slanted over the water. This girl of his climbed up and perched on that mimosa tree, so that she could get some breeze. And when that girl had been there for some time, a certain woman who lived across the river told her child, "Run, my child. Go and dip some water for me at the river. I'm thirsty; I've been working the fields with my hands."

The child refused, she utterly refused. But in the end, she went. And when she looked into the water, this child, she said, "*Yhu!* My mother has no right to send me on an errand, since I'm so beautiful! I can't submit to that! Let her die of thirst!"

And so she went home with her billycan.

"Where's the water?"

The child said, "I didn't realize that I am so beautiful! No one has a right to send me on such an errand. I refuse to consider it! Never again will I go to the river—because I'm so beautiful!"

So her mother took a bucket and went to the river. When she got there, she looked into the water, said, "*Yhu!* What's happened to me? I have never been aware that I look so young! I didn't know that I was still so beautiful!"

She dipped and dipped. And when she regarded this face that was reflected in the water, it was, she noted, really quite unlike her own face concerning its complexion. She noticed that this face was light in color. Because she was mature, she realized that it was not her own reflection.

"There's someone here!" she said. "Hello, my child!"

"Yes."

"Whose child are you?"

This girl said, "I might as well be yours!"

She said, "Come down."

So she came down.

When she had done so, the mother asked, "Whose child are you?"

She said, "You may adopt me, Mother! I am lost. I don't know who I am."

"Come with me."

And the two of them went home.

They reached her home, and the girl became the woman's child. She was given as a gift two little fowls, a hen and a cock. And this girl began to teach them to talk, she continually taught them how to speak.

Then one day she said, "Mother."

"Yes."

"My fowls are able to talk."

"What do they say?"

She said, "Bring me some maize, and I'll show you how they do it."

[A brief interruption.]

The woman brought some maize, and she gave it to them. They ate and ate.

Then the hen said,

> "*Tyhini le!* You eat and eat, and then attack me!
>   Aren't you the one to whom my father said,
>   'Cut down the forest'?
>   Then I came and found you weeping and helped
>   you!"
> *Go go go go xho!*[48]

> "*Tyhini le!* You eat and eat and then attack me!
>   Aren't you the one to whom my father said,
>   'Shoot crows on the veld'?
>   I came and found you crying, and helped you!"
> *Go go go go go xho!*

> "*Tyhini le!* You eat and eat, and then attack me!
>   Aren't you the one to whom my father said,
>   'Bring my daughter's needle from the deep pool'?
>   Then I came and found you crying, and I helped
>   you!"
> *Go go go go xho!*

> "*Tyhini le!* You eat and eat, and then attack me!
>   Aren't you the one to whom my father said,
>   'Bring my daughter's engagement ring from the deep
>   pool'?
>   I came and found you crying, and came to your
>   aid!"
> *Go go go go xho!*

> "*Tyhini le!* You eat and eat, and then attack me!
>   Aren't you the one to whom my father said,

'Gather a bagful of sorghum from the undergrowth'?
Then I came and found you weeping, and came to
    your aid!"
Go go go go xho!

"*Tyhini le!* You eat and eat, and then attack me!
Was it not you to whom my father said,
'Bring my fiery horse'?
I came and found you crying, and assisted you!"
Go go go go xho!

"*Tyhini le!* You eat and eat, and then attack me!
Aren't you the one to whom my father said,
'Bring my life [secret] from the willow tree'?
Then I came and found you weeping, and assisted
    you!"
Go go go go go xho!

"*Tyhini le!* You eat and eat, and then attack me!
Aren't you the one who said
I should kill my father on the veld?
I came and found you crying, and I came to your aid!"
Go go go go xho!

"*Tyhini le!* You eat and eat, and then attack me!
Was it not you who abandoned me on the veld?
Left me alone on the veld?
I came and found you crying, and I came to your aid!"
Go go go go xho!

Her mother then said, "Stop now, my child!"

In another homestead, a wedding was taking place. That young man had arrived and had gone courting in speedy fashion with the help of that heap of money he had brought from—Sathana's place.[49]

So these fowls also went to that man's wedding. The woman went too, and she and her adopted mother took these fowls with them to that wedding. They had arrived just before the ceremony was to take place, and this child was carrying both of the fowls.

Her adopted mother said that the marriage could not go on. She whistled: *viiiiiityo!* "I have a child here with some talking fowls! If you want them to talk, just say so!"

The response was a calm of anticipation. Everybody was ready to listen to these fowls. Someone suggested that maize be brought. It was brought and fed to them. They ate and ate and ate—*go go go go xho!*

> "*Tyhini le!* You eat and eat, and then attack me!
> Was it not you to whom my father said,
> 'Cut down the forest'?
> I came and found you crying, and came to your aid!"
> *Go go go go xho!*

> "*Tyhini le!* You eat and eat, and then attack me!
> Was it not you to whom my father said,
> 'Shoot the ravens on the veld'?
> I came and found you crying, and assisted you!"
> *Go go go go xho!*

> "*Tyhini le!* You eat and eat, and then attack me!
> Was it not you to whom my father said,
> 'Bring my daughter's needle from the deep pool'?
> I came and found you crying, and came to your aid!"
> *Go go go go xho!*

> "*Tyhini le!* You eat and eat, and then attack me!
> Was it not you to whom my father said,
> 'Retrieve my daughter's engagement from the pool'?
> I came and found you crying, and assisted you!"
> *Go go go go xho!*

> "*Tyhini le!* You eat and eat, and then attack me!
> Was it not you to whom my father said,
> 'Scatter a bagful of sorghum over the undergrowth'?
> I came and found you crying, and assisted you!"
> *Go go go go xho!*

> "*Tyhini le!* You eat and eat, and then attack me!
> Was it not you to whom my father said,

'Bring my fiery horse'?
I came and found you crying, and came to your aid!"
Go go go go xho!

"*Tyhini le!* You eat and eat, and then attack me!
Aren't you the one to whom my father said,
'Bring my life [secret] from the willow tree'?
I came and found you crying, and assisted you!"
Go go go go xho!

"*Tyhini le!* You eat and eat, and then attack me!
Aren't you the one who said
I should kill my father on the veld?
I came and found you crying, and assisted you!"
Go go go go xho!

"*Tyhini le!* You eat and eat, and then attack me!
Aren't you the one who said
I should remain in the wilderness?
And then you abandoned me!"

Suddenly that man remembered! He threw the wedding proceedings into confusion. The ceremony was nullified. The bridal party was driven away.[50]

He made a fresh start now. He initiated the procedure for marrying the first girl, the daughter of Sathana. He asked for her hand in marriage from that woman who had adopted her.[51] Then there was a wedding ceremony, and she actually became his wife.

That's how the *intsomi* ends.

COMMENTARY

The plotting of imagery in this tale depends on two related motifs having to do with marriage. The first describes a place from which no one returns—an image in African oral tradition often having to do with the wresting of a bride from a reluctant, even menacing, father-in-law. The second motif has to do with the father-in-law's daughter, who becomes the means of the suitor's salvation. The father-in-law takes on a duality: his death-dealing qualities are obvious enough; his daughter, as his extension, becomes his life-giving part. The narrative involves a struggle between those two forces, with the young suitor caught in their strange web. The antagonist, disguised as a friend and helper, is, in this version of the tale, given a Christian name, Satan, so that emotions attendant on his villainy are intensified, drawn as they are from two distinct traditions, the Xhosa and the Christian. He is truly evil: "Do you see those seven heads?" his daughter asks. "The seventh is the head of my mother! My father wants to have eight heads, that's why he wants yours!" Motivations grow out of these motifs—a youth's hopes to obtain a job evolve into a bride-quest and a struggle with the father-in-law.

But these motifs do not establish the theme; that is left to a highly evocative image that suffuses the narrative imagery and provides a means of organizing it, complementing the more obvious plotting of conflict and resolution. While the story could be told without this mythic element, it takes on mystery with it, the familiarity of dreams: this strong emotional component is the foundation for the generation of the more enduring message of the performance. There is utility in distinguishing between those motifs from which the narrative is developed and those that elicit (then hold and manipulate) extraordinary audience responses. They can be the same; often, as in this tale, they are not. Because mythic and narrative images differ here, the members of the audience are moved from an obvious theme to a startling insight.

The mythic significance of this story of Sathana versus the young man, of evil against good, is found in the curious relationship that exists among three characters—for the pivotal character is the young woman, Sathana's daughter. She comes from that same never-never land as Sathana, the land from which no one returns, and she moves into the world of the suitor. This is the singular force of the tale—the representative from the unknown world now forever implanted in the world of the living, the realm of the real. As the offspring of the eternal Sathana, she has his supernatural abilities: he uses them for evil purposes, she for obscure ends. She will not allow the human to neglect his ties to her.

Once the young man enters the forbidden world, he becomes irreversibly tied to her, whatever she represents. When he brings her back from that prohibited realm, his life can never be the same. He might briefly forget her, immersing himself in the world of memory and involving himself with the personae of his past: his mother, his dog, and later a bride from his human society. But this remembered world can no longer be. The devil-daughter reveals to him that his relationship with her has irrevocably altered his routine experiences. Having saved the young man, she remains a vivid and constant force in his life. Her extraordinary beauty is the image selected by the storyteller to dramatize her detachment from the human world. The might and mystery of Sathana continue to exert themselves through the daughter. The young man has passed through a period of his life now irretrievably lost.

It is, seemingly, a story of the struggle between a malevolent being and his offspring, with the young man simply the conduit for the expression of this conflict. But as the tale develops, the earlier antagonistic relationship between the youth and Sathana imposes itself on the apparently more benign link between the youth and Sathana's daughter and raises unsettling questions about that linkage. He remains in the end dogged by a persistent pursuer—is it Sathana or Sathana's daughter? Is she a force for good or a force for evil? She marks the change in the life of a youth who has moved into the land from which no one returns—at least, not in the same way that he entered.

The element of myth and the narrative plotting of the struggle are joined by the patterning of imagery. The rhythmical union of narrative segments weaves the mythic image into a tale pitting supernatural force against mortal intuition. The haunting tone of the story is created by this combination. The pattern is repeated in pristine and more obviously poetic fashion when Sathana's daughter later recalls what happened—telling, first, her new friend, then a larger group that includes her forgetful husband.

Myth elicits emotional responses from the members of the audience, tying the present to the past and addressing ancient fears, hopes, and dreams. Sathana's daughter is the carrier of the mythic motif in this tale; she becomes the means of tension and connection between the human youth and the eternal Sathana. Father and daughter, denizens of this land from which no one returns, are the polar reaches of a set of forces into which this young man from the human world blunders—the innocent abroad. He can never get rid of that experience; this is the power of the performance. He is changed, permanently harnessed to the forces that he has unleashed.

A Xhosa Story

THE GIRL AND THE *IMBULU*

By Nontsomi Langa

It happened . . .

There were a man and his wife. They bore only two children, girls.

The older girl got married. Her name was Mabele-ngambonga.

These people began to age, and they were without a son. All they had were these two daughters. They aged, they aged and aged and aged.

They aged, and then these two daughters: the older one got married to a king in a far-away country.

When the man and his wife had aged, they died. They died at the same time. One died one day, the other died the next day.

Then this younger girl was told, "You see now, you should gather all the livestock that is at home here, all of it. Take all of it, and go to the home of your sister: take horse and cow, take goat and sheep, and fowl and pig. Take with you everything, even the grinding stone for ochre. Leave nothing behind. And when you leave, set these houses on fire. Burn them."

"Oh."

Well, then, friends, this child did all of this when her mother and father had died.

The next day, she set the houses on fire.

It was said, "Take this stick with you. As you travel, the livestock will be coming along under the ground. When you are a long distance off, when you want to rest, and so that the livestock too should be able to eat, strike the ground with the stick, and say, 'Open up, Ground! I have neither mother nor father.'"

So this younger girl set out. She went on and on and on.

When she was a way off, she rested. She struck the ground with the stick, and the stock began to graze. She too sat down, and the stock grazed and grazed.

This tale (1S-621) was narrated by Nontsomi Langa, a Gcaleka woman about fifty-five years old, on September 13, 1967, about 3:30 pm, outside, in the kraal of Nontsomi Langa, in Mboxo (Nkanga) Location, Gatyana District, to an audience of about twenty women, six or seven men, fifteen teenagers, and thirty children, all Gcaleka.

When they were full, she struck the ground with the stick, and the stock disappeared. Then this child proceeded, she proceeded on her way.

When she had gone a long way, she again rested. Before she struck the ground, she leaned against an anthill. There was movement in this anthill: an *imbulu* appeared.

It said,[52] "Hello, Sister!"

"Yes."

"Oh, please come in and let us eat. Swallow this lot of millipedes."

"No, I don't eat them."

"Oh. Where are you going?"

"I am going to my sister's place."

"Why?"

"To visit."

"Oh. Let's go together. I shall accompany you!"

So they went on then; they walked and walked.

Eventually, they came to a small river.

This *imbulu* said, "No one crosses here before one washes. Before crossing this river, one has to undress and wash."

Then the *imbulu* dipped its tail into the water and sprayed water around. It said, "You've gotten a taste of the water. Now, wash."

They got to the river, and the girl undressed.

The *imbulu* said, "When someone washes here, the practice is to remove all one's clothing in order to wash."

So the girl undressed completely. She even removed her bangles and leg ornaments. Then she washed and washed and washed.

Meanwhile, that *imbulu* was over there putting on all the clothes of that girl; it put on her skirts. Then it said to the girl, "Please put on these rags of mine."

Well, then, friends, she put them on. She put them on.

"When will you give my clothes back to me?"

"Well, I shall give them back to you when we get to the stream that is ahead of us."

"Give me back my clothes!"

"No, wait a while. I'll give them back to you soon."

Then, suddenly, the girl took mud and smeared herself with it, she smeared herself, she smeared herself, and went on.

Then they arrived at her sister's place.

The *imbulu* greeted them: "*Yho yho yho!* Hello, Brother-in-law! Hello, In-laws!"

"Hello. Oh! Where have you come from, Sister-in-law?"

"Well, I have come from home, Sister-in-law. I have come from home, I have come from home. I have come to visit."

"Oh. Say, why is it that you lisp?"

"Well, I was once very ill, I became very ill."

"Oh."

In the meantime, this girl remained inconspicuous by the doorpost.

"And where did you meet this person who is in your company?"

The *imbulu* said, "I met her over there, over the hill, this wretched thing of patches."

It was almost harvest time, and the birds had to be kept from the sorghum fields.

This was the royal residence, so there was also a councillor here. His name was Sigadanko.

People said, "Well, Sigadanko, you have got someone now who will help you to ward off the birds."

Well then, friends, the next day came. It was suggested that this person was to be made to eat with the dogs. But the girl refused.

The king left her a portion of food from his dish. He said, "No, let her eat from my dish."

So the king fed her.

In the morning, they went to keep the birds from the sorghum fields. The girl was positioned on one side, this wretch. And Sigadanko stood on the other end of the field.

A name was given to this girl: She became Ngodowanja, Dogshit.[53]

Sigadanko said,

> "Here they come!
> The birds are coming your way, Ngodowanja!
> *Tsa' tsayi bo!*
> There they come, there they come, Ngodowanja!
> *Tsa' tsayi bo!*
> There they come, there they come, Ngodowanja!"

She said,

> [sings:] "What do you suggest I do, Sigadanko?
> All this is the doing of my mother and father,
>   Sigadanko!
> They said I should go to my sister's place,
>   Sigadanko!
> To Mabele-ngambonga's place, Sigadanko!
> On the way, I met a little *imbulu*, Sigadanko!
> It dispossessed me of my garments, Sigadanko!"

"Oh!" said Sigadanko. "There is a human being! Hey! *Mha!*"

"I swear by my mother, Nkobe-zamazimba!"[54]

When it was midday, after they had eaten, this girl went to the river. She washed and washed and washed. Then she struck the ground with her stick.

"Open up, Earth! I have neither father nor mother."

Suddenly, the livestock from her home emerged from the earth right there in the fields, and they grazed and grazed and grazed.

Sigadanko saw all this.

The stock grazed and grazed while this girl washed. She anointed herself; she cleaned her ornaments.

Then again she took mud, and she smeared herself with it, she smeared herself, she smeared herself with mud.

They went home.

Sigadanko said, "King, that is a human being, not a dog! She is the real sister of this wife of yours! She was dispossessed of her garments by this *imbulu!*"

"No!"

"Yes!"

The king said, "Do not worry. I shall go and observe."

So it was that, the next morning, the king went down to the fields.

And Sigadanko and the girl arrived in the fields.

The girl wondered, "Whose tracks are these that we are following?"

Sigadanko said, "Well, they are the tracks of wild game. There is much wild game in this country."

"Oh."

Well, they traveled on and arrived.

Sigadanko took his position at one end, anxious that the king should come.

> "There they come,
> The birds are coming, Mgodowanja!
> *Tsa' tsayi bo!*
> There they come, they are coming, Mgodowanja!
> *Tsa' tsayi bo!*"

She said,

> [sings:] "What do you suggest I should do,
>   Sigadanko?
> All this is the doing of my mother and father,
>   Sigadanko!
> They said I should go to my sister's place,
>   Sigadanko!
> To Mabele-ngambonga's place, Sigadanko!
> On the way, I met a little *imbulu*, Sigadanko!
> It dispossessed me of my garments, Sigadanko!"

"Hey! *Mha!*"

"I swear by my mother!"

"I knew I was right! That is a person!"

The girl went down to the river. She got there and washed, she washed and washed. Then she anointed herself and greased her bangles. She took out her pipes and smoked.

In the meantime, the cattle were grazing here. So much stock! There emerged from the earth everything, including pigs and fowls, and so on. And the livestock drank here.

Well, then, she finished smoking, she put away her pipes, and she struck the ground once more. And the livestock disappeared.

Then she soiled herself with mud, and she came up to the fields from the river.

The next day, the king again went down and positioned himself closer to this place by the river, so that he could seize her, so that he could capture her more readily. *Mh mh,* they waited and waited.

Then, when it was midday, this girl again went down to the river. She arrived at the river, and she washed, she washed and washed, and she anointed herself.

Then the king surprised her.

The girl said, "No! Do not seize me! These two oxen will gore you."

"Just speak! What is the matter?"

"My mother and father died on me. I was told to come and live with you, to bring this livestock with me, that you would look after me. But I encountered an *imbulu,* and it dispossessed me of my garments. That is why I soil myself with mud. I am trying to hide my nakedness."[55]

"Oh!"

On the next day, the king said, "No one will go to the fields today! What will be done is this: boil some water. I want to clean up the pits that are at my father's old site."

Well, then, water was transported to that site, water was transported there. Water was boiled, and when it was boiling, the women were told that they must go through an ordeal: the jump.

The *imbulu* said, "What an extraordinary thing to have women do!"

It was said, "No matter. Undress. Undress, undress. You will do the jump in your underwear."

So they all undressed.

The *imbulu* gathered up its tail like this and simulated buttocks here.

The proceedings began, the jump commenced, and the women leapt.

As the *imbulu* jumped, its tail dragged it down to the bottom, into the old corn that smelled down in the bottom of the pit.[56] The pit was then filled with boiling water. It was filled, it was filled.

When the *imbulu* emerged from the pit, from the boiling water, it was without a skin. It slipped past the people; it went in and out among them, slipping through their grasp.

And it said, "I really did take advantage of the little thing! I really did take advantage of the little thing!"

It ran in and out among the people. By the time it disappeared, it was already meat.

Then this girl came into view. She went to wash, then came to reclaim her garments. She girded herself.

Then she explained, "I have come to stay here. All of my people have perished."

The story is over.

COMMENTARY

The *imbulu* is a fantasy figure, usually playing a role in stories having to do with girl's puberty rites of passage. It is a betwixt and between transformational character, embodying the girl's movement into womanhood. The *imbulu* typically and deceptively obtains the girl's identity, then plays her role while she must move about in the rags or muck of the *imbulu*. During this identity crisis, the girl is undergoing a change. In the end, when her transformation is complete, the society, in the form of its leader, steps in, and the *imbulu* is destroyed.

This is the normal means of change in traditional society. During that period of change, the *imbulu* becomes a fantasy replication of the real-life character. When the transformation from *imbulu* is not completed, stories such as this one become a commentary on intrusions from without, intrusions that interfere with normal cultural transformations.

DRAWING THE MYTHIC WORLD IN SPACE

Emotions are at the core of storytelling. Ashton Ngcama,[57] born in 1923 in Ngqeleni District in the Transkei, argues that he stores the images of his poetry in his mind; when he composes, he subconsciously brings them to the surface: "They simply come," he says, as if he had been in a trance. And the success of his poetry? "It's a *feeling!* It's a feeling!" he exclaims.[58]

The storyteller is like the San artist who, in an ancient rock painting, depicted a youth's quest for birds by dramatically emphasizing the pattern.[59] This is also what happens in the spoken tale. One author recalled, "[W]hen my father first told it [a story] to me many years ago, he added: 'Stories are like a tree growing on the horizon. March towards the tree, and it will keep you in a straight line. But the tree itself is not your goal. When you reach it, you will have to let it go, and pick another point further on."[60]

Unlike painting, unlike sculpture, however, the story or poem is a work always in process. When it is complete, it disappears, leaving its traces in the imagination and memory of each member of the audience but never surviving intact. The story, the poem is always being constructed, trailing behind it memories. The words appear and then dim, as the storyteller, the poet, gradually shapes and reshapes the imagination of the audience member. The words never remain, so that the work of art can be appreciated by repeated visits. Nor are the story and poem ever complete, all the words remaining so that they may be viewed, inspected, and analyzed by the audience member. With the imagination and memory of the members of the audience, and heavily dependent on those, the storyteller constructs the verbal work. It is there, yet it is not there. It is always passing, temporary, never permanent. It can be reconstructed, but the reconstruction will never be what it was before: it will be a new construction. Images are familiar, for they are the stuff of verbal arts, and the form that engages and connects those images will be remembered. But the work is always new: memorization cannot duplicate it, because much of the stuff of the performance is the ever-changing psyche, memory, imagination of the members of the audience. They never stand still but are ever shifting, ever moving, the product of memory and imagination. This evanescence is what characterizes the oral story and poem: we have it for the moment, and then it is gone, produced by memory and become a product of memory. The storyteller and poet construct their works out of air, the voice of the performer providing the daring acrobatic airborne work, formed of words and sounds and movements and unified memories, the primary imagination of the artist shaping a host of secondary imaginations—all in the air, all evanescent, a feat of the memory and the imagination. The artist has a repertory of images, a limited number of rhythmic organizers: everything else is dependent on that artist's daring and inventiveness, his play with the remembered.

The line creates the outline of a figure and so transposes it. It is a line but not the literal movement of the story, not the outline of the sculpted figure. The music of the line is what we discuss here: the dancing line, the rhythmical and thready line. The bounding line moves unbroken, creating and connecting the parts of each of the two sculptural works, at once constructing the circular patterns, then moving decisively to the fearful destruction of those patterns, the circularity established by the depiction of the human bodies, the lineal element that is a continuation of the artists' unbroken line moving in concert with the circularity even as it turns to undermine that poetic roundness, so that both works are tense and alive with the balance of the roundness and the destructiveness of the linear. In the process, there is a mirroring—of the real and that which is rendered in the windowpane—and that metaphorical pairing deepens the emotional aspects, the pain and the beauty of these works. Masking is the crucial factor: in the process of the windowpaneing, the humans are re-created in the serenity of roundness, and the archetypal lineal serpent is set to alter this; it is an alteration that has already begun in both of these works. The force and meaning of these works is found in the dynamic interplay between opposing forms, set free from a molded mound of clay. With words and patterns of words, the poet creates a metaphor in the process of becoming, the back-and-forth movement, from man to bird to man; he is simultaneously the two, man and bird, as he moves from the one to the other, a dancing metaphor, and there seems to be no permanent identity. The man is a bird; each is composed of the other.

The artist takes the familiar and masks it with the tenacious line, takes words and creates a story, as a sculptor takes wood and establishes a metaphor, creating a story. The raw material is words and wood: those are a part of reality. With words and wood, masks are created, artists' windowpane views of reality. But the words are now more than words, the wood more than wood. Out of those something new is created, but the new is always familiar—the words are still there, the wood still present. If the observer looks hard enough, he can see the words and the wood, but when he looks in that way he has lost the effect of the poetic line; he converts the story to words, the mask to wood, and he ignores the windowpane. With those elements of the real, the artists reshape, reform, reassemble the familiar and render it jarringly unfamiliar, with new planes, shapes, forms. That is the effect of the artist's wily line. The observer is never far from the original raw data of the real: the familiar must always be present. The tension between the real and its reordering is what reforms our emotions, takes one to an essence, with unfamiliar surfaces and volumes derived from surfaces and volumes that are a part of routine existence. A world is drawn in space, rooted in the real yet stretching beyond the real. The artistic experience is narrowed in any attempt to look through this windowpane of the artist to the real words, the wood, the clay—that is one view, but it is not the view of the artist, the view that evokes the emotions.[61]

"Ah, happy, happy boughs! that cannot shed / Your leaves, nor ever bid the Spring adieu."[62] In stories, there is always a frozen inner image: like Keats's urn, it is eternal. All around it are the evanescent images of the real world. The shimmering relationship between the frozen image and the evanescent image creates metaphor, myth. But another layer, a third layer, is needed, for the evanescent images are also frozen in the written work but not in the work that is created before a live audience. As a result, we have two layers of frozen imagery, and then the outer set—the audience's world, which is made real, given form, by the double layering in the story. Art needs the two layers so that we, the third layer, can see them: we, the audience and the reader, constitute that third layer. In this way, we find the connection between two events or images that seem eternally unconnected.

From a Notebook

The mechanics of connection: how it is done in the oral tradition, how it is done in literary works (poems and stories), (and how it is done in physics?). How the mythic center becomes connected to the evanescent real world: the mechanics of this are the poetic essence of storytelling, making the connections

Conversation with a Poet

Ngcama: It [the poem] simply came by itself.
Scheub: You don't go to school—
N: No, not for it.
S: No other *imbongi* [poet] sits down and tells you how to do it—
N: No. No, I have not been taught by any person to do it.
S: Your son will not necessarily be an *imbongi.*
N: *E—*
S: Even if he wants to be?
N: Even if my son wants to be an *imbongi,* he can't learn to be an *imbongi.* It's just—It's a *feeling!* It's a feeling. You see, if a preacher preaches, now you have a feeling—it's the same thing, it comes to the same thing. You see, when we say our prayers, we don't know what we have said. And we can't repeat it. It comes like that. That's how it comes to me. You see, I have been asked by many chiefs to create *izibongo* [heroic poetry], but I *can't,* because I don't remember—even what I've been saying now, I can't say it. It's not mine. It belongs to *ithongo.*[63] That's what I think.
S: Would you explain that?
N: This thing, we think that it comes from a dream. There is nothing that we speak to ourselves. When a person arrives who is sick, it happens that I know how to tell him he is sick, a certain thing, yet I don't know him. . . .
S: The art of the *imbongi:* will this go on, or will it die now, do you think?

The conversation (2S-520) was with Ashton Ngcama, a Bhaca *imbongi,* on Friday, August 25, 1972, on the veld in Mount Ayliff District, the Transkei, before a mixed audience.

N: I don't know whether it will die, because if *ithongo* has picked someone among the family to have the same *umoya*[64] as we have, I think it will be something that will still [----] a particular person. Because you know, a witch-doctor—we have got witch-doctors and they are called "witch-doctors" because they have not learnt to be doctors, because they can't say what they have discovered in a person.

S: When did you learn that you have the *umoya*?

N: This—I was in school.

S: How old were you?

N: I was about sixteen years old.

S: And how did you know this? What were the circumstances of this?

N: Of—?

S: Of knowing that you had the *umoya* of the *ithongo*.

N: I did not know; I have been told by people. I did not know that I had *umoya* that came from *ithongo*.

S: Is that the first time—when you were sixteen, is that the first time you created an *izibongo*?

N: Oh, yes!

S: What was the occasion? Was there a chief at the school? or what?

N: It was—you see, people were playing. Yes. You see, there were uniforms of the children, and when I looked at these people, and—there was something in my mind about them. . . .

S: When you create *izibongo* . . . , do you find that some of the same poetry that you used at one time will find its way into another *izibongo*?

N: It happens that when—you see, if one is praising the same chief, another time when I come, I will say other things in connection with what I have said today, because all these things that I am saying are connected with the chief. I always praise a chief with some things connected to him.[65]

S: Do you memorize anything?

N: Not as such. Yes, I can't memorize.

S: Do you remember things when you're actually in the process of creating *izibongo*?

N: Yes. Yes, I remember some things. Very few. Not in the same order that I have given. Yes. Yes, because it comes of itself. . . .

S: And how would you compare *izibongo* and *iintsomi*?[66] Are these similar?

N: No, they are not similar. *Intsomi* is a tale; an *intsomi* is a narrative, something narrated. This could be narrated, you see; it's followed by one, step by step by step. Even if the children were here, could listen to *intsomi,* could say it, as the other person has said it.

S: But not an *izibongo.*

N: Not *izibongo.* Unless I repeat the same poetry—

S: —again and again—

N: —again and again and again. Some *iimbongi*[67] are of that nature. That is why you say that mine are excellent, because I can't say the same thing. Tomorrow, if I'm giving *izibongo,* I'll give another thing. Because it's not mine. I don't think. If I sit down to think, I fail to write *izibongo,* I fail to write *izibongo,* I fail to write *izibongo.*

≠KÁGÁRA AND |HAŨNU, WHO FOUGHT EACH OTHER WITH LIGHTNING

They formerly, ≠kágára[68] formerly went to fetch his younger sister, he went to take her away; he went to take her away from |haũnu;[69] and he took (her) back to her parents.

|haũnu gave chase to his brother-in-law, he passed along behind the hill.

The clouds came, clouds which were unequaled in beauty;[70] they vanished away.

≠kágára said:[71] "Thou must walk on."

His younger sister walked, carrying (a heavy burden of) things, (her) husband's things. ≠kágára said: "Thou must walk on; for, home is not near at hand."

|haũnu passed along behind (the hill).

The clouds came, the clouds vanished away.

≠kágára said: "Thou must walk on, for, thou art the one who dost see." And he, because the house became near, he exclaimed: "Walk on! Walk on!" He waited for his younger sister; his younger sister came up to his side. He exclaimed:

From Bleek and Lloyd, *Specimens of Bushman Folklore,* 112–19.

"What things[72] can these be, which thou dost heavily carry?"

Then |haũnu sneezed, on account of it;[73] blood poured out of his nostrils; he stealthily lightened at his brother-in-law. His brother-in-law fended him quickly off,[74] his brother-in-law also stealthily lightened at him. He quickly fended off his brother-in-law. His brother-in-law also lightened at him. ≠kágára said: "Thou must come (and) walk close beside me; for, thou art the one who dost see that husband does not allow us time; for, he does not singly lighten."

They (≠kágára and |haũnu) went along angry with each other. |haũnu had intended that he should be the one lightening to whisk away ≠kágára. ≠kágára was one who was strong,[75] he continued to fend off his younger sister's husband |haũnu. His younger sister's husband was also lightening at him; he was lightening at his brother-in-law. Then he stealthily lightened at his younger sister's husband with black lightning,[76] he, lightening, whisked him up and carried him to a little distance.

His younger sister's husband, in this manner, lay dying; he, in this manner, he thundered,[77] while ≠kágára bound up his head[78] with the net, he, returning, arrived at home.

He went to lie down in the house, while |haũnu lay thundering;[79] he thundered there, while ≠kágára went to lie down, when he had rubbed them[80] with buchu,[81] buchu, buchu, buchu, he lay down.[82]

POSTLUDE

Surviving 350 Years

*I*t was in 1976, when Desmond Tutu, who would later be awarded the Nobel Peace Prize, had just been appointed the first black Anglican Dean of Johannesburg in South Africa, that he wrote a letter to then Prime Minister John Vorster, an Afrikaner, who had, as minister of justice, passed a law allowing for indefinite detention in solitary confinement without charge or trial. Tutu wrote, "We all, black and white together, belong to South Africa and blacks yield place to no one in their passionate love for this our beloved land. We belong together—we will survive or be destroyed together." That was on May 6, 1976: in no way would Vorster's white regime ever countenance such an audacious scheme. But twenty years later, in 1994, echoing Tutu, the African National Congress called for establishment by the Government of a "commission of truth" to investigate abuses of power by state officials as well as by others. In 1995, the South African government initiated a Truth and Reconciliation Commission to investigate political crimes by all parties between 1960 and December 1993. It would consider violations of human rights, amnesty, and reparations for and rehabilitation of victims. And it would do this by hearing the stories of those who had suffered, by those who had inflicted the suffering.

We have to be able to *tell* our story. Speaking of one petitioner who appeared before South Africa's Truth and Reconciliation Commission, a supplicator who failed in his quest to communicate his experience, an observer wrote, "It was a pity—and an irony—that George Dube, the victim in question, failed to seize the dramatic moment afforded by the present occasion. The man simply couldn't tell a story."[1] When I was conducting research in Swaziland, a Swati storyteller was performing a story, but he was having a difficult time ordering the various parts of the story, and after a time, the audience interrupted, sounding the closing formula of the story to let the storyteller know that his awkward performance was at an end.

Time collapses, and we are in the presence of history . . . it is a time of masks. Reality, the present, is here, but with these explosive, emotional images giving it a context. This is the storyteller's art: to mask the past, making it mysterious, seeming inaccessible. But it is inaccessible only to our present intellect. It is always available to our hearts and souls, our emotions. The storyteller combines our present waking state and our past condition of semiconsciousness, and so we walk again in history, we join our forebears. And history, always more than an academic subject, becomes our collapsing of time, our memory and reliving of the past. We never live wholly in the present—much of our temperament, our nature, our character is rooted in the past, for our emotional life has its origins in and its impetus from the experiences and images of history. The storyteller brings us unerringly into those spiritual centers of our lives, making us for the moment consciously aware of something that is a constant part of our unconscious lives. This emotional core is what largely dictates our actions and our thought, our decision making, our vision. Storytelling contains the humanism of the people, and it keeps them and their traditions alive despite life's daily vicissitudes. Time obliterates history. The storyteller arrests time and brings her audience into the presence of history, the heart and substance of the culture.

We are all storytellers: we all have our stories, each one of us. Our stories unfold within the embrace of storytelling traditions that have been with us for centuries. Our world and our lives make no sense outside the framework of story. Apartheid in South Africa is one moment in history, a moment the significance of which is revealed through stories—stories by professional storytellers and stories by those who lived that event. This storytelling instant is a moment in all time, in all of the world's cultures and people. We hear the storytellers, people who lived the moment, people who reported it, and people who renewed it in fiction. It is a moment during which an entire people are defined on the basis of the color of their skin. Consider the power of the written word and the spoken word, consider the effect of stories, think of how stories work to communicate the dimensions of any one moment in history, in the process revealing storytelling as a means of vaulting linguistic, geographical, and temporal boundaries: the storyteller making the world one. We are in the company of storytellers as residents of South Africa tell their stories of hate and of guilt, brought about by the judgment of some who considered African people inferior. Now, those who judged are themselves being judged—ironically, by their own stories. Story is the way we remember, the way we make judgments. And perhaps, because they touch the heart, stories point the way to forgiveness and understanding. "The storyteller," said Walter Benjamin, "is the figure in which the righteous man encounters himself."[2]

Stories touch us, and storytellers and their audiences know that narratives are not simply tales with obvious meanings—a message goes deeper than that. But too frequently, when people ponder stories and storytellers, they think of simple stories that point to facile morals.

Storytellers know that narratives are not simply tales with obvious meanings. At a Zulu performance I attended some years ago, I was expressing an opinion about the symbolism in one of the stories we heard; the Zulu performer stopped me and explained to me that the meaning of a story is the totality of performance, not a simple message. Performance is the thing. The Zulu performer told me, "If I am to tell you what this story means, I must tell it again."

We know that thousands of years of humanity—of great civilizations and peoples, of complex institutions and sophisticated art, religious, and philosophical systems—have done far more than merely create an oral tradition, the essence of most of the world's thought, that contains merely Aesop's fable-like morality.

These stories encapsulate the most deeply felt emotions of the world's peoples, and they pass on to those of us who care to listen the thoughts and ideals of our forebears. The same story, from a number of vantages, with a different view, takes on a different cast each time it is told. Whose story is truth? All we have is the story: Ryunosuke Akutagawa writes that beyond the story "was only darkness, . . . unknown and unknown."[3] So it has ever been; so it will ever be.

We tell stories from tradition, and we cast our own lives into the frame of those ancient narratives, all of us having stories to tell. History, autobiography, fiction—we stand on the brink of all of these when we create our own stories. And what do our stories reveal about our world? After all, social scientists argue, it's only "anecdotal evidence." But anecdotal evidence is all we have—all that counts. Such anecdotal evidence always flows from the emotions. Truth and emotions are always an explosive mix . . . and in the end, whose story is it?

During every age, there is a renewed interest in story, and there is so today, in history, in law, and in psychology, as well as in literature and the arts.[4] Storytellers have been around from the beginning: they are the artists who give shape and meaning to our world, to our lives. They reproduce fragments of reality; coupling these fragments with the images of the past, they reconstruct reality. In fact, there is no reality without the storyteller, whether that storyteller be a historian, the evening news broadcaster, the writer of the soap opera, or a person recounting his or her daily experiences. Reporters of the mass media tell their stories, then behave like the traditional storytellers who say, "I was there, it's true, every word of it!" The difference is that the traditional storytellers are being ironic. Story is the only way we can understand our world. Does this mean that story is truth? Put it this way: story is the only truth that we have.

South Africa's history is blemished by fearful instances of hatred based on skin color. And I speak here not only of the past: the problem remains very much one of the present in South Africa and also in the United States, where people cannot shake its hold on the way one acts, the way one lives, and so the continued movement of the historical journey remains fraught with violence and shame. The reason America cannot get out of its terrible shadow is because the nation has never come to terms with it, has never faced its stories. Consider this historical guilt, then think of how the world acquiesced in what unfolded in the reaches of the United States and South Africa—how attitudes, perspectives, practices, and assumptions locked the whites of those countries and the rest of the world into patterns of incivility that led to unthinkable violence. It is today too late to undo this historical tragedy. "History has to live with what was here," wrote Robert Lowell in 1973 (in a poem called "History"):

> History has to live with what was here,
> clutching and close to fumbling all we had—
> it is so dull and gruesome how we die,
> unlike writing, life never finishes.[5]

But story can help us to understand. More than that, it can show the way to wholeness. Story is not the entire answer, but it is the beginning of a necessary return to things past. Guilt, judgment, and forgiveness: story chronicles our way in the world, logs the trajectory as we make life's corrections and move through our personal and national rites of passage—it seeks to make sense of those journeys. By means of story, we can learn the terrible and noble dimensions of what happened, that is, we can put names to faces, add continuum to places and events, gain a sense of the humanity of the victims and the victimizers, and relive the events of history in their fearsome detail: story provides that.

At the explosive center of the storyteller's art can be found our deepest hopes and dreams, the quintessence of the society. Here also lurk our hates and nightmares, the underside of the human condition. These venerable images, never forgotten and routinely recalled, with their compressed emotional potential, are meticulously arranged by storytellers in such a way that they organize and shape images from the contemporary world. Cees Nooteboom asks, "What is a fairy tale? An intensified form of story, while a story is, or ought to be, not a copy but an intensified form of reality, history torn out of its slow chronology."[6]

Behind the diversity of human societies is a unity that makes brothers and sisters of us all. This is the great lesson of the world's storytellers, a lesson that is craftily kept hidden in the parliaments of the world. The human image in the storytelling tradition is an image of unity: as Joseph Campbell put it, a hero with a thousand faces; as Carl Jung put it, we all have similar experiences and find similar images with which to express these. This common element in human experience binds us irrevocably as members of the family of man.

Storytelling contains the essential humanism of the people; it keeps the people and their traditions alive despite life's daily vicissitudes. In South Africa, the traditions, frequently in the process of change, had hardened against the fevered onslaught of racist apartheid: traditions and the storytelling that carried them, remembered them, and cherished and nurtured and communicated them were weapons in the war against racism.

Sallust, the Roman historian and politician who lived from 86 to 34 BC, observed in his *Of Gods and the World,* "These things [stories] never happen, but are always." We can do worse than heed the advice and the example of the world's storytellers, whose weapon and ploughshare is the word and who, with the word and memory and the ideal that shows from the one to the other, reinvent our worlds, always reminding us of our essential humanity, of our necessary community, of our ever-elusive goal of unity. All of my experiences in Africa and elsewhere have convinced me that the significance of culture, while not to be understated, is nothing when put beside that which binds us together as humans.

Storytelling chronicles our great transformations and helps us to undertake periodic transfigurations. During the momentous rites of passage—birth, puberty, marriage, death—and all of the other crises that erupt in life, storytellers are there to provide imaged explanations and emotional cushioning: the stories become our means of making those corrections in movement through our life cycles. The earliest story that we know of—the spare, splendid Gilgamesh epic of Babylon, from 2000 BC—takes us even today into the anguished soul of a man confronting his mortality. Stories have to do with transitions, as humans move from one milestone in their lives to another: storytellers help us to move through these great human crises.

They make space for us, enabling us to experience topics that are not normally discussed. They take us into the innermost recesses of our souls and, by means of their luminous images, cast soul-shattering light into our deepest and most secret places. Storytellers are the mirrors of our nature, the guardians of our ideals, the means whereby we find our connections. They move us into new worlds, into realms blushed in cardinal colors, into domains of fantasy in which we will be shorn of our identities and be recast, reborn, re-emerging into our reality refurbished, rejuvenated, revitalized, restored. They make possible the transformation of members of audiences into unique and rare entities with new and daunting responsibilities. Storytellers form our children and remind us of who we are.

In South Africa, the result of judgments made on people for centuries because of the color of their skin was the establishment of separate nations of people—unhappily, uncomfortably, and sometimes violently coexisting. Africans in South Africa were made to feel guilt for who they were, their historical roots, their African past. That sense of guilt has ironically now come to settle on the victimizers, as South Africa's whites have been forced to relive their ugly past. Where, in this unhappy mixture of judgment and guilt, is forgiveness? Where is reconciliation? South Africa is attempting, through its Truth and Reconciliation Commission, to find an answer through storytelling. During the 1990s, thousands of stories were told by victims of apartheid to the Truth and Reconciliation Commission: "The gory and heartbreaking stories the victims have told," reported the *New York Times*, "usually between sobs, have gripped this country and may well have enlightened those who had failed to see the extent of the brutality of the former Government."[7]

These compelling stories include that of Singqokwana Ernest Malgas, arrested and tortured in 1963; his house was burned down, his son Simphiwe died after police poured acid on him, and a man was stabbed to death because he was Malgas's brother.[8] We now know their story.

Four youths from a place called Cradock were abducted and assassinated, their bodies burned and mutilated, on June 27, 1985. We know the story now of the Cradock Four.

Cornish Mmeko Makhanya, in June 1986, suffered electric shock to the nipples and frog-marching, had wires connected to the penis and the sides of his head, and had his head flushed in a toilet. We have heard his terrible story.

A mother saw on television the dead body of her child being dragged by a rope tied around his waist, and she and other mothers were told by the police to "bury their dogs" on a specific day. This is one of a group of stories about seven youths, known as the Guguletu Seven. We have their stories now.

Sizwe Kondile was arrested on June 26, 1981; he was poisoned, then shot, his body burned while those responsible drank beer. His story has now been told.

Is storytelling one grand mirage? Story has always been used to provide connections between the present and the past, to examine and explain the past within the context of the present. The past has never been frozen in time: it has always been a restless repository of images, the flotsam and jetsam of human existence, brought to life in contemporary times by storytellers who have agendas of their own, and so it is that history is always revisionist history. Does story provide an index to the past in the sense that the past can be perfectly reconstructed—as it happened? Surely the way it happened and what happened depends on the point of view. Still, imperfect as it may be, in the end, story is all we have.

If we are to understand ourselves and our world in these early years of a new millennium, we have to understand our past, and that means that we must take a fresh look at the storyteller and at story. Here is the greatest, the most revolutionary and startling conclusion that we will reach: when we understand the art of the storyteller, we will also understand our brotherhood and our sisterhood with the peoples of the world, because the human image in world folklore is splendidly, magnificently the same universally.

In a world in which diversity of cultures is being heralded and celebrated, in which multiculturalism is central and people persistently cut themselves and their cultures off from others, we are once again, and to our great detriment, turning a deaf ear to the storytellers. This is detrimental because the storytellers will reveal to us the one great lesson, the only thing that is really worthy of learning: the storytellers will reveal to us our oneness, our universality.

This is what happens when we turn ourselves into Us and Them categories: we marginalize, then demonize, then terrorize, then eliminate, using the euphemism "ethnically cleanse." Storytelling at its worst aids in this process, but—and this is the dizzying, even annoying, irony of the oral tradition—at its most sublime it does not allow this Us and Them categorization to occur but instead champions our oneness. When societies come into contact, one of the first things they exchange is their stories. We understand each other, we speak the same language. At a time when intercultural, ethnic, and religious disputes would threaten to separate us, storytellers unite us. Storytelling assures us of our common humanity: it is our shield against the forces that would divide us.

"The music just takes over": the storyteller has us in thrall, and we revel in the experience. With the English poet Coleridge, there is a willing suspension of disbelief as we move into the magical world of the performer, as our emotions are unknotted, then worked into evanescent, shimmering vessels of form.[9] "The song gets inside you and makes you move, and then you understand its meaning," says the Egyptian singer Umm Kulthum: "The song makes you so happy that you feel you're dancing with it, you're living with it."[10]

Our steps have truth, says the San storyteller. The English poet laureate Alfred Lord Tennyson wrote,

> I am a part of all that I have met;
> Yet all experience is an arch wherethrough
> Gleams that untraveled world, whose margin fades
> For ever and for ever when I move.
> How dull it is to pause, to make an end,
> To rust unburnished, not to shine in use![11]

The venerable storytellers of history provide those of us who are struggling with contemporary issues a way to survive, a path to fullness.

When stories are told, they are never cut out of whole cloth; they are always derivative of stories from the past, ever familiar, as tale-tellers construct contemporary images around motifs in which are lodged compressed cores of those ancient narratives. *The Thousand and One Nights,* observed Jorge Luis Borges, "appears in a mysterious way. It is the work of thousands of authors, and none of them knew that he was helping to construct this illustrious book, one of the most illustrious books in all literature."[12] Borges concluded, "It is a book so vast that it is not necessary to have read it, for it is a part of our memory."[13] The American poet Ralph Waldo Emerson suggested a similar phenomenon: "His own secret biography he finds in lives wonderfully intelligible to him, dotted down before he was born."[14]

It is the task of the storyteller to forge the fantasy images of the past into masks of the realistic images of the present, enabling the performer to pitch the present to the past, to visualize the present within a context of and therefore in terms of the past. Flowing through this potent emotional grid is a variety of ideas that have the look of antiquity and ancestral sanction. Story occurs under the mesmerizing influence of performance—the body of the performer, the music of her voice, and the complex relationship between her and her audience. It is a world unto itself, whole, with its own set of laws. Unlike images are juxtaposed, then the storyteller reveals—to the delight and instruction of the members of the audience—the linkages between them that render them homologous. In this way, the past and the present are blended: ideas are thereby generated, forming our conception of the present. Performance gives the images their context and assures the audience of a ritual experience that bridges past and present and shapes contemporary life. It was the situation one thousand years ago; so it shall be one thousand years hence.

Storytellers are the repositories of the memories of the people. The North African writer Assia Djebar, describing the art of the storyteller, writes of people "[r]etaining their role of story-teller, figurehead at the prow of memory. The legacy will otherwise be lost—night after night, wave upon wave, the whispers take up the tale, even before the child can understand, even before she finds her words of light, before she speaks in her turn and so that she will not speak alone."[15]

Connections: story provides the connections, revealing our oneness with our worlds, communicating our experiences, the zenith and the nadir . . . And so the python uncoils.

> "Well, maybe every guy has his own Africa."
> Saul Bellow, *Henderson the Rain King*

> . . . but man, proud man,
> Drest in a little brief authority,
> Most ignorant of what he's most assured,
> His glassy essence, like an angry ape,
> Plays such fantastic tricks before high heaven
> As make the angels weep.
>
> William Shakespeare, *Measure for Measure*, 2.2.117–20

> Methinks you are my glass, and not my brother:
> I see by you I am a sweet-faced youth.
> Will you walk in to see their gossiping?
>
> William Shakespeare, *Comedy of Errors*, 5.1.418–20

The White Man and the Slave

UmLungu neKhoboka

By S. E. Krune Mqhayi

One day, there arrived in Nompondwana's court an Englishman who accused his slave of disobedience. A writer, Charles William, briefly related the case:

A certain white man, an Englishman, who was traveling, peddling goods among the Xhosa, with his wagon and his slaves, and he was not satisfied with the progress of his slave whom he had brought with him to the Xhosa, coming from Cape Town; after beating him vigorously with a sjambok,[16] he proceeded to go to accuse him at Maqoma's court. These men arrived and stood at the court and gave the report: this white man arrived and pointed the slave out to them at the hearing, told of his indolence, laziness, lack of respect, and finally it was seen that he must truly be beaten with a whip, according as even this meeting could now see.

Before the case was decided, His Excellency Maqoma proclaimed, "Here, among the Xhosa, there are no slaves." This case would be seen as a case of two men accusing each other. Then he called for the slave that he should tell his side of the story. The slave said he was punished for nothing by his master, and then he produced witnesses to testify. When the defendant and plaintiff were sent out, the men went aside to consult at the court. Then the plaintiff and the accused were called, and the chief made this speech to the plaintiff:

"It is clear that you, I accuse, beat this man and you dealt with him badly, as everyone in the court can see, and you have no bruise, you have no scratch that might reveal that this person was violent in his dealings with you. You should have brought him here before you did this to him. That is what the court says to you. This man is released, to go where he wishes. That thing

S. E. Krune Mqhayi, *Ityala Lamawele* (Lovedale, South Africa: Lovedale Press, 1914), 95–97.

is scattered which you brought this court together for, what you call slavery. And there is a second matter: pay one ox, the expenses of this court."

The white man was enraged when he heard this decision, and he stood up contentiously, saying, "I will not pay even that ox, because even this case has not been adjudicated properly; the way things of civilization are done. You, Maqoma, you do not even know the purpose of property rights of a person, like this slave you took from me. I will also report you to Colonel Somerset, the overseer of the forces of the council, who will show you the difference between an outlaw and a ruler."

When the white man became calm, Maqoma instructed him, saying, "Now, the thing that I waited for, from the morning until the setting of the sun, was to decide between man and man, when their disputes were made, that finally they find the truth. If it is thus and people secretly over there exert power over others, instead of coming to tell their stories to the judge and the important people of the court, we would be meeting in vain in this court.

"This Somerset, I know that he is strong—yes, he is elephantine; but I have never been called an outcast,[17] and also my father. You boast that you people and wiser than our people—a thing but that you leave behind discussions/consultations in order to avoid fights does not communicate that thing—what makes human force intellectual power."

Then the chief ended by saying, "When you return to Phakathi, you may bring this case up again; but now if it is fitting that you pay that ox." The white man paid the ox—and the meeting ended.

COMMENTARY

Mqhayi's 1914 story of black-white relations in apartheid South Africa is a much more direct example of those relations than Africans were generally permitted in the racist country. African storytellers found much more subtle but no less potent weapons in their traditional stories and poems. As a result, a study of how Africans survived 350 years of racist rule requires that one become familiar with a tradition that has often been dismissed as insignificant, fairy tales, and the like.

Henry Callaway was close to the truth at the same time that he was mangling it when, in 1868, he wrote,

Children's tales *now;* but not the invention of a child's intellect; nor all invented to gratify a child's fancy. If carefully studied and compared with corresponding legends among other people, they will bring out unexpected relationships, which will more and more force upon us the great truth, that man has every where thought alike, because every where, in every country and clime, under every tint of skin, under every varying social and intellectual condition, he is still man,—one in all the essentials of man,—one in that which is a stronger proof of essential unity, than mere external differences are of difference of nature,—one in his mental qualities, tendencies, emotions, passions. . . . In reflecting on the tales of the Zulus the belief has been irresistibly fixed upon my mind, that they point out very clearly that the Zulus are a degenerated people; that they are not now in the condition intellectually or physically in which they were during "the legend-producing period" of their existence; but have sunk from a higher state. Like the discovered relics of giant buildings in Asia and America, they appear to speak of a mightier and better past, which, it may be, is lost for ever. But though by themselves they may be powerless to retrace the footsteps of successive generations, yet is it unreasonable to suppose that under the power of influences which may reach them from without, they are not capable of regeneration? Far otherwise. For it appears to me that this Zulu legendary lore contains evidence of intellectual powers not to be despised; whilst we have scattered every where throughout the tales those evidences of tender feeling, gentleness, and love, which should teach us that in dealing with these people, if we are dealing with savages, we are dealing with savage *men,* who only need culture to have developed in them the finest traits of our human nature.[18]

The fact is that the intellectuals in Zulu society were not given their due, and when they turned to traditional storytelling as a means of protecting themselves and their families from the destructive assaults of racism, they were seen as children, animists, noble savages, "a degenerated people."

Christian missionaries in Africa, in an effort to convert Africans by using the stories in the oral traditions of the people, would often affix at the end of the stories Christian morals, homilies, that had the effect of dissolving the power of the stories. Oral stories are not obvious preachments: they are much more complex. And as major means of combating the racist system of apartheid, they were, for 350 years, splendidly effective. These stories were the force within the uncoiling python.

Sigcau Sarili:

Ndith' ovuk' emini akabonanga nto,
Kub' akayibonang' inamb' icombuluka.
I say the one who rises late has seen nothing,
For he has not seen the python uncoil.[19]

NOTES

The book epigraph is from Alfred Lord Tennyson, "Ulysses," in *The New Oxford Book of English Verse, 1250–1950,* ed. Helen Gardner (New York: Oxford University Press, 1972), 645.

PREFACE AND ACKNOWLEDGMENTS

1. "The South African Truth and Reconciliation Commission (TRC) was set up by the Government of National Unity to help deal with what happened under apartheid. The conflict during this period resulted in violence and human rights abuses from all sides. No section of society escaped these abuses" (http://www.doj.gov.za/trc/trc_frameset.htm).

2. *Truth and Reconciliation Commission of South Africa Report* (London: Macmillan, 1999), 1:1.

3. Ibid., 1:16.

4. Author unknown, "Historical Resume & Statistical and Other Vital Information Relating to Mount Ayliff District," typescript, n.d., 9; W. Power Leary, resident magistrate, Mount Frere, September 27, 1904, untitled typescript; Captain G. D. Ward, comp., "Historical Record of the Mount Ayliff District, Cape Province, Union of South Africa, 1878 to 1937," compiled from notes by Mrs. I. B. Hunter and from other sources (Kokstad, South Africa: Kokstad Advertiser, 1937), 2.

PRELUDE: THE UNCOILING PYTHON

The chapter epigraph is from the King James Version of the Bible, ed. Robert P. Carroll and Stephen Prickett (Oxford: Oxford University Press, 1997).

1. Axel-Ivar Berglund, *Zulu Thought-Patterns and Symbolism* (London: C. Hurst, 1976), 60–61.

2. Ibid.

3. W. B. Rubusana, *Zemk' Inkomo Magwalandini* (Frome: Butler and Tanner, 1906), 262–63. "Ofisi Kona, ukunene. Uzalwa ngoNobhesi intokazi kaBikitsha yasemaQocweni Izibongo" (of Ofisi Kona, the right-hand. He is born of Nobhesi, the daughter of Bikitsha of the Qoco clan).

4. Ibid., 266.

5. This praise-poem (1S-451) was narrated by Magagamela Koko, a Mfengu man about eighty years old, in a home overlooking the Kei River valley, Nqancule, Ngqamakhwe District, the Transkei, on August 31, 1967, before an audience of ten women, two men, and ten children.

6. *Into yam enkulu* means "thing, my senior son."

7. *UBantwana bayaxathula:* "[He who is] Children-walk-in-shoes."

8. This description was given by Nongenile Masithathu Zenani in 1972 in Willowvale District in the Transkei, when a group of narrative performers and poets discussed poetry. See also note 58 to chapter 3. Nongenile Masithathu Zenani delivered this praise imagery (2S-15) on August 2, 1972, at 2:15 pm, outside, along the side of a ridge near her home, to an audience of three teenagers, three women, and three children.

9. Rubusana, *Zemk' Inkomo Magwalandini,* 347–48.

10. Ibid., 231. Hintsa (c. 1790–1835) was a major Gcaleka king (the Gcaleka are a Xhosa-speaking people).

11. Ibid., 252.

12. Harold Scheub, *Story* (Madison: University of Wisconsin Press, 1998); Harold Scheub, *The Poem in the Story* (Madison: University of Wisconsin Press, 2002); and Harold Scheub, *Shadows: Deeper into Story* (Madison, WI: Parallel Press, 2009).

13. Harold Scheub, *The Tongue Is Fire* (Madison: University of Wisconsin Press, 1996).

14. The materials for this study include transcripts of field recordings of approximately nine thousand Xhosa, Zulu, Swati, and Ndebele performances of stories, histories, biographies, and poetry in 1967–68, 1972–73, 1975–76; five thousand color slides of storytellers, historians, and various other people, along with scenery and communities (mainly in the rural areas of southern Africa); thirty-five hundred black and white photographs of storytellers, historians, and various other people; and Super 8 mm motion pictures, both silent (about ten hours) and sound (about five hours).

15. Kafir: "*inkawu: in-Kau.* the Vervet monkey . . . fig. an albino native. *Isi-kau:* That which is little, insignificant, unimportant." Albert Kropf, *A Kafir-English Dictionary,* 2nd ed., ed. Robert Godfrey (Lovedale, South Africa: Lovedale Mission Press, 1915), 184. Xhosa: "*inkawu,* an ape, monkey; an albino. *isikhawu:* something insignificant; a short cut. *ubunkawu:* monkey nature." J. McLaren, *A New Concise Xhosa-English Dictionary* (Cape Town: Longman, 1963), 70.

16. Scheub, *The Tongue Is Fire,* xvi.

17. Harold Scheub, review of *Towards an African Literature: The Emergence of Literary Form in Xhosa* by A. C. Jordan, *Journal of American Folklore* 90, no. 357 (July–September 1977): 347–52.

18. Jon Stewart, the American comedian, said about his storytelling, "It's a wonderful feeling to have this toxin in your body in the morning, that

little cup of sadness, and feel by 7 or 7:30 that night, you've released it in sweat equity and can move on to the next day." Quoted in Michiko Kakutani, "Is This the Most Trusted Man in America?" *New York Times,* August 17, 2008, Arts and Leisure section, 19.

19. The persistence of these ideas can be seen in some contemporary views of the world: in the late 1960s, David Brooks argues, "The old hierarchy of the arts was dismissed as hopelessly reactionary. Instead, any cultural artifact produced by a member of a colonially oppressed out-group was deemed artistically and intellectually superior." Brooks, "Lord of the Memes," *New York Times,* August 8, 2008, p. A19.

20. Wilhelm Heinrich Bleek (1827–1875) began his study of San language and vocabulary in Cape Town in 1857, continuing his work with |xam speakers in the 1860s. Bleek and his sister-in-law, Lucy Lloyd (1834–1914), who carried on the work after Bleek's death, recorded |xam and !kun folklore and personal narratives. Bleek and Lloyd's collections of texts and artwork (hereafter referred to in the source notes as Bleek Archive) are held by the National Library, Iziko South African Museum, and the University of Cape Town. Digital scans of Lloyd's and Bleek's notebooks, as well as other material from the archives, are accessible online at http://www.lloydbleekcollection.cs.uct.ac.za.

21. Pippa Skotnes, *Claim to the Country* (Johannesburg: Jacana; Athens: Ohio University Press, 2007).

22. The *goura* is an instrument made of a bamboo rod across which a string is drawn. The quill is placed between the lips of the performer. See Henry Balfour, "The Goura and the Kite Bows," in "The Goura, a Stringed Wind Musical Instrument of the Hottentots," *Journal of the Anthropological Institute of Great Britain and Ireland* 32 (1902): 170–73 and pl. VII, pic. 5+6+7.

23. A word is omitted here in the manuscript.

24. Aristotle, *Poetics,* trans. Gerald F. Else (Ann Arbor: University of Michigan Press, 1967), 57.

25. George Lakov and Mark Johnson, *Metaphors We Live By* (Chicago: University of Chicago Press, 1980), 244.

26. Zoltán Kövecses, *Metaphor: A Practical Introduction* (New York: Oxford University Press, 2002), 4.

27. Michael Spitzer, *Metaphor and Musical Thought* (Chicago: University of Chicago Press, 2004), 221.

28. See "The Trope Laboratory," in Scheub, *Story,* 131–44.

29. "Anthropologists . . . have persuasively argued that the trance dance [of the San] affirms and strengthens kinship relations, which for their part serve to shape the relationship between people and available resources. They have also argued that trance dances are one of the most important mechanisms that Bushmen have for coping with the vortex of change that is sweeping them off their feet." Robert J. Gordon and Stuart Sholto Douglas, *The Bushman Myth: The Making of a Namibian Underclass,* 2nd e   ⟨   de CO: Westview Press, 2000), 234.

CHAPTER 1: METAPHOR

1. Meeting in the mythic center.

2. See Harold Scheub, *Storytelling Songs of Zulu Women: Recording Archetypal Rites of Passage and Mythic Paths* (Lewiston, NY: Edwin Mellen Press, 2006), 62–64.

3. For a fuller analysis of this story, see ibid., 74–76.

4. Mamba: "The-snake-man."

5. Nhlamvu-yobuthlalu: "Bead-woman."

6. Nhlamvu-yetusi: "Brass-bead-woman."

7. "The man who goes to wait for the marriage party is called Umkhongi [the bridegroom's negotiator] or Umhlaleli [marriage medium]. His office is to urge on the friends of the bride to hasten the marriage; he stays at the bride's kraal and there is guilty of all kinds of mischief until they get tired of him, and the wedding party sets out." Henry Callaway, *Nursery Tales, Traditions, and Histories of the Zulus* (Springvale, Natal: John A. Blair, 1868), 330n. Compare Nongenile Masithathu Zenani, "The Necessary Clown," in Scheub, *The Tongue Is Fire,* 61–77.

8. The head-ring is a headdress or headband.

9. The *imamba* is a "species of very venomous snakes." Clement M. Doke, *Lamba Folk-Lore* (New York: American Folk-Lore Society, 1927), 167.

10. The *ithongo* is an "ancestral spirit." Ibid., 299.

11. *Amasi* refers to curdled milk.

12. The *idlozi* is a "spirit, soul; departed spirit; guardian spirit." Doke, *Lamba Folk-Lore,* 48.

13. Some of these comments are in Scheub, *Storytelling Songs,* 74–76.

14. José Ortega y Gasset, *La deshumanizacion del arte* and *Ideas sobre la novela* (Madrid: Revista de Occidente, 1928); translated by Helene Weyl as *The Dehumanization of Art* and *Notes on the Novel* (Princeton: Princeton University Press, 1948).

15. Samuel Taylor Coleridge, "Frost at Midnight," in *The New Oxford Book of English Verse,* ed. Helen Gardner (New York: Oxford University Press, 1972), 524–25, lines 21–22.

16. The *zim* is a folkloric character, a swallowing monster.

17. The *imbulu* is "an imaginary animal that has the power of assuming human shape, but is continually hampered by its tail which it persistently endeavors to hide. It is an arch-deceiver." Kropf, *Kafir-English Dictionary,* 233.

CHAPTER 2: SAN METAPHOR

The chapter epigraph is from Elias Canetti's posthumously published collection of notes, *Aufzeichnungen, 1992–1993* (Munich: Carl Hanser, 1996), 23. The reference is to Wilhelm Heinrich Immanuel Bleek and Lucy Catherine Lloyd, *Specimens of Bushman Folklore* (London: G. Allen, 1911).

1. ||kábbo was born in 1810. His name means "dream."

2. ||kábbo, "||kábbo's Intended Return Home," in Bleek and Lloyd, *Specimens of Bushman Folklore*, 302–3. I have made a few alterations in the translation. The translation by Bleek and Lloyd reads, "I must first sit a little, cooling my arms; that the fatigue may go out of them; because I sit. I do merely listen, watching for a story, which I want to hear; while I sit waiting for it; that it may float into my ear."

3. In a footnote (ibid., 303), the translators wrote, "||kábbo explains that when one has travelled along a road, and goes and sits down, one waits for a story to travel to one, following along the same road."

4. Ibid., 302–3. The Bleek and Lloyd translation of this passage is as follows: "These are those to which I am listening with all my ears, while I feel that I sit silent. I must wait, listening, behind me, while I listen along the road; while I feel that my name floats along the road. . . . I will go to sit at it, that I may listening turn backwards, with my ears, to my feet's heels, on which I went; while I feel that a story is the wind."

5. A Xhosa story of the origin of the mantis states, "One day, there was a big thunderstorm in a certain village. A big house on one homestead was struck by lightning. People were asked to come and extinguish the blaze. They tried and tried, but gave up. Suddenly, there appeared a thin, weak, green insect. It perched on the burning house, and the fire immediately subsided. The people at once called that insect the Child of Heaven." Garvey Nkonki, "The Traditional Prose Literature of the Ngqika," MA thesis, University of South Africa, n.d., 52–53. Translated from Xhosa by Garvey Nkonki.

6. See the bibliography for San and Khoi oral materials.

7. Although the collecting techniques of Wilhelm Heinrich Immanuel Bleek, the German philologist for whom he worked, did not emphasize the performance itself—"He was an excellent narrator," Bleek noted, "and patiently waited until a sentence had been written down before proceeding with what he was telling" (Bleek and Lloyd, *Specimens of Bushman Folklore*, x)—||kábbo was able to reveal in the fifteen thoughtful pieces that he provided for Bleek and Lloyd's *Specimens of Bushman Folklore* the ambiguous nature of |kággen, enabling the storyteller to bridge the realism of the world of the San hunters and the eternal realm of the gods.

8. Dorothea F. Bleek, *The Mantis and His Friends* (Cape Town: T. Maskew Miller, [1923]), 30–40.

9. Karosses are rugs made of skins.

10. An ichneumon is either a mongoose or a wasp.

11. The term *dassie* means hyrax.

12. This behavior of Mantis, bestriding godly heaven and mortal earth, becomes the model for the hero, who will later become identified as the human who bestrides the old order and the new, leading the people from the one to the other.

13. A. R. Willcox, *The Rock Art of South Africa* (Johannesburg: Thomas Nelson and Sons, 1963), plate 6, facing page 34; George W. Stow, *The Native Races of South Africa* (London: S. Sonnenschein and Co., 1905), 81–84.

14. Willcox, *Rock Art*, pl. 7, facing p. 34.

15. J. M. Orpen, "A Glimpse into the Mythology of the Maluti Bushmen," *Cape Monthly Magazine* 9 (July 1874); reprinted in *Folk-Lore* 30 (1919): 141.

16. Dorothea F. Bleek, *The Naron: A Bushman Tribe of the Central Kalahari* (Cambridge: Cambridge University Press, 1928), 23–24; I. Schapera, *The Khoisan People of South Africa: Bushmen and Hottentots* (London: Routledge and Kegan Paul, 1930), 119–26.

17. Quoted in James David Lewis-Williams, *Believing and Seeing: Symbolic Meanings in Southern San Rock Paintings* (London: Academic Press, 1981), 118.

18. Monica Wilson, "The Hunters and Herders," in *The Oxford History of South Africa*, ed. Monica Wilson and Leonard Thompson (Oxford: Oxford University Press, 1969), 1:54.

19. Elizabeth Marshall Thomas, *The Harmless People* (New York: Alfred A. Knopf, 1965), 59.

20. George B. Silberbauer, *Report to the Government of Bechuanaland on the Bushman Survey* (Gaborone: Bechuanaland Government, 1965), 47.

21. Stow, *Native Races*, 89–92.

22. Ibid., 82.

23. Wilson, "Hunters and Herders," 54.

24. Stow, *Native Races*, 97.

25. L. Fourie, "The Bushmen of South West Africa," in *The Native Tribes of South West Africa*, ed. C. H. L. Hahn, L. Fourie, and H. Vedder (Cape Town: Cape Times, 1928), 96.

26. Stow, *Native Races*, 111.

27. J. R. R. Tolkien, "On Fairy-Stories," in *Tree and Leaf* (London: George Allen and Unwin, 1964), 20.

28. Dorothea F. Bleek, *Mantis and His Friends*, 41–44.

29. "The Young Man of the Ancient Race, Who Was Carried Off by a Lion, When Asleep in the Field," in Bleek and Lloyd, *Specimens of Bushman Folklore*, 174–91. See also Paul Radin, ed., *African Folktales and Sculpture* (New York: Pantheon Books, 1964), 161–64, where the tale appears under the title "The Young Man Who Was Carried Off by a Lion."

30. |háň‡kass'ō, "The Son of the Wind," in Bleek and Lloyd, *Specimens of Bushman Folklore*, 100–107. See also Radin, *African Folktales and Sculpture*, 49–50.

31. Quoted in Lewis-Williams, *Believing and Seeing*, 118.

32. Dorothea F. Bleek, *Naron*, 26.

33. Willcox, *Rock Art*, 35.

34. Stow, *Native Races*, 130. In a footnote, he writes, "Communicated to the writer by Mr. William Coates Palgrave, Special Commissioner to the Tribes on the West Coast, and obtained by him many years ago, in one of his first visits to that part of the country." When the San were asked how they knew this

story, they said that it was "what they had learnt from their fathers, and . . . what their fathers' great-great-grandfathers had told them" (130).

35. Ibid., 129–31.

36. Ibid., 132–34.

37. Wilson, "Hunters and Herders," 54.

38. Jalmar Rudner and Ione Rudner, *The Hunter and His Art: A Survey of Rock Art in Southern Africa* (Cape Town: C. Struik, 1970), 205.

39. Rudner and Rudner, *Hunter and His Art,* 205.

40. Ibid., 205.

41. Ibid., 206.

42. Stow, *Native Races,* 81–84.

43. Ibid., 122.

44. Ibid., 123.

45. James David Lewis-Williams, "The Syntax and Function of the Giant's Castle Rock Paintings," *South African Archaeological Bulletin* 27 (1972): 61.

46. Ibid., 63–64.

47. That is, he went to fetch bushes, to make a shelter for her, not knowing that she had no house.

48. "On account of it" is a reference to the rain.

49. Her house was in the ground and had a lid.

50. No one brings his things; they come of themselves.

51. Each felt that the other had taken his things away from him.

52. For a similar reference to strings, see "The Broken String" in Bleek and Lloyd, *Specimens of Bushman Folklore,* 236–37. This is a lament sung by Xaatting after the death of his friend, the magician and rain maker !nuing|kuiten, who was shot "when going about, by night, in the form of a lion." The lament is narrated by Díä!kwäin:

> People were those who
> Broke for me the string.
> Therefore,
> The place became like this to me,
> On account of it,
> Because the string was that which broke for me.
> Therefore,
> The place does not feel to me,
> As the place used to feel to me,
> On account of it.
> For,
> The place feels as if it stood open before me,
> Because the string has broken for me.
> Therefore,
> The place does not feel pleasant to me,
> On account of it.

The editors note, "[N]ow that 'the string is broken,' the former 'ringing sound in the sky' is no longer heard by the singer, as it had been in the magician's lifetime."

53. I.e., the elder sister.

54. The purpose of the thong was to tie their forelegs.

55. By *sawa* they meant "making no noise."

56. "The stage is that apparatus in the background of the house (built of mats) opposite the door, upon which the Hottentots hang their bamboos, bags of skins, and other things, and under which the women generally keep their mats." Wilhelm Heinrich Immanuel Bleek, *Reineke Fuchs in Afrika: Fabeln und Märchen der Eingeborenen* (Weimar: Böhlau, 1870); translated as *Reynard the Fox in South Africa; or, Hottentot Fables and Tales* (London: Trübner and Co., 1864), 56.

57. Compare this with Lydia umkaSethemba's 1868 Zulu tale, "Combecantsini," in Callaway, *Nursery Tales*, 105–30:

> There was an old woman who lived at that village. She had no legs, only arms. She remained at home, doing nothing. Her name was Thlese. She was so called because when walking she rolled along with her body only.
>
> The people had gone to dig. When they were gone, the bridesmaids again turned into human beings, and came to that place.
>
> They went to Thlese and said, "Will you say that you have seen any young women here at home?"
>
> Thlese said, "No, my children. I will say, how could I see people here since I am but Thlese?"
>
> They went out and took all the vessels from one side of the village, and they went to fetch water. They came with the water. Then they crushed maize for making beer for the whole village. They fetched water again and again, and boiled it for the beer. They fetched water, and daubed the floors of the houses of the whole village. They went and fetched firewood, and placed it in the whole kraal.
>
> Then they went to Thlese and said, "Thlese, who will you say has done all this?"
>
> She said, "I will say that I did it."
>
> They went to the open country, and on their arrival again became birds.
>
> In the afternoon, when the people returned, all the women of the village said, "*Hawu!* Who has been daubing the floors here at home? And who has fetched water? and firewood? and crushed maize for beer? and heated the water?"
>
> All went to Thlese, and asked her by whom it was done.
>
> She said, "It was done by me. I shuffled and shuffled along, and went and fetched water. I shuffled and shuffled along, and went and fetched firewood. I shuffled and shuffled along, and crushed the mealies, and I shuffled and shuffled along, and heated the water."
>
> They said, "*Hawu!* Was all this done by you, Thlese?"
>
> She said, "Yes."
>
> They laughed and were glad, saying, "Thlese has helped us by making beer for the whole village."
>
> They retired to rest.
>
> On the following morning, they went to dig.
>
> All the bridesmaids came to the village, carrying firewood.
>
> Thlese said, "Ye, ye, ye! See the daughters-in-law of my father. It is well that the wedding party should come home."

They placed the firewood for the whole kraal. They ground the maize that they had crushed the day before for the beer, and they made beer in every house in the kraal. They fetched water. They ground malt, being about to make beer, they mixed the malt with the maize-mash.

They went to Thlese and said, "Goodbye, our grandmother."

She replied, "Yes, bridal party of my mother's mother."

So they departed.

In the afternoon, all the women came home, and they again went to Thlese, and said, "Who has ground the mash? who has cooked?"

Thlese said, "I shuffled and shuffled, and went and fetched wood. I shuffled and shuffled, and ground the mash. I shuffled, and fetched water. I shuffled, and boiled water. I shuffled and shuffled, and ground malt. I shuffled, and mixed it with the maize-mash. I shuffled, and came back here to the house, and sat down."

They laughed, saying, "Now we have got an old woman who will work for us."

They sat down, they retired to rest.

On the following day, when no one was there, the bridesmaids arrived. Thlese was sitting outside. They went to her, and said, "You are a good creature, Thlese, because you do not tell anyone."

They went into the houses, they ground malt, they mixed the mash, they strained the beer they had set to ferment rapidly on the day before, they poured the grains into the mash they had mixed, that it might quickly ferment. They collected into large earthen vessels that which they had strained. They took another vessel, and went with the beer that was in the vessel to Thlese. When they came to her, they drank, and gave also to Thlese.

She laughed and was joyful, and said, "I will never tell, for my part. You shall do just as you like."

Again, they departed and went into the open country, again turning into birds.

In the afternoon, all the women came and saw that all the mash was mixed. They said, "Thlese is wearied with us for asking by whom it was done. Let us just say nothing. There is something wonderful which is about to happen here at home."

But in the evening, Kakaka went to Thlese and earnestly asked her, "*Hawu!* Grandmother, tell me by what means this is done."

Thlese replied, "By me, child of my child."

He said, "*Hawu*, grandmother! You could not do it. Tell me by whom it has been done!"

She said, "At noon, when every one of you are gone, there come many women. But among them there is one most beautiful, her body is glistening. It is they who make beer here at home."

Kakaka said, "Grandmother, did they not say they would come tomorrow?"

Thlese replied, "Oh, they will come."

Kakaka said, "I too will come at noon, and see the women." He said, "But do not tell them, grandmother."

She replied, "No, I will not tell them."

So they retired to rest.

58. Bleek note: "The lion putting his tail into his mouth, talks like a man."

59. Bleek note: "If she had answered he would have come and killed her; she lay and listened, but replied not."

60. Bleek note: "The mother ordered the children never to call out when alone in the veld."

61. Bleek note to page 4026: "The lions, R. says, used to be very numerous in the Bushmen's country; but are so no longer."

62. The reference is to deep pits, like a well.

63. *Buchu* is an oil made from an aromatic shrub.

64. *Veldschoens* are shoes.

65. "!kwéiteṇ ta ||kēn has not seen these things herself, but she heard that they were beautiful, and striped like a |hábba, i.e., zebra. The water was as large as a bull, and the water's children were the size of calves, being the children of great things." Bleek and Lloyd, *Specimens of Bushman Folklore*, 199.

66. "All the women and all the children but one." Ibid.

67. "All the family and their mats and all their things were carried into the spring by the whirlwind." Ibid., 203.

68. "These things that grew by the spring belonged to the first San, who preceded the present race, !kwéiteṇ ta ||kēn says. Her mother told her this." Ibid., 205.

69. "That part of him with which he still thinks of us is that [in] which he comes before us, at the time when the sorcerers are taking him away. That is the time when he acts in this manner. My mother and the others used to tell me that when we die we do as the |nū people do, they change themselves into a different thing." Ibid., 369.

70. "My sister Tā-kkumm's husband told us that he had perceived a child who was afraid of him. It wanted to run away." Ibid.

71. "At one time, when he looked at it, it was not like a person, it was different looking, a different thing. The other part of it resembled a person." Ibid., 371.

72. "The ǂnèrru, now a bird, was formerly a person; a man of the early race was the one who married her." Ibid., 207. "The ǂnèrru's bill is very short. The male ǂnèrru is the one whose plumage resembles that of the ostrich; it is black like the male ostrich. The female ǂnèrru is the one whose plumage is white like that of the female ostrich. They resemble the ostriches." Ibid., 213. "They eat the things that little birds usually eat, which they pick up on the ground. They make grass nests on the ground, by the root of a bush. When not breeding, they are found in large numbers." Ibid., 215.

73. I.e., earthy.

74. Literally, "had killed."

75. "I do not know well about it, for my people were those who spoke thus: they said that the ǂnèrru's entrails were formerly upon the little kaross." Bleek and Lloyd, *Specimens of Bushman Folklore*, 211.

76. I.e., sang.

77. "Her daughter was the one of whom she spoke, of her singing." Bleek and Lloyd, *Specimens of Bushman Folklore*, 211.

78. *Keeries* are stout sticks, or clubs.

79. A. W. Buckland discusses *canna* in "Ethnological Hints Afforded by the Stimulants in Use among Savages and among the Ancients," *Journal of the Anthropological Institute of Great Britain and Ireland* (1879): 239–54. On page 251, Buckland writes, "The Kon or Canna-root (*mesembryanthemum emarcidum*) chewed by the Bushmen and Hottentots, of which Thunberg says: 'The Hottentots come far and near to fetch this shrub, with the root, leaves and all, which they beat together and afterwards twist them up like pigtail tobacco; after which they let the mass ferment and keep it by them for chewing, especially when they are thirsty. If it be chewed immediately after fermentation it intoxicates." Adding, "the Hottentots who traverse the dry carrow-fields (*Karoo*) use several means, not only to assuage their hunger, but more particularly to quench their thirst. Besides the above-mentioned plant called Kon or Gunna, they use two others, namely, one called Kameká or Barup, which is said to be a large and watery root; and another called *Ku*, which is likewise, according to report, a large and succulent root."

Buckland cites Carl Peter Thunberg's "Account of the Cape of Good Hope . . . ," in *A General Collection of the Best and Most Interesting Voyages and Travels in All Parts of the World,* ed. John Pinkerton (London: Longman, Hurst, Rees, and Orme, 1808–14), 17 vols.

80. *Assegais* are spears.

81. Bleek note: "Or her brother."

82. Bleek and Lloyd, *Specimens of Bushman Folklore*, 96–98.

83. These grubs are ant larvae.

84. The lynx is a wildcat.

85. "This is a dance or game of the San, which |háñ‡kass'ō has not himself seen, but has heard of from Tɣai-an and ‡kᶐmmì, two of Tsátsi's wives. They used to say that their fathers made a *!kù* and played. Their mothers were those who clapped their hands, clapped their hands for the men; the men nodded their heads." Bleek and Lloyd, *Specimens of Bushman Folklore*, 91.

86. It is not so much a bridge as a *process*. "Our present interest in metaphor seems appropriate to our intermediary position; we see ourselves in transit between life and art, or life and death." Richard Shiff, "Art and Life: A Metaphoric Relationship," in *On Metaphor,* ed. Sheldon Sacks (Chicago: University of Chicago Press, 1978), 120.

87. Parts of this section appeared in Harold Scheub, "A Review of African Oral Traditions and Literature," *African Studies Review* 28, nos. 2/3 (June/ September 1985): 1–72.

CHAPTER 3: THE NGUNI ARTIST

The chapter epigraph is a line from a story narrated in 1879 (Bleek and Lloyd, *Specimens of Bushman Folklore,* 86–87).

1. Nongenile Masithathu Zenani, *The World and the Word: Tales and Observations from the Xhosa Oral Tradition,* ed. Harold Scheub (Madison: University of Wisconsin Press, 1992), 7.

2. Edwin W. Smith and Andrew Murray Dale, *The Ila-Speaking Peoples of Northern Rhodesia* (London: Macmillan, 1920), 2:336. See p. 335 for a photograph of a storyteller.

3. John Keats, "On First Looking into Chapman's Homer," in *The Poems of John Keats,* ed. Jack Stillinger (Cambridge, MA: Harvard University Press, 1978), lines 1–2.

4. See, for example, "The Story of Mr. Lion-Child and Mr. Cow-Child," in Doke, *Lamba Folk-Lore,* 15–23.

5. Walter Benjamin, *Illuminations,* trans. Harry Zohn (Glasgow: William Collins, 1973), 90.

6. Archibald Campbell Jordan, *Towards an African Literature: The Emergence of Literary Form in Xhosa* (Berkeley: University of California Press, 1973), 3.

7. Such translation has been attempted, for example, in some of the Julliard/Armand Colin publications in the 1960s and 1970s, such as Amadou Hampâté Bâ, *Kaïdara: Récit initiatique peul,* ed. Amadou Hampâté Bâ and Lilyan Kesteloot, Classiques africains 7 ([Paris]: Julliard, 1969); Alfâ Ibrâhîm Sow, ed., *La femme, la vache, la foi: Écrivains et poètes di Foûta-Djalon,* Classiques africains 5 ([Paris]: Julliard, 1966); Tierno Mouhammadou-Samba Mombéyâ, *Le filon du bonheur éternel,* ed. Alfâ Ibrâhîm Sow, Classiques africains 10 (Paris: Armand Colin, [1971]); and Tinguidji, *Silâmaka & Poullôri: Récit épique peul,* ed. Christiane Seydou, Classiques africains 13 ([Paris]: A. Colin, [c 1972]).

8. Smith and Dale, *Ila-Speaking Peoples,* 2:334, 336.

9. The groom later says, "This dead man's regiment was Nokhenke."

10. I.e., his bride.

11. The phrase "smelled you out" indicates the detection of a culprit by occult means. See Shakespeare's *Romeo and Juliet,* act 1, scene 4, in *The Annotated Shakespeare:* "Sometimes she gallops o'er a courtier's nose, / And then dreams he of smelling out a suit." Eileen Jensen Krige writes of "a 'smelling out' in which the doctor uses his occult powers to find the culprit." She notes, "Before 'smelling out,' the doctor or doctors shut themselves up in a hut in order to prepare themselves for the work before them by concentrating power within them." Krige, *The Social System of the Zulus* (Pietermaritzburg, South Africa: Shuter and Shooter, 1936), 225. Joseph Shooter, in *The Kaffirs of Natal and the Zulu Country* (London: E. Stanford, 1857), writes that the doctor "affects to examine them [the suspects] by means of his olfactory sense" (174):

> "When he does point out the 'evil-doer,' it is sometimes done in the following manner. Sufficient people being assembled, and the suspected person among the number, he disposes them around him in a circle. To the shaggy ornaments of a Kafir's ordinary full dress he has probably added the skins of serpents; small inflated bladders are tied to his hair; in one hand he carries a short stick with a gnu's tail affixed to it, and in the other a trusty assagai. Thus equipped the prophet begins to dance, accompanying

his movements with a song or chant; and, becoming gradually excited, he appears at length like a phrenzied being; 'his eyes roll with infernal glare,' tears run down his face, loud cries interrupt his chanting, and he seems as if an evil spirit really possessed him. The spectators, who believe that he is receiving inspiration, behold him with dismay; but their attention is turned from the prophet to themselves, when he proceeds to discover the culprit. Dancing towards several individuals in succession, he affects to examine them by means of his olfactory sense; and, when he has found the real or supposed offender, he touches him with the gnu's tail and immediately leaps over his head." (174)

12. Mavumabi: "He-who-agrees-to-a-bad-thing."

13. Dolosikuhlumba: "Big-knee."

14. See "Mbulukazi and the Raven Wife," in Zenani, *The World and the Word*, 41–60.

15. A traditional weekend entertainment of young men and women of their age group where men dance to the accompaniment of the women's singing and clapping; this lasts all night.

16. The audience responds, "*Chosi.*"

17. The audience responds, "Ohh!"

18. The storyteller snickers.

19. The audience joins in the ideophone.

20. The audience joins in.

21. His father's youngest brothers.

22. A member of the audience says, "Oh!"

23. Literally, "come out."

24. Ngangazulu: "As-great-as-the-sky."

25. Ndlel' ethusini: "Way-that-is-in-the-shadows."

26. Gabadul' imilibo: "Overreaching-clan-relationships."

27. She laughs.

28. Rondavel: cylindrical house with a thatched roof.

29. Literally, "You bore a thing that is not present."

30. The doves serve as the mythic center.

31. A member of the audience comments, "Oh! You are saying so, fellows!"

32. Literally, "I deliver toward the ground."

33. A member of the audience responds, "Oh!"

34. The real world.

35. The mythic center.

36. The real world of Mbengu.

37. This is where the real world of Mbengu and the mythic world of Nqunuse connect, with the wresting of the elixir from the ogres.

38. The audience laughs.

39. The audience laughs.

40. The audience laughs.

41. For a similar theme, see "The Magician's Daughter."

42. Nontsomi Langa laughs here and says, "I will leave out *hlonipha* language today." The term *hlonipha* "describes a custom between relations-in-law, and is generally but not exclusively applied to the female sex, who, when married, are not allowed to pronounce or use words which have for their principal syllable any part or syllable of the names of their chief's or their husband's relations, especially of their fathers-in-law; they must also keep a distance from the latter. Hence, they have the habit of inventing new names for those persons; for instance: if one of these persons is called *uMehlo*, which is derived from *amehlo* (eyes), the women will no longer use *amehlo*, but substitute *amakangelo* (lookers)." Kropf, *Kafir-English Dictionary*, 161.

43. I.e., by that single blow.

44. Nontsomi Langa coughs and says, "Well, this cough of mine might even get into the tape, lords! *Ehee! ehee!*"

45. She lapses into *hlonipha* language here.

46. "I'm using *hlonipha* language now; I'm mixing up vocabulary. I forgot myself."

47. Again she lapses into *hlonipha* language.

48. The hen ate the maize, and the one attacked the other—*xho!*

49. Aside: "What's all this *isicelo?*"—profuse smoking.

50. For a similar play-within-the-play, see *Hamlet,* in *The Annotated Shakespeare*, 3:188–267.

51. This was a neat and tidy ending—because he need not ask Sathana now for her hand.

52. Lisping.

53. Laughter.

54. Nkobe-zamazimba, "Boiled-sorghum."

55. Laughter.

56. These were pits in which corn was stored after the harvest.

57. The poems and interviews of Ashton Ngcama took place in 1972.

58. Nongenile Masithathu Zenani, in 1967, recalled how, in the old times among the Xhosa, a certain king would, when trying cases and conducting affairs of state, appear at the royal residence carrying a handsome skin mat, which would be spread in the courtyard. Here, the king would sit, garbed in a cape fashioned of the skins of game animals and joined to form a splendid kaross. His headgear was also constructed of the pelts of animals and sometimes of the feathers of elaborately plumed birds. Then the poet would appear; he excelled in poetic skills and knew well how to perform the praises of a king. On one such occasion, the poet began his poem; as he spoke, his images dramatic and vivid, he walked in pomp toward the royal residence where the king sat. The bard, still rhythmically creating his images, slowly worked his way to the motionless figure of the king. Then, the poem at an end, he stopped before his leader and put his hand on the ground. The poet's body was not covered; a poet did not wear his cape over his body in those days but draped it over one shoulder.

This description was given in 1967 in Willowvale District in the Transkei, when a group of narrative performers and poets discussed poetry.

59. "The first two-dimensional images were thus not two-dimensional representations of three-dimensional things in the material world, as researchers have always assumed. Rather, they were 'fixed' mental images. In all probability the makers did not suppose that they 'stood for' real animals." David Lewis-Williams, *The Mind in the Cave* (London: Thames and Hudson, 2002), 193.

60. Saira Shah, *The Storyteller's Daughter* (New York: Alfred A. Knopf, 2003), 253–54.

61. For discussions of stories and sculpture, see Scheub, *Storytelling Songs*, 29–37 and following.

62. John Keats, "Ode on a Grecian Urn," in *The Poems of John Keats*, 372–73, lines 21–22.

63. The term *ithongo* means "a trance, a dream."

64. *Umoya* means "spirit."

65. See also Nongenile Masithathu Zenani's description of performing praises for a king, in note 58 to this chapter.

66. *Intsomi* are fantasy stories.

67. *Imbongi* are poets.

68. ǂkágára is "a little bird, resembling the *Lanius Collaris*, a butcher-bird." Bleek and Lloyd, *Specimens of Bushman Folklore*, 113.

69. "A man (it) is; the rain (it) is. I think that a rain's sorcerer (he) seems to have been. His name resembles (that of) the mucus which we are used to blow out of our nose, which is thick, that which the San call |hãu|hãuṅ." Ibid.

70. Literally, "clouds which not beautiful like them." Ibid.

71. "To his younger sister." Ibid.

72. "The things which the wife carried, they resembled water; they, in this manner, were pushing at her; while they felt that they were not hard, they did in this manner (i.e., swayed forward), behind her back." Ibid., 115.

73. "|haũnu was the one from whose nostrils blood came out, when he intended to sneeze. He sneezed on account of his things, to which ǂkágára did in this manner (i.e., felt at roughly)." Ibid.

74. "In the word ||khábbe(t) the *t* is barely pronounced. The meaning of this word is explained by the narrator as follows: (He) fends off his brother-in-law (by motioning with his arm). Fending off (it) is, when other people are fighting their fellows with their fists. Fending off is that which they are wont to do." Ibid.

75. Literally, "was not light," or "did not feel light." Ibid., 117.

76. "Black lightning is that which kills us, that which we do not perceive it come; it resembles a gun, we are merely startled by the clouds' thundering, while the other man lies, shriveled up lies." Ibid.

77. "As he lay." Ibid.

78. "His head ached; his head was splitting (with pain)." Ibid.
79. "To thunder is |kuérrīten; but the narrator explained that |kĕ|kéya tà here means 'to lie thundering'; and illustrated the expression by saying that 'the San are wont to say that the springbok is one which goes to lie bleating; it is not willing to die quickly.'" Ibid.
80. "I.e., himself and his younger sister." Ibid.
81. *Buchu* is a low shrub native to the Cape region of South Africa. The dried leaves are harvested during the flowering season.
82. "Note by the Narrator. My grandmothers used to say: '≠kágára and his companion are those who fight in the East, he and |haũnu.' When the clouds were thick, and the clouds, when the clouds were thick, and the clouds were at this place, and the clouds resembled a mountain, then, the clouds were lightening, on account of it. And my grandmothers used to say: 'It is ≠kágára, with |haũnu.'" Bleek and Lloyd, *Specimens of Bushman Folklore,* 119.

POSTLUDE

A previous version of the first half of this chapter was delivered as the keynote address, titled "The Storyteller: Making the World One," on Friday, March 12, 2004, for the international education conference "Education across Six Continents: Teaching and Curriculum for a Global Society," March 12–13, 2004, at the Pyle Center, University of Wisconsin–Madison.

1. Adewale Maja-Pearce, "Binding the Wounds," *Index on Censorship* 5 (1996): 50.
2. Benjamin, *Illuminations,* 109.
3. Ryunosuke Akutagawa, "To a Grove," in *Rashomon and Other Stories,* trans. Takashi Kojima (New York: Liveright, 1952), 44.
4. See, for example, Peter Brooks and Paul Gewirtz, eds., *Law's Stories: Narrative and Rhetoric in the Law* (New Haven, CT: Yale University Press, 1996).
5. Robert Lowell, "History," in *History* (London: Faber and Faber, 1973), 24.
6. Cees Nooteboom, *In Nederland* (Netherlands: Uitgeverij De Arbeiderspers, 1984); translated by Adrienne Dixon as *In the Dutch Mountains* (New York: Harcourt Brace, 1987), 62–63.
7. Suzanne Daley, "In Apartheid Inquiry, Agony Is Relived but Not Put to Rest," *New York Times,* July 17, 1997, A5.
8. Unless otherwise indicated, the cases noted in this postlude are based on material provided by the Truth and Reconciliation Commission (www .truth.org.za).
9. From *Biographia Literaria* (1817).
10. From the video *Umm Kulthum, A Voice Like Egypt,* Arab Film Distribution, Seattle, Washington, 1996. Directed by Michal Goldman. Based on Virginia Danielson, *"The Voice of Egypt": Umm Kulthum, Arabic Song, and Egyptian Society in the 20th Century* (Chicago: University of Chicago Press, 1997).

11. Tennyson, "Ulysses," pp. 644–46, lines 18–23.

12. "Las mil y una noches surgen de modo misterioso. Son obra de miles de autores y ninguno pensó que estaba edificando un libro ilustre, uno do los libros más ilustres de todas las literaturas." Jorge Luis Borges, *Siete Noches* (Mexico City: Fondo de Cultura Económica, 1980), 64; translated by Eliot Weinberger as *Seven Nights* (New York: New Directions, 1984), 48.

13. "Es un libro tan vasto que no es necesario haberlo leído, ya que es parte previa de nuestra memoria." Borges, *Siete Noches,* 74; *Seven Nights,* 57.

14. Ralph Waldo Emerson, "History," in *Ralph Waldo Emerson: Essays and Lectures,* ed. Joel Porte (New York: Library of America, 1983), 251.

15. Assia Djebar, *Fantasia: An Algerian Cavalcade,* ed. Dorothy S. Blair (Portsmouth, NH: Heinemann, 1985), 177.

16. A *sjambok* is a whip made of hippopotamus or rhinoceros hide.

17. Literally, "a hartebeest."

18. Callaway, *Nursery Tales,* preface (unpaginated).

19. Rubusana, *Zemk' Inkomo Magwalandini,* 233.

BIBLIOGRAPHY

Abu-Manga, Al-Amin. "Baakankaro, A Fulani Epic from Sudan." *Africana Marburgensia* 9 (1985): 9-11.

Adler, Jeremy, Richard Fardon, and Carol Tully. "Franz Steiner." In *From Prague Poet to Oxford Anthropologist: Franz Baermann Steiner Celebrated; Essays and Translations,* edited by Jeremy Adler, Richard Fardon, and Carol Tully, 256-57. Munich: Idicium, 2003.

Akivaga, S. Kichamiu, and A. Bole Odaga. *Oral Literature.* Nairobi: Heinemann, 1982.

|a!kunta. "The Resurrection of the Ostrich." In Bleek and Lloyd, *Specimens of Bushman Folklore,* 136-45.

Akutagawa, Ryunosuke. *Rashomon and Other Stories.* Translated by Takashi Kojima. New York: Liveright, 1952.

Arbousset, Jean Thomas, F. Daumas, and John Croumbie Brown. *Narrative of an Exploratory Tour to the North-east of the Colony of the Cape of Good Hope.* Cape Town: Robertson, 1846.

Aristotle. *Poetics.* Translated by Gerald F. Else. Ann Arbor: University of Michigan Press, 1967.

Bâ, Amadou Hampâté. *Kaïdara: Récit initiatique peul.* Edited by Amadou Hampâté Bâ and Lilyan Kesteloot. Classiques africains 7. [Paris]: Julliard, 1969.

Balfour, Henry. "The Goura and the Kite Bows." In "The Goura, a Stringed Wind Musical Instrument of the Hottentots." *Journal of the Anthropological Institute of Great Britain and Ireland* 32 (1902): 170-73 and pl. VII, pic. 5+6+7.

Basden, George Thomas. *Niger Ibos.* London: Cass, 1938.

Baumann, Chr. "Nama-Texte." *Zeitschrift für Kolonialsprachen* 6 (1915-16): 55-78.

Bellow, Saul. *Henderson the Rain King.* New York: Penguin, 1987.

Benjamin, Walter. *Illuminations.* Translated by Harry Zohn. Glasgow: William Collins, 1973.

Berglund, Axel-Ivar. *Zulu Thought-Patterns and Symbolism.* London: C. Hurst, 1976.

Bible. King James Version. Edited by Robert P. Carroll and Stephen Prickett. Oxford: Oxford University Press, 1997.

Biebuyck, Daniel P., and Kahombo C. Mateene. 1969. *The Mwindo Epic from the Banyanga (Congo Republic)*. Berkeley: University of California Press, 1969.

Biesele, Megan. "Aspects of !Kung Folklore." In *Kalahari Hunter-Gatherers, Studies of the !Kung San and Their Neighbors*, edited by Richard B. Lee and Irven DeVore, 302–24. Cambridge, MA: Harvard University Press, 1976.

——. "The Black-Backed Jackal and the Brown Hyena: A !Kung Bushman Folktale." *Botswana Notes and Records* 4 (1972): 133–34.

——. "Religion and Folklore." In *The Bushmen: San Hunters and Herders of Southern Africa*, edited by Phillip V. Tobias, 162–72. Cape Town: Human and Rousseau, 1978.

Bisele, Marguerite Anne. "Folklore and Ritual of !Kung Hunter-Gatherers." Ph.D. dissertation, Harvard University, 1975.

Bleek, Dorothea F. "Bushman Folklore." *Africa* 2 (July 1929): 302–13.

——, ed. *The Mantis and His Friends*. Cape Town: T. Maskew Miller, [1923].

——. *More Rock-Paintings in South Africa*. London: Methuen, 1940.

——. *The Naron: A Bushman Tribe of the Central Kalahari*. Cambridge: Cambridge University Press, 1928.

Bleek, Wilhelm Heinrich Immanuel. Archives. University of Cape Town Library.

——. *A Brief Account of Bushman Folk-Lore and Other Texts*. London: Trübner and Co., 1875.

——. "The Bushman Language." In *The Cape and Its People, and Other Essays*, edited by Roderick Noble, 269–84. Cape Town: J. C. Juta, 1869.

——. "Bushman Researches." *Cape Monthly Magazine* 11 (August 1875): 107.

——. *Reineke Fuchs in Afrika: Fabeln und Märchen der Eingeborenen*. Weimar: Böhlau, 1870. Translated as *Reynard the Fox in South Africa; or, Hottentot Fables and Tales*. London: Trübner and Co., 1864.

——. *Report of Dr. Bleek Concerning His Researches into the Bushman Language and Customs, Presented to the Assembly*. Cape Town: Printed by Order of the House of Assembly, May 1873. Reprinted in Bleek and Lloyd, *Specimens of Bushman Folklore*, 443.

——. *Second Report Concerning Bushman Researches, with a Short Account of Bushman Folk-Lore*. Cape Town: Saul Solomon, 1875.

Bleek, Wilhelm Heinrich Immanuel, and Lucy Catherine Lloyd. *A Short Account of Further Bushman Material Collected*. London: David Nutt, 1889.

——. *Specimens of Bushman Folklore*. London: G. Allen, 1911.

Bleek and Lloyd Archive. The Digital Bleek and Lloyd. National Library, Iziko South African Museum, and University of Cape Town collections, http://www.lloydbleekcollection.cs.uct.ac.za/index.jsp.

Borges, Jorge Luis. *Siete Noches*. Mexico City: Fondo de Cultura Económica, 1980. Translated by Eliot Weinberger as *Seven Nights*. New York: New Directions, 1984.

Broderick, Modupe. *Go Ta Nan* 1 (1980): 7–8.

Brooks, David. "Lord of the Memes." *New York Times,* August 8, 2008, A19.

Brooks, Peter, and Paul Gewirtz, eds. *Law's Stories: Narrative and Rhetoric in the Law.* New Haven, CT: Yale University Press, 1996.

Buckland, A. W. "Ethnological Hints Afforded by the Stimulants in Use among Savages and among the Ancients." *Journal of the Anthropological Institute of Great Britain and Ireland* (1879): 239–54.

Butcher, H. L. M. "Four Edo Fables." *Africa* 10 (1937): 342.

Callaway, Henry. *Nursery Tales, Traditions and Histories of the Zulus.* Springvale, Natal: John A. Blair, 1868.

——. *The Religious System of the Amazulu.* Springvale, Natal: J. A. Blair, 1870.

Campbell, Joseph. *The Hero with a Thousand Faces.* Princeton: Princeton University Press, 1949.

Cancel, Robert. *Allegorical Speculation in an Oral Society.* Berkeley: University of California Press, 1989.

Canetti, Elias. *Aufzeichnungen, 1992–1993.* Munich: Carl Hanser, 1996.

——. *Nachträge aus Hampstead, Aus Den Aufzeichnungen, 1954–1971.* Munich: Carl Hanser, 1994.

"Cat and the Lynx, The." Bleek and Lloyd, *Specimens of Bushman Folklore,* 220–23.

Chimenti, Élisa. *Tales and Legends from Morocco.* Translated by Arnon Benamy. New York: I. Obolensky, 1965.

Clark, John Pepper. *The Ozidi Saga.* Ibadan, Nigeria: Ibadan University Press, 1977.

Coetzee, J. M. *Life and Times of Michael K.* London: Secker and Warburg, 1983.

Coleridge, Samuel Taylor. "Frost at Midnight." In Gardner, *New Oxford Book of English Verse,* 524–25.

Conrad, Joseph. *Youth, a Narrative; and Two Other Stories.* London: W. Blackwood and Sons, 1902. Includes *Youth, Heart of Darkness,* and *End of the Tether.*

Daley, Suzanne. "In Apartheid Inquiry, Agony Is Relived but Not Put to Rest." *New York Times,* July 17, 1997, A5.

Danielson, Virginia. *"The Voice of Egypt": Umm Kulthum, Arabic Song, and Egyptian Society in the 20th Century.* Chicago: University of Chicago Press, 1997.

Díä!kwäin. "Concerning Two Apparitions." In Bleek and Lloyd, *Specimens of Bushman Folklore,* 364–71.

——. "A Man Becomes Clouds." In Bleek and Lloyd, *Specimens of Bushman Folklore,* 396–401.

——. "The Scapegoat." In Bleek and Lloyd, *Specimens of Bushman Folklore,* 364–65.

——. "Young Girls." Bleek Archive, http://lloydbleekcollection.cs.uct.ac.za/data/stories/126/index.html, 2609–18

Djebar, Assia. *Fantasia: An Algerian Cavalcade.* Edited by Dorothy S. Blair. Portsmouth, NH: Heinemann, 1985.

Doke, Clement M. *Lamba Folk-Lore*. New York: American Folk-Lore Society, 1927.

Elliot, Geraldine. *The Long Grass Whispers*. New York: Schocken Books, 1968.

Emerson, Ralph Waldo. "History." In *Ralph Waldo Emerson: Essays and Lectures*, edited by Joel Porte, 251. New York: Library of America, 1983.

Enright, D. J. "The Thing Itself." *Times Literary Supplement*, September 30, 1983, 1037.

Evans-Pritchard, E. E. *The Zande Trickster*. Oxford, UK: Clarendon Press, 1967.

Fourie, L. "The Bushmen of South West Africa." In *The Native Tribes of South West Africa*, edited by C. H. L. Hahn, L. Fourie, and H. Vedder, 81–105. Cape Town: Cape Times, 1928.

Gardner, Helen, ed. *The New Oxford Book of English Verse, 1250–1950*. New York: Oxford University Press, 1972.

Gordimer, Nadine. "The Idea of Gardening." *New York Review of Books* 31 (February 2, 1984): 6.

———. *July's People*. New York: Viking Press, 1981.

Gordon, Robert J., and Stuart Sholto Douglas. *The Bushman Myth: The Making of a Namibian Underclass*. 2nd ed. Boulder, CO: Westview Press, 2000.

Hahn, Theophilus. *Tsuni-||goam: The Supreme Being of the Kho-Khoi*. London: Trübner and Co., 1881.

|háñ‡kass'ō. "Lynx, Wife of the Dawn's-Heart Star." In Bleek and Lloyd, *Specimens of Bushman Folklore*, 84–98.

———. "A Man Becomes a Bird." In Bleek and Lloyd, *Specimens of Bushman Folklore*, 106–9.

———. "The ‡nèrru and Her Husband." In Bleek and Lloyd, *Specimens of Bushman Folklore*, 206–13.

———. "Thinking Strings." In Bleek and Lloyd, *Specimens of Bushman Folklore*, 86–87.

Helser, Albert D. *African Stories*. New York: Fleming H. Revell, 1930.

"Historical Resume & Statistical and Other Vital Information Relating to Mount Ayliff District." Typescript, author and date unknown.

Jablow, Alta. *Yes and No: The Intimate Folklore of Africa*. New York: Horizons Press, 1961.

Jacottet, Édouard. 1908. *The Treasury of Basuto Lore*. Morija, Lesotho: Sesuto Book Depot, 1908.

Jordan, Archibald Campbell. *Towards an African Literature: The Emergence of Literary Form in Xhosa*. Berkeley: University of California Press, 1973.

Jordan, Pallo. "Zemk' Inkomo Magwalandini: The Life and Times of W. B. Rubusana (1858–1936)." *Sechaba* (January 1984): 4–13.

|||kábbo. "*!khwe-/na-ssho-!kui*" ("Darkness between Two Houses. The Dog Which Is Not a Dog"). Bleek Archive, http://lloydbleekcollection.cs.uct.ac.za/data/stories/283/index.html, 2320–25, 2326–2412, 2413–26.

———. "A Man Becomes a Tree." Bleek Archive, http://lloydbleekcollection.cs.uct.ac.za/data/stories/184/index.html, 295–305.

Kabira, Wanjiku Mukabi. *The Oral Artist.* Nairobi: Heinemann, 1983.

Kabira, Wanjiku Mukabi, and Kavetsa Adagala. *Kenyan Oral Narratives.* Nairobi: Heinemann, 1985.

Kakutani, Michiko. "Is This the Most Trusted Man in America?" *New York Times,* August 17, 2008, Arts and Leisure 1, 18–19.

Keats, John. *The Poems of John Keats.* Edited by Jack Stillinger. Cambridge, MA: Harvard University Press, 1978.

Kholekile. "Umambakamaqula, The Bewitched King." Collected by O. Stavem. *Folk-Lore Journal* 1, no. 5 (September 1879): 102–9.

Kolb, Peter. *Caput Bonae Spei Hodiermum, das ist, Vollständige Beschreibung des africanischen Vorgegürges der Guten Hofnung.* Nuremberg: Peter Conrad Monath, 1719.

Kövecses, Zoltán. *Metaphor: A Practical Introduction.* New York: Oxford University Press, 2002.

Krige, Eileen Jensen. *The Social System of the Zulus.* Pietermaritzburg, South Africa: Shuter and Shooter, 1936.

Kropf, Albert. *A Kafir-English Dictionary.* 2nd ed. Edited by Robert Godfrey. Lovedale, South Africa: Lovedale Mission Press, 1915.

!kwéitẹn ta ||kēn (Rachel). "The Girl's Story, The Frogs' Story." In Bleek and Lloyd, *Specimens of Bushman Folklore,* 198–205.

———. "The Rain's Story." Bleek Archive, http://lloydbleekcollection.cs.uct.ac.za/data/stories/374/index.html, 3930–41.

———. "Tākkŭmm Called by a Lion." Bleek Archive, http://lloydbleekcollection.cs.uct.ac.za/data/stories/385/index.html, 4026–33.

Lakov, George, and Mark Johnson. *Metaphors We Live By.* Chicago: University of Chicago Press, 1980.

Lang, Andrew, ed. *The Violet Fairy Book.* London: Longmans, Green, 1901.

Leary, W. Power. "History of the Xesibes." Typescript. September 27, 1904.

Lee, Richard B., and Irven DeVore, eds. *Kalahari Hunter-Gatherers: Studies of the !Kung San and Their Neighbors.* Cambridge, MA: Harvard University Press, 1976.

Lewis-Williams, James David. *Believing and Seeing: Symbolic Meanings in Southern San Paintings.* London: Academic Press, 1981.

———. *The Mind in the Cave.* London: Thames and Hudson, 2002.

———. "The Syntax and Function of the Giant's Castle Rock Paintings." *South African Archaelogical Bulletin* 27 (1972): 49–65.

Llosa, Mario Vargas. *El hablador.* Barcelona: Biblioteca de Bolsillo, 1987. Translated by Helen Lane as *The Storyteller.* New York: Penguin, 1990.

Lloyd, Lucy Catherine. *A Short Account of Further Bushman Material Collected.* London: David Nutt, 1889.

Lowell, Robert. "History." In *History,* 24. London: Faber and Faber, 1973.

Maja-Pearce, Adewale. "Binding the Wounds." *Index on Censorship* 5 (1996): 50.

Mangoaela, Zakea Dolphin. "Joele Molapo." In *Lithoko tsa Marena a Basotho,* 118–28. Morija, Lesotho: Morija Sesuto Book Depot, 1977. (Originally published in 1921.)

Marshall, Lorna. "!Kung Bushman Religious Beliefs." *Africa* 32 (1962) 222.

Maugham, Reginald Charles F. *Zambezia*. London: J. Murray, 1910.

Mbiti, John S. *Akamba Stories*. Oxford, UK: Clarendon Press, 1966.

McLachlan, Geoffrey Roy, and Richard Liversidge. *Roberts Birds of South Africa*. Rev. ed. Cape Town: Central News Agency, 1958.

McLaren, J. *A New Concise Xhosa-English Dictionary*. Cape Town: Longman, 1963.

"Mditshwa Diko." In Rubusana, *Zemk' Inkomo Magwalandini*, 347–48.

Mofolo, Thomas. *Pitseng*. Morija, Lesotho: Sesuto Book Depot, 1910.

Mombéyâ, Tierno Mouhammadou-Samba. *Le filon du bonheur éternel*. Edited by Alfâ Ibrâhîm Sow. Classiques africains 10. Paris: Armand Colin, [1971].

Mqhayi, S. E. Krune. *Ityala Lamawele*. Lovedale, South Africa: Lovedale Press, [1931].

—— (Mbongi YakwaGompo). "Lifile Madoda." In Rubusana, *Zemk' Inkomo Magwalandini*, 491–95.

Nasr, Ahmad Abd-al-Rahim. "Maiwurno of the Blue Nile: A Study of an Oral Biography." Ph.D. dissertation, University of Wisconsin-Madison, 1977.

Nkonki, Garvey. "The Traditional Prose Literature of the Ngqika." M.A. thesis, University of South Africa, n.d.

Nooteboom, Cess. *In Nederland*. Netherlands: Uitgeverij De Arbeiderspers, 1984. Translated by Adrienne Dixon as *In the Dutch Mountains*. New York: Harcourt Brace, 1987.

Noss, Philip A. "Gbaya Traditional Literature." *Abbia*, nos. 17–18 (1967): 35.

Ntsikana, William Kobe. "Nokhonya, the Son of Nyanga" (*"UNokhonya into KaNyanga"*). In Rubusana, *Zemk' Inkomo Magwalandini*, 167–69.

Orpen, J. M. "A Glimpse into the Mythology of the Maluti Bushmen." *Folk-Lore* 30 (1919): 139–56. (Originally published in *Cape Monthly Magazine* 9 [July 1874].)

Ortega y Gasset, José. *La deshumanizacion del arte* and *Ideas sobre la novela*. Madrid: Revista de Occidente, 1928. Translated by Helene Weyl as *The Dehumanization of Art and Notes on the Novel*. Princeton: Princeton University Press, 1948.

Ozick, Cynthia. "A Tale of Heroic Anonymity." *New York Review of Books* (December 11, 1983): 26.

Pager, Harald, Revil J. Mason, and Robert G. Welbourne. *Ndedema: A Documentation of the Rock Paintings of the Ndedema Gorge*. Graz, Austria: Akademische Druck- u. Verlagsanstalt, 1971.

Pessoa, Fernando. *Selección de textos y análisis de su persamiento, Anthropos, Revista de documentación científica de la cultura*. Barcelona: Anthropos, 1987.

Pityana, N. Barney, Mamphela Ramphele, Malusi Mpumlwana, and Lindy Wilson, eds. *Bounds of Possibility: The Legacy of Steve Biko and Black Consciousness*. Cape Town: D. Philip; Atlantic Highlands, N.J.: Zed, 1991.

Qing. "Qwanciqutshaa—A Love Story." In "A Glimpse into the Mythology of the Maluti Bushmen" by J. M. Orpen. *Cape Monthly Magazine* 9 (July 1874). Reprinted in *Folk-Lore* 30 (1919): 139–56.

Radin, Paul, ed. *African Folktales and Sculpture.* New York: Pantheon Books, 1964.

Ross, Mabel H., and Barbara K. Walker. *"On Another Day . . . ," Tales Told among the Nkundo of Zaire.* Hamden, CT: Archon Books, 1979.

Rubusana, W. B. *Zemk' Inkomo Magwalandini.* Frome: Butler and Tanner, 1906.

Rudner, Jalmar, and Ione Rudner. *The Hunter and His Art: A Survey of Rock Art in Southern Africa.* Cape Town: C. Struik, 1970.

Rureke, Shé-kárịsị Candi. *The Mwindo Epic.* Edited and translated by Daniel Biebuyck and Kahombo C. Mateene. Berkeley: University of California Press, 1969.

Samatar, Said S. *Oral Poetry and Somali Nationalism.* Cambridge: Cambridge University Press, 1982.

Schaar, W. "Nama-Fabeln." *Zeitschrift für Kolonialsprachen* 8 (1917–18): 81–109.

Schapera, Isaac. *The Khoisan People of South Africa: Bushmen and Hottentots.* London: Routledge and Kegan Paul, 1930.

Scheub, Harold. *African Oral Narratives, Proverbs, Riddles, Poetry, and Song.* Boston: G. K. Hall and Co., 1977.

———. *The African Storyteller.* Dubuque, IA: Kendall/Hunt, 1999.

———. *A Dictionary of African Mythology: The Mythmaker as Storyteller.* New York: Oxford University Press, 2000.

———. "Narrative Patterning in Oral Performances." *Ba Shiru* 7, no. 2 (1976): 10–30.

———. *The Poem in the Story.* Madison: University of Wisconsin Press, 2002.

———. "A Review of African Oral Traditions and Literature." *African Studies Review* 28, nos. 2/3 (June/September 1985): 1–72.

———. Review of *Towards an African Literature: The Emergence of Literary Form in Xhosa,* by A. C. Jordan. *Journal of American Folklore* 90, no. 357 (July–September 1977): 347–52.

———. *Shadows: Deeper into Story.* Madison, WI: Parallel Press, 2009.

———. *Story.* Madison: University of Wisconsin Press, 1998.

———. *Storytelling Songs of Zulu Women: Recording Archetypal Rites of Passage and Mythic Paths.* Lewiston, NY: Edwin Mellen, 2006.

———. "Telling Michael K's Story." *West African Research Association Newsletter* (Spring 2001): 15–19.

———. *The Tongue Is Fire.* Madison: University of Wisconsin Press, 1996.

Schultze, Leonhard. *Aus Namaland und Kalahari.* Jena, Ger.: G. Fischer, 1907.

Senghor, Léopold Sédar. *Negritude et civilsation de l'universel.* Paris: Seuil, 1977.

Shah, Saira. *The Storyteller's Daughter.* New York: Alfred A. Knopf, 2003.

Shakespeare, William. *The Annotated Shakespeare.* Edited by A. L. Rowse. New York: Clarkson N. Potter, 1978.

Shiff, Richard. "Art and Life: A Metaphoric Relationship." In *On Metaphor,* edited by Sheldon Sacks, 105–20. Chicago: University of Chicago Press, 1978.

Shooter, Joseph. *The Kaffirs of Natal and the Zulu Country.* London: E. Stanford, 1857.

Silberbauer, George B. *Report to the Government of Bechuanaland on the Bushman Survey.* Gabarone: Bechuanaland Government, 1965.

Skotnes, Pippa. *Claim to the Country.* Johannesburg: Jacana; Athens: Ohio University Press, 2007.

Smith, Edwin W., and Andrew Murray Dale. *The Ila-Speaking Peoples of Northern Rhodesia.* 2 vols. London: Macmillan, 1920.

Sow, Alfâ Ibrâhîm ed. *La femme, la vache, la foi: Écrivains et poètes di Foûta-Djalon.* Classiques africains 5. [Paris]: Julliard, 1966.

Spitzer, Michael. *Metaphor and Musical Thought.* Chicago: University of Chicago Press, 2004.

Staven, O. "Umambakamaqula." *Folk-Lore Journal* 1, no. 5 (September 1879): 102–9.

Stephens, Jean B. "Tales of the /Gwikwe Bushmen." M.A. thesis, Goddard College, 1971.

Stow, George W. *The Native Races of South Africa.* London: S. Sonnenschein and Co., 1905. Reprinted, Cape Town: C. Struik, 1964.

Tennyson, Alfred Lord. "Ulysses." In Gardner, *New Oxford Book of English Verse,* 644–46.

Thomas, E. W. *Bushman Stories.* Cape Town: Oxford University Press, 1950.

Thomas, Elizabeth Marshall. *The Harmless People.* New York: Alfred A. Knopf, 1965.

Thunberg, Carl Peter. "An Account of the Cape of Good Hope, and Some Parts of the Interior of Southern Africa." In *A General Collection of the Best and Most Interesting Voyages and Travels in All Parts of the World,* edited by John Pinkerton. 17 vols. London: Longman, Hurst, Rees, and Orme, 1808–14.

Tinguidji. *Silâmaka & Poullôri: Récit épique peul.* Edited by Christiane Seydou. Classiques africains 13. [Paris]: A. Colin, [c 1972].

Tolkien, J. R. R. *Tree and Leaf.* London: George Allen and Unwin, 1964.

Truth and Reconciliation Commission of South Africa Report. 5 vols. London: Macmillan, 1999.

Van Gennep, Arnold. *Les rites de passage.* Paris: É. Nourry, 1909.

Ward, G. D. "Historical Record of the Mount Ayliff District, Cape Province, Union of South Africa, 1878 to 1937." Compiled from notes by Mrs. I. B. Hunter and from other sources. Kokstad, South Africa: Kokstad Advertiser, [1937].

Wickenden, Dorothy. "South African Specter." *New Republic* (December 19, 1983): 35.

Willcox, A. R. *The Rock Art of South Africa.* Johannesburg: Thomas Nelson and Sons, 1963.

Wilson, Monica, and Leonard Thompson. *The Oxford History of South Africa*. 2 vols. Oxford: Oxford University Press, 1969.

Yeats, William Butler. "A Woman Young and Old." In *The Collected Poems of W. B. Yeats*, 266–72. New York: Macmillan, 1933.

Zenani, Nongenile Masithathu. *The World and the Word: Tales and Observations from the Xhosa Oral Tradition*. Edited by Harold Scheub. Madison: University of Wisconsin Press, 1992.

INDEX

Aesop's fables, xiii, 115, 196
African National Congress (ANC), xv, 194
Afrikaans, xiv
Afrikaners, xiv, xv
|a!kunta, 53; "The Resurrection of the Ostrich," 72–75
Akutagawa, Ryunosuke: "To a Grove," 196
Algeria, 115
allegory, 112
Anglo-Boer War, xiv
animals, kinship with, 48–51
anti-pass demonstrations, xv
apartheid laws, xv
Aristotle: Poetics, 13
Asians, xv

Bâ, Amadou Hampâté: Kaïdara, 218n7
Babylon, 198
Baikie, William Balfour, 52
Balfour, Henry: "The Goura . . . ," 209n22
Bantu Education Act (1953), xv
Bantu speakers, xiv, 5, 52
Barkly, Henry, 53
Bellow, Saul: Henderson the Rain King, 202
Benjamin, Walter: Illuminations, 107–8, 196
Berglund, Axel-Ivar: Zulu Thought Patterns and Symbolism, 1–2
Berlin University, 52
Bhaca, 127, 147
Bible, King James Version, 207n
Bleek Archive, 55–57, 58–59, 65–66, 69–71
Bleek, Dorothea F.: Customs and Beliefs of the |xam Bushmen, 54; The Mantis and His Friends, 46, 54; The Naron, 43, 54; A Survey . . . of Rock-Paintings in South Africa, 54
Bleek, Friedrich, 52

Bleek, W. H. I., 7, 9–13, 40, 52–53, 54, 209n20, 211n7, 216nn58–61, 216n77; "The Bushman Language," 53; A Comparative Grammar of African Languages, 53; Reineke Fuchs in Afrika, 60–64, 214n56; Report . . . , 53
Bleek, W. H. I., and Lucy C. Lloyd: Specimens of Bushman Folklore, 7, 9–13, 40, 52–54, 57–58, 102–3, 209n, 210nn2–4, 211n7, 213n52, 216nn65–72, 222n82; "Concerning Two Apparitions," 78–81, 216nn69–71; "Girls Become Stars," 81; "The Girl's Story, the Frog's Story," 75–77, 216nn65–68; "‡kágára . . . ," 192–93, 221–22nn68–82; "Lynx . . . ," 88–93, 217nn82–85; "A Man Becomes Clouds," 81–82; "The ‡nèrru and Her Husband," 83–85, 216nn72–77; "The Resurrection of the Ostrich," 72–75; "The Scapegoat," 77–78
Boers, xiv
Bonn, University of, 52
Borges, Jorge Luis: Siete Noches, 201, 223nn12–13
Breakwater, 53
British, xiv, 8, 31
British Museum, 103
Brooks, David, 209n19
Brooks, Peter, and Paul Gewirtz, eds.: Law's Stories, 222n4
Bubesi Location, 135
Buckland, A. W.: "Ethnological Hints . . . ," 217n79

Callaway, Henry: Nursery Tales . . . , 24–31, 205, 210n7, 214–15n57
Campbell, Joseph: The Hero with a Thousand Faces, 198